A CULTURAL HISTORY OF
CHILDHOOD AND FAMILY

VOLUME 1

A Cultural History of Childhood and Family

General Editors: Elizabeth Foyster and James Marten

Volume 1

A Cultural History of Childhood and Family in Antiquity
Edited by Mary Harlow and Ray Laurence

Volume 2

A Cultural History of Childhood and Family in the Middle Ages
Edited by Louise J. Wilkinson

Volume 3

A Cultural History of Childhood and Family in the Early Modern Age
Edited by Sandra Cavallo and Silvia Evangelisti

Volume 4

A Cultural History of Childhood and Family in the Age of Enlightenment
Edited by Elizabeth Foyster and James Marten

Volume 5

A Cultural History of Childhood and Family in the Age of Empire
Edited by Colin Heywood

Volume 6

A Cultural History of Childhood and Family in the Modern Age
Edited by Joseph M. Hawes and N. Ray Hiner

A CULTURAL HISTORY OF CHILDHOOD AND FAMILY

IN ANTIQUITY

Edited by Mary Harlow and Ray Laurence

BLOOMSBURY

LONDON · NEW DELHI · NEW YORK · SYDNEY

Bloomsbury Academic

An imprint of Bloomsbury Publishing Plc

50 Bedford Square	1385 Broadway
London	New York
WC1B 3DP	NY 10018
UK	USA

www.bloomsbury.com

Hardback edition first published in 2010 by Berg Publishers, an imprint of
Bloomsbury Academic
Paperback edition first published by Bloomsbury Academic 2014

British Library Cataloguing-in-Publication Data
A catalogue record for this book is available from the British Library.

ISBN: HB: 978-1-84788-794-8
PB: 978-1-4725-5473-4
HB Set: 978-1-84520-826-4
PB Set: 978-1-4725-5474-1

Library of Congress Cataloging-in-Publication Data
A catalog record for this book is available from the Library of Congress.

Typeset by Apex CoVantage, LLC, Madison, WI, USA
Printed and bound in Great Britain

CONTENTS

ILLUSTRATIONS

MAPS

INTRODUCTION

CHAPTER 1

CHAPTER 8

CHAPTER 9

CHAPTER 10

GENERAL EDITORS' PREFACE

The literature on the histories of children and the family has reached a critical mass. The proliferation of encyclopedia, conferences, and professional associations reflects the vitality of these closely related but independent fields. The two subjects are naturally linked; Western conceptions of the family have virtually always included children, and children and youth are irrevocably shaped by their time growing up in families.

A Cultural History of Childhood and Family aims to bring order to these sometimes disparate histories and historiographical traditions with original material written especially for these volumes. More than six dozen editors and authors from five continents and thirteen countries were commissioned to take a comprehensive look at the subject from a Western perspective with more than casual glances at the world beyond. Based on deep readings of the secondary literature and on representative primary sources, each of the chapters is an original work of synthesis and interpretation.

It is our hope that imposing a standard table of contents on a project covering literally thousands of years and hundreds of ethnicities, religious faiths, and communities will help us find otherwise hidden patterns and rich contrasts in the experiences of children and families and in humankind's attitudes about them. There is inevitably a bit of overlap; issues related to children and the family do not form and develop according to convenient beginning and ending dates. But there is also a variety of viewpoints, even on similar topics. Indeed, as general editors we embrace the divergence of interpretations, emphases, and even writing and organizational styles that emerge from these five dozen chapters. Some of the diversity follows naturally from the vastly different conditions facing children and their families in different eras, while in other cases it is inspired by the authors' expertise and personal approaches to the field.

There have always been many childhoods and many families in the West. The purpose of these volumes is not only to look at the constructions of childhood and the family, particularly as they reflect evolving ethnic, gender, religious, national, and class assumptions, but also the lived experiences of children and of the families in which they spend so much of their lives. The symbiotic relationship between child and parent, between brother and sister, and between the individual and the family to which he or she belongs is reflected in the intertwined historical literature on children and families. By studying both, we can learn more about each.

Elizabeth Foyster
Clare College, University of Cambridge

James Marten
Marquette University

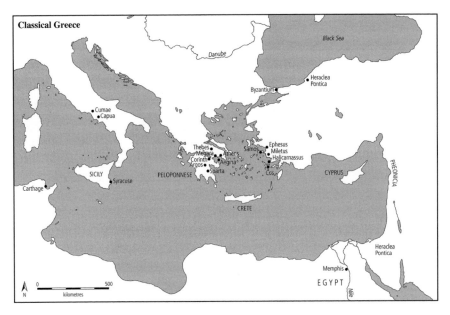

MAP 1: *Classical Greek world fifth through fourth centuries* B.C.E. *(illustration: Henry Buglass).*

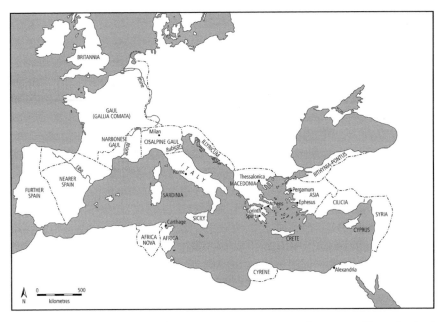

MAP 2: *Roman world at the death of Julius Caesar 44* B.C.E. *(illustration: Henry Buglass).*

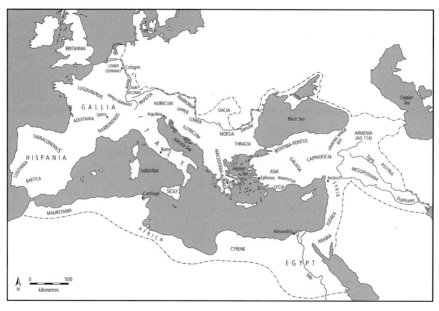

MAP 3: *Roman Empire at the start of second century* C.E. *(illustration: Henry Buglass).*

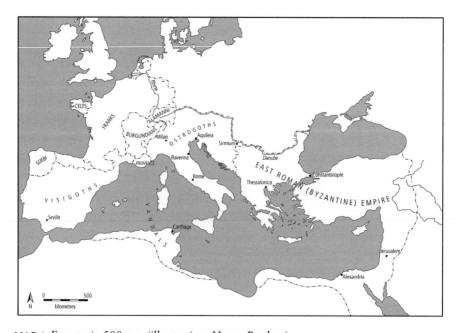

MAP 4: *Europe in 500* C.E. *(illustration: Henry Buglass).*

Introduction

MARY HARLOW AND RAY LAURENCE

Every adult today, and in the past, experienced a childhood and family life of some description, but our experiences can be wildly different and our expectations of family behavior consequently highly diverse. This position is also slanted by age and gender. The editors of this volume, while only seven years apart in chronological age, come from very different family backgrounds and are even now at different stages of family life: one has two young sons, aged only five and three; the other is already a grandparent. Our own experiences of parenting are separated by over twenty years, and our children have experienced or are experiencing very different childhoods. Our life courses reflect personal choices, it is true, but these choices are a product of circumstance, upbringing, and wider social expectations and pressures. This reflects a pattern not only unique to the modern age but that also existed in antiquity—early marriage for women and later marriage for men—but at this point the similarities cease. Each individual's experience of family life is particular and temporally and culturally specific.

There is a methodological distinction between the life of a child and the construction of this phase of life known by adults simply as childhood. Every adult has experienced being a child, but only those adults with children gain direct experience of childhood through being parents. The study of the family in the past is particularly difficult because there is no direct access to the inner workings of the choices made by individuals. In antiquity, the sources (literary, epigraphic, visual, and archaeological) tend to present an idealized or normalizing image of one particular social group—the adult elite—and a representation of male voices that results in a female silence.[1] Even the individual choices of adult males appear unclear, but what can be accessed today is the overall pattern (including female silence) that permits a history of childhood and the family to be constructed for the period 800 B.C.E. to 800 C.E.

Antiquity covers an extensive period of human history stretching over more than a millennium and accounting for social and political contexts across the Mediterranean and what is now Western Europe. The surviving evidence is eclectic and fragmentary. Vast amounts of literature do survive and range across a variety of genres from the philosophy of Aristotle to the poetry of Virgil or the medical writings of Soranus, onto the theologically driven texts of St. Augustine and the church fathers, and ending with early medieval texts such as Isidore of Seville's *Etymologies*. All of these exist today due to chance survival, selection, and transcription in the Middle Ages and the Renaissance. Not all parts of the ancient world are covered by this selection of texts, and inevitably some societies fare better than others, most notably Athens (500–300 B.C.E.); Sparta (500–300 B.C.E.); Rome (100 B.C.E.–250 C.E. and 330–550 C.E.); and a number of barbarian kingdoms (600–800 C.E.). Not surprisingly, prior to the second half of the twentieth century archaeological interest was strongly allied to the recovery of societies familiar from textual evidence. This means that much of the information derived from excavations concentrates on the very same periods from which the famous authors of antiquity are drawn. More importantly, archaeology as a discipline has only very recently focused on the recovery of children and, in so doing, has come to recognize that as a discipline it has often been blind to the presence of children in the material record.[2]

It can be argued that some of the most immediate evidence for family relationships in antiquity is drawn from funerary inscriptions and commemorations. These often poignant reminders of the brevity of life for many in antiquity appear at first sight to speak directly to us. The surviving examples are unevenly distributed with a far greater number surviving from the first two centuries C.E. than any other time. The doyenne of the study of Roman childhood, Beryl Rawson, recently admitted that when confronted by this testament to the fragility of life as a young researcher, she was both reduced to tears and determined to recover the history of children who had lived such short lives in the past.[3] The modern perception of Roman childhood is shaped by the personal statements found on tombstones and their sheer numbers (about fifty thousand from the city of Rome). Faced with such overwhelming evidence, historians are in danger of not reading the historical phenomenon of childhood in a detached or objective manner. Instead, there is a temptation to empathize with the existence of childhood mortality on a scale that no historians living in the modern West have ever experienced and to internalize the evidence, wondering how as parents we might deal with the deaths of our own children. This emotive response, combined with knowledge of the Roman practice of infant exposure, can lead historians to a denial of parental attachment to these children, a denial of the relevance of the modern conception of childhood to a premodern world, or an attempt to read into the evidence a role for sentiment in the face of death.[4] When examining the history of human demography, the high childhood mortality in antiquity was a far more normative demographic pattern.

It is striking that many of the key concepts that later periods of Western history associate with a cultural understanding of childhood and the family have their foundations in antiquity. In the medical field, an understanding of the body of the child as quite different from that of an adult shaped the nature not just of pediatrics but of the understanding of the wider social connotations of puberty.[5] The patterns associated with biological development were mapped onto the mental sphere by ancient authorities then allied to an astrological fascination with the movement of the seven planets. The astrological dimension creates some major differences in terms of *mentalité*, but the other factors result in a series of broad life stages: from birth to seven and from seven to fourteen, fourteen to twenty-one, twenty-two to forty-one, forty-two to fifty-six, and so on.[6] Gender distinctions can be found in the medical literature, but, as with most texts from antiquity, the focus is on the male rather than the female. When women are mentioned it is usually in association with gynecological matters. These physical differences were mapped onto mental and emotional states: men were strong in mind and body where women were weak; men were rational, women irrational; men were active and natural rulers while women were passive and needed ruling. These physical and mental characteristics were further mapped onto gendered social roles: women did not have active political roles in the state as they were ideally confined to the domestic and family sphere. Children were raised in the gendered expectations of their society. Of course, idealizations of age or gender can be subverted, but they are still strong forms of social control.

The problem that historians of antiquity face is how to deal with evidence that is both of such relevance to later times and at the same time so patchy. The 1980s saw a phenomenal increase in scholarly interest in the Roman family. This was in part generated by Beryl Rawson's series of conferences beginning in 1981 with a reappraisal published in 1986 followed by further edited collections of essays.[7] Summing up the reappraisal in 1986, Rawson defined the Roman family as small, encompassed within a single household in the format of a nuclear family but sometimes extended via slaves, ex-slaves,

FIGURE 0.1: *Ara Pacis*. The Ara Pacis (dedicated 9 B.C.E.), or Altar of Augustan Peace, in Rome is the earliest public monument that includes children. Here, the children of the emperor's family are seen in procession with their parents (photo courtesy of Alex Williams).

and fostering.[8] Historical research approaches to the family tended to focus on the delineation and definition of it as a social institution, but at all times there was an awareness that the issue was more complex than it seemed: actual Roman practice did not appear to conform to stated ideals.[9] Literary texts and legal evidence were mined to establish a series of cases that might help to determine an overall pattern. However, contradictions existed (especially when examining Roman case law), and these begged the question of how representative or atypical any piece of evidence was.[10] What holds true for Roman law also holds true for all literary texts from antiquity. More importantly, it is almost impossible methodologically to move from the reporting of a child-rearing practice—for example, wet-nursing or the exposure of infants—to deducing from its presence (or absence) an understanding of attitudes toward children.[11]

In 1986, it was accurate to say "little has been written specifically on children in Roman society."[12] Over twenty years later, there is a wealth of material not just on the Roman family but also Roman childhood—including an all-embracing 2003 study of the subject by Rawson. Credit has also to be given to a number of scholars mostly based in Australia and North America who, in the 1980s and 1990s, began to explore the Roman family.[13] No single approach dominates, but the majority of authors have been trained in classics—a subject that until the 1980s put particular emphasis on the accumulation of examples in texts with a view to an empirical explanation of social practices and at the same time looked to shift the emphasis in the social history of antiquity from an antiquarian or daily life approach to one more in line with trends in the study of other historical epochs.[14] Many of these studies were informed by the development of demographic models and reading material written on the history, anthropology, and sociology of the family in other time periods, but most of the researchers involved did not have any formal training in these areas. As a result, these publications were written within a tradition of logical positivism (or common sense) associated with the study of classics, which looks to sources while accumulating bibliography.[15] This approach can produce some unusual myths of its own—for example, the ritual of a father lifting up his child as a symbol of the child's acceptance into the family or of a father indulging in the right to kill his offspring, both of which have now been exposed as a muddling of evidence and a conflation of instances to create a universal Roman social practice.[16] From another direction, the study of childhood and the family needs to be subjected to the level of literary critique associated with the current understanding of women in antiquity.[17] Until recently, this approach has been absent. In these varied approaches to children and/or childhood there is not a reconstruction of a child's view of the world but rather the place to which adults assigned children and the place of children in an adult's social world.[18] Inevitably, all historians of childhood in antiquity cannot escape the fact that the source material concerned with the lives of children was written by adults (and nearly all male adults, at that) and was shaped by the writers' experiences of both their own childhoods and their experiences of children as adults. Intriguingly, the industrious search for sources to extend the study of childhood and the family in the Roman period has not been matched with a similar proliferation of publications in the earlier periods of classical and Hellenistic Greece or the early Middle Ages. This may simply be related to the amount of available evidence. For example, thousands of those who died young are commemorated by surviving inscriptions in the Roman Empire, but this type of evidence is much rarer for other periods of antiquity.[19]

Childhood as a concept is an adult construction that was, and still is, naturalized as a stage of life with reference to biological growth and sexual capacity.[20] In antiquity, the concept of childhood served as a focal point for the empowerment of adult men and the disempowerment of children and women, who could be associated with childlike qualities.[21] Intriguingly, there seems to be more surviving evidence for relations between parents and their adult children than for their relations with their children in early childhood.[22] When early childhood is explicitly discussed, the focus tends to shift away from the child to the actions of his or her parents: mothers in birth or parents in mourning, for instance.[23] Both literature from antiquity and modern scholarship, which constructs a history of childhood in antiquity, are involved in a methodological phenomenon by which the category of "the child" is inherently dependent on a defined sense of adulthood; at the same time, "the child" was, and still is, a means of creating identity and selfhood in the adult author—ancient or modern.[24] Not surprisingly, the dialectical examination of identity expressed by parents about children did not cease when their children became adults and is well established with reference to antiquity.[25] Writing a history of the experience of childhood in antiquity will nearly always lead both author and reader to consider parenting (biological and social) and the role of adults.[26] To discuss the child in antiquity is also by implication to discuss adulthood and the family.[27] The dialectical relationship of child and adult cannot be broken down into its constituent elements and is not fractured with the death of either party.

The study of childhood and the family in antiquity presents challenges not associated with other volumes in this series. Is it possible to characterize childhood and family life across such a long temporal period, which encompasses profound political, social, legal, religious, and cultural changes? More importantly, perhaps, how should historians account for childhood and the family in the many different societies and historical contexts across the geographical spread of the Mediterranean and Western Europe? Most authors in this volume have played it safe by covering Athens in the fifth and fourth centuries B.C.E. with an excursus on Sparta, followed by a more extensive treatment of Rome from 200 B.C.E. through to 300 C.E., before finally looking at late antiquity—300 to 600 C.E. Readers need to be aware of the numerous differences of context involved in this long temporal period.[28] Childhood and the family in Athens in the fifth century B.C.E. involved quite different social institutions from a Visigothic childhood in Seville in the eighth century C.E. Roman family history in itself encompasses a whole variety of time periods; it is becoming increasingly clear that even relatively short time frames of one hundred years made a huge difference in terms of, for instance, the availability of goods for consumption, the presence of philosophical ideas, or the wholesale conversion to Christianity.[29] Across the geographical spread of *Romanità*, the experience of growing up in Rome (with an urban population of seven hundred and fifty thousand by the end of the first century c.e.) was utterly different from growing up in the newly founded Roman colony of Mérida in Spain made up of a few thousand loyal veteran soldiers. Yet some common ground is established through a similar repertoire of symbols (found in architecture, coins, statues, mythology, etc.) that link the two experiences. This is also true of the long temporal frame of the Roman period (which can in some cases be extended to include the barbarian kingdoms of late antiquity); there was a sense in which children grew up with an inherited set of cultural images of a past.[30] It was a cultural framework that encouraged the incorporation of new ideas. This is distinct from the deliberate characterization of difference between Athenian and Spartan institutions and social practices or the cultural space that separated Greco-Roman traditions and those of the barbarians—so alien not just in speech but also in customs. Yet, by the sixth century, barbarian and Roman traditions were melded together to create a new system of values that saw both cultures having a respectable longevity, a fusion overlain by a more important cultural context: Christianity.[31] The creation of shared traditions through cultural reinvention allows the categorization of the long temporal period 600 b.c.e. to 800 c.e. as a single entity—antiquity. Here, some ideas of childhood and the family were maintained, even if the realities of the lives of children and their families were quite distinct from period to period and varied across geographical space.

The emphasis on cultural reinvention creates an illusion of stability and continuity in the concept of childhood and the idea of a family. There is some variation to the construction of the stages of the human life course from the earliest examples in the sixth century b.c.e. to the formats found in late antiquity.[32] There is, however, remarkable consistency in the overall conception of the young and old. Underpinning these concepts was an intellectual rhetoric that set out to create the adult male in a dominant position in terms of both age and gender. The young and the old were seen to be inferior to adult men, as were all women. Children were recognized for their potential to develop into adults and fill the dominant position of adult males in their turn.[33] However, the ability of the child or young adult male to act rationally or take on positions of responsibility was limited in the eyes of older adults. The articulation of power relations was structured and centered upon men who perceived themselves to be in their prime—no longer young, but not yet old. Like the governmental ideals of ancient democratic and republican constitutions, this age of power was transitory and briefly held. In the Roman imperial period there was criticism of rulers whose actions and motivations were determined or hindered by their age; some rulers were considered too young or too old

FIGURE 0.2: *Girls playing*. Fragment from a sarcophagus showing children playing ball games. Roman. Louvre, Paris: Bridgeman Art Library.

to rule effectively (for example, Nero in his late teens and early twenties was too young, and Nerva in his mid-sixties was too old). The ancients conceived power as associated with a small minority of their population: males from about twenty-five to forty-five. It is this group who were written into history (and were often the authors of that history) and are most easily recovered by historians of antiquity. However, the actions of this group had a direct impact on the lives of the rest of the population. This is most clearly seen in relation to warfare. Cities were sacked and plundered, and inhabitants of any age or gender were tortured and killed.[34] Civil war affected the entire family, not just men but women and children; civil conflicts took warfare right to the heart of the state, into the homes of its citizens, onto the streets, and into public spaces and sacred sites.[35] The antithesis of the chaos of warfare is represented in the altar of peace (Ara Pacis) set up in Rome between 13 and 9 B.C.E. (figures 0.1, 7.2, 8.1, 10.1). This monument is iconic for our understanding of the history of childhood and Augustus's active reframing of the concept of family values. It is the first public monument to include sculptural images of adult males, adult females, and children of both sexes—for the most part members of the emperor's family.[36] As in other public sculpture of the

Augustan Age, the civil wars were alluded to by an absence of military imagery and the creation of distance. The images of children were incorporated into the state's repertoire of representations of stable government promised by Augustus as based on peace rather than civil war. Yet underpinning this imagery was a knowledge that civil war affected all regardless of age or gender.

The difficulty of recovering childhood and the family is not unique to their representation in sculptures and texts. Archaeologists have been relatively slow to recover the child within the archaeological data set.[37] Recently, a number of archaeologists have considered the presence of children at sites that include relatively well preserved sets of artifacts, such as those at Pompeii.[38] However, the problem of interpretation remains: the artifacts cannot be read in a straight-forward manner and mapped onto identities associated with age or gender. The dialectical relationship of child and adult that exists in texts also exists in material culture. For example, dolls are created for children by adults. Societies might attribute gender and age associations to certain objects (e.g., toys), but the overall distribution of objects is the key to understanding the intersection of children and adults in houses, within the city, and in landscapes. Our means to interpret archaeological evidence of this nature remains relatively under-theorized at present.[39] Sadly, those who died in childhood reveal rather more about this stage of life than those who survived. For much of antiquity, however, societies engaged in the archaeologically inconvenient habit of cremating their dead, resulting in huge variations in the availability of skeletal remains for analysis by osteoarchaeologists. There also tends to be an overall under-representation of children (or in the recovery of children) in the excavations of cemeteries (e.g., at Metaponto).[40] Where skeletons do survive, however, it is possible to begin to build an appraisal of health and disease in the population, but it is necessary to remember that a skeleton informs us about the diseases associated with an individual who did not survive.[41] As a consequence, skeletons may not be the best guide to the overall health of a population during childhood or any stage of life. Yet this is the best evidence from which to deduce long-term changes and regional variations in the lives of individuals across the span of antiquity in time and space. What is less clear at present is how to read back from the results of osteoarchaeology onto the construction of childhood and the actual lives of children who survived to become adults.

Over the last three decades, the study of childhood and the family in antiquity has developed from being associated with a spurious depiction of daily life to a demographically informed sociological study of adult-child relations. At the same time, temporal parameters have expanded to reach the later phases of antiquity, and the geographical range has also expanded from Athens and Rome to include a far greater number of cultures. The scholarly world of the history of childhood in antiquity has evolved and now includes new disciplines with new bodies of evidence (osteoarchaeology), a greater sophistication of analysis (especially in the study of inscriptions), and a far greater number of active research scholars. There is, of course, room for further development—not least the entire evaluation of the place of the child in the genres of classical literature; and, perhaps, with so much focus on the study of childhood (and women) in antiquity, there might be a need to re-evaluate the unspoken reference point for this work: the adult male, who remains somewhat undefined (or defined by opposition) but essential for our understanding of childhood.[42] As readers will see in the following chapters, authors write about children and childhood, but they do so with reference to adults—the wider family. It is impossible to speak of one without the other, however much agency is given to the children who constituted the majority of the population in antiquity.

In antiquity, the context for any discussion of adult-child relationships tends to lie in the study of the family, a social institution that was defined not just as a building block of the community but also of the state. Recent work on the family has, in many ways, mirrored or been closely associated with that on children. It shares a similar outlook and draws on a very similar constituency of scholars. Hence, many of the same phenomena can be observed in its study: an emphasis on definition of the family; its variation due to death, remarriage, and adoption; and the explicit discussion of patriarchy and the unevenness of gendered relationships in antiquity. Interestingly, these are topics that have received attention from historians of antiquity, whereas archaeologists have tended to be less concerned with the family as a social institution, though much work has been done in connection with the physical setting of the family—the house and its associated artifacts and decoration. The material world does not easily provide evidence for social institutions unless studied in conjunction with written evidence that might delineate the parameters of interpretation, which are set by the availability of evidence. As a result, our picture of the family tends to be legalistic, frequently focusing more on the processes of family continuity associated with inheritance and the transfer of wealth across generations (including via marriage in connection with dowry payments) rather than sentiment, affection, or emotions, which can also be associated with family structures in our modern societies.[43] Underpinning the family as a social institution was the patriarchal supremacy of the adult male, in his roles as father or husband, whose power within the family was legally defined—even if he chose not to exploit the law in order to affirm his position.

If the father/husband died, the law and society restructured the roles of the individuals within his family via inheritance to create a new series of social identities for its members and to distribute his possessions and wealth. The regulation of this process by law was a matter that ensured not just the continuity of lineage but also the maintenance of property holdings, the economy, the community, and the state.

CHAPTER ONE

Family Relationships

MARY HARLOW

The family was regarded as the key social institution in antiquity. It was seen as fundamental for the continuation of society and, in its composition, a reflection of the wider state.[1] The danger for historians is that it is easy to make assumptions about what a family is and, further, to assume any working definition is both universal and normalizing. In order to create a framework for thinking about the family and childhood in the past, this chapter looks at the ideas, ideologies, assumptions, and anxieties that framed domestic life in antiquity. In the history of the family in all periods there is a tension between the way lives and emotions are portrayed in various types of evidence and the lived experience of family life. This is more acute in antiquity than in later periods as our view is dependent on fragmentary statements from a diverse range of sources (literary, epigraphic, visual, and archaeological), nearly all of which privilege the viewpoint of the upper-class father or husband. There is little direct access to the views of children or adult women, their mothers, or the lower classes. The historian has to look behind and between the lines of the evidence to examine the lives of those who did not write their own history or leave much material evidence. Readers will find this caveat a constant but necessary refrain throughout this volume.

THE STRUCTURE OF THE ANCIENT FAMILY

For modern readers, the word *family* tends to have two meanings: the immediate group of mother, father, brothers, and sisters (a nuclear family) and the larger group of kin—grandparents, aunts, uncles, and cousins. For those living in antiquity, however, even defining "mom, dad, and the kids" was more complex. The Greek and Latin words for family, *oikos* and *familia*, embraced a much wider grouping than just a husband and wife and their children. In strictly legal terms, *oikoi* and *familiae* were ruled by the father figure (*kyrios* in Greek and *paterfamilias* in Latin) and included not only the immediate biological family but also slaves; the wider kin group, often only through the father (agnates); and property and landholdings. As such, these terms are far better translated as "household" rather than "family." That said, the desire to come together and have children—to form families—was considered a natural part of human nature.[2] As only a man could legally hold power over those in the household, the whole idea of the Greek and Roman family was inherently patriarchal. A head of a household would be judged by his ability to control his wife, children, and slaves and his ability to sustain and ideally increase the household's landholdings and property, providing for the future of the family. An Athenian household of the fifth or fourth century B.C.E. would normally contain the husband, wife, and children and, at first sight, would appear to be a nuclear family residing in its own dwelling. However, single households were rarely autonomous and were part of a much wider kin group (*anchisteia*) that played an important role in family life. Athenians looked to these kin groups for the provision of marriage partners (endogamous marriage was common at Athens), to undertake legal responsibilities including dealing with inheritance, to share burial practices, and to exact vengeance on each other's behalf.[3] In classical Greek society, the continuation of the family line was dependent on sons, and it was ideal for a parent to have at least one son to carry on the family name and cult and maintain the family into the future. A household without sons or only a single daughter could face extinction, so several measures were put in place to ensure the survival of the *oikos* in such circumstances: if only an underage son survived his father, an adult guardian would be appointed until the son came of age; if a single daughter survived, the rules governing *epikleroi* would come into play; if there were no natural heirs, a *kyrios* could provide for the survival of his *oikos* through adoption.[4] In the case of a single daughter, her father could marry her to a male relative whom he would then adopt as his son, or he could adopt a male grandson if he survived long enough to see the child's birth. In legal and ideal terms, women played very little role in the maintenance and continuation of the family outside their key position as bearers of the next generation. However, while legal definitions give us an insight into the ideological framework in which society placed the family, they are not the whole story.

In Rome, the *familia* was defined in law as all those people and property in the power (*potestas*) of the *paterfamilias* (the oldest living male).[5] By the late first century B.C.E., the legal definition of the *familia* did not include his wife but did include his children and grandchildren by his sons as well as his slaves and freedmen. The father had control over all the economic assets of the household, and his children, even those of adult age, could not own property or do business on their own account or receive inheritances until either officially liberated by their father or, more likely, deemed legally independent (*sui iuris*) by his death. Roman law also gave a father the power of life and death over all in his *potestas*. Prior to the first century B.C.E., Roman wives, like their Athenian counterparts, left their natal homes and joined the families and inheritance networks of their husbands, who become their *paterfamilias*. By the late republic, this tradition had been superseded by a system that kept married women in the power of their own fathers. This meant they did not legally belong to the *familia* of their husband or their children, who were in the power of another.[6] This legal definition did not, of course, reflect the functioning of daily life: a married woman resided with her husband and their mutual offspring for the duration of the marriage. However, its implications in the case of marriage breakdown had consequences for the children, who would normally remain with their father's family rather than in the custody of their mothers.

To describe the conjugal group, Romans would not use the term *familia*, from which the modern word *family* is derived, but rather *domus* (which could also refer to the physical house) or simply terms like *mei* ("my people").[7] The underlying structure of the family in antiquity has many fundamental differences from that of the modern family in the West, but there are some common elements. Research undertaken by Richard Saller and Brent Shaw has demonstrated that funerary commemorations, for instance, were far more likely to be between husbands and wives or parents and children or brothers and sisters and even unrelated associates (patrons, freed slaves, and friends) than kin from the extended family network. This suggests that the primary focus of obligations, loyalty, perhaps affection (but this is harder to track), and duty of commemoration lay with the close family group, centered on what is now called the nuclear family.[8] As in Athens, the focus on the nuclear-type family does not preclude attention to the wider kin group. The Roman sense of family was also embedded in their ancestry and networks of support in which kinship relations were given priority over outsiders. One of the changes that came about in the Roman period was that men as often used their ancestry through their mother's family (cognates) as through their father's—depending on which put them in a better light or was more favorable to the occasion.

The definition of family as set out here has depended on ancient legal definitions that tend to simplify the complex interpersonal relationships that are the reality of family life. As a social institution the family was neither simple nor static. In both Greece and Rome, most homes contained slaves as well as the husband and wife and their offspring; during the life course of the household, children might grow up and leave, and aged parents (especially widowed mothers) might return. Over time, relationships between the conjugal group shifted as children grew and parents aged. Households might also alter through the death or divorce of a partner, remarriage, or the arrival of stepchildren or adopted sons. It should also be noted that this definition did not fit all the cultures of antiquity. For example, in Greco-Roman Egypt, the census data of the first to third century C.E. offers a view of a quite different set of family structures: brother-sister marriage was practiced, and evidence points to highly complex multiple and extended family groups where brothers and sisters were also husbands and wives who lived with each other, their parents and siblings, and all their offspring.[9] Over the long-term, however, the evidence of antiquity and the early medieval periods suggests that the nuclear family (albeit a fluid version) remained a common feature of both upper and lower classes in areas previously controlled by Rome.[10] Demographics supported by mortuary evidence suggest that a three generational family would be very rare, while testamentary evidence rarely mentions family outside of widows and children. Even by the seventh century C.E., demographics would have militated against anything like an extended grouping of three generations cohabiting.[11]

POWER DYNAMICS WITHIN THE FAMILY

Aristotle described the hierarchy of family relationships thus: the head of the *oikos* was the *kyrios*, governing his slaves as their master, his children as a sort of king because of their affection for him and his greater age, and his wife as a political leader. Several centuries later, early Christian texts expressed a similar hierarchy in the "household codes."[12] It was expected that the power structure of the public world would be mirrored in the private life of the family. Children would learn about the power dynamics of both family and the wider social world by observing relationships within the household. Sons and daughters would observe the subtle interactions between their parents and between parents and gradations of slaves; they would absorb the implicit gender roles and learn how to negotiate the social politics of adult lives as well as recognize their own position in the hierarchy. In antiquity, a hierarchy of power was based on a presumption of a natural order in which male was superior to female and the young should defer to their elders.

This deference was encouraged by the large age gap common between husband and wife. In Athens, girls were usually married between the ages of fourteen and eighteen to a young man of around thirty; in Rome, girls could legally be married at twelve and boys at fourteen, but the norm was rather different: girls married in their late teens to young men in their late twenties. Marriages were arranged by parents, guardians, or the wider kin group, and romance played little or no part in the process. Grooms, older and perhaps without fathers by the age they came to marry, may have had some say in the choice of partner, but daughters were likely to have to acquiesce to their parents' (or guardian's) wishes.[13] For both cultures, the point of marriage was the production of legitimate offspring in order to maintain the family into the future.

An Athenian wife who married moved, with her dowry, to a new *oikos*. Her husband replaced her father as her guardian (*kyrios*), and she became a member of his family. As the practice in Athens favored endogamous marriage, it is likely the bride and groom may have had some prior knowledge of each other from family occasions. For the young wife, this was the moment she left childhood behind and became an adult; she lost her virgin status to become a wife. She would also leave the *oikos* in which she had grown up to move to her

FIGURE 1.1: *Married couple.* Funerary relief of Publius Aiedius and his wife Aiedia from a monument on the Via Appia, Rome, ca. 99–50 B.C.E. Pergamum Museum, Berlin: image from Bridgeman Art Library.

husband's house, where she would most likely spend the rest of her life. This rather abrupt status change and the disparity in age between husband and wife would certainly have encouraged the sense of superiority and paternalism of the husband. The extent of this subordination can only be speculated about and may have been internalized by the young wife, causing the phenomenon to be invisible to men (and thus to us today): evidence from Greek comedy certainly shows that men could envisage a topsy-turvy world where women might take charge or subvert the social order by having affairs, but, on the whole, women were meant to be kept under control by their husbands and live their lives in private.[14] Husbands, ideally, would instruct their young wives on the running of the household and continue their wives' social education.[15] In Athens, women came completely under the power of their husbands, and their subordinate status was reinforced by a social system that excluded them from public life and an ideal that required them to live relatively segregated lives.[16] However, there was also a strong idea that husbands and wives should act in partnership for the mutual benefit of the *oikos*. In antiquity, romance might not play a part in the arrangement of a marriage, but companionship and harmony (*concordia* and *homonoia*) were meant to develop over time. Xenophon (430–350 B.C.E.) quoting Socrates (469–399 B.C.E.) states: "I believe that a wife who is a good partner plays an equal role with her husband in benefiting the household. Possessions come into the household mainly as a result of the husband's efforts, but most of the outgoings are under the wife's stewardship. If both do their jobs well, the household prospers, but if they do them badly the household is diminished."[17] The idea of equal roles needs some nuancing as some roles in antiquity were clearly not as equal as others, and not all commentators would agree with Xenophon: women were considered to be inferior in all sorts of ways, both physically and mentally. Like children, they required guidance and training in order to fulfill their social role and position. In material from Athens, the names of wives are rarely mentioned, but according to Isomachus, his new young wife (aged fourteen) welcomed her duties of supervising and training servants, organizing supplies both into and out of the house, tending sick slaves, kneading dough, and weaving. In his view, his wife demonstrated her innate intelligence by responding well to her husband's training.[18]

It is too easy to be taken in by the dominant discourse; other sources suggest not all Athenian wives fit into the submissive mold and not all Athenian husbands were overbearing masters. Speeches from orators and law courts offer views of partnerships that do not fit the ideal and of partnerships outside marriage. This material is not unproblematic—as it no more offers a direct reflection of daily life than the idealizing texts of the philosophers or the comedic world of the dramatists—but it does present alternatives worth taking into account as situations understood by society. In this material, women appear in control of the household finances and display competent knowledge of such matters, they act as witnesses, and they ferociously look after the interests of their children. Less-than-perfect wives are also seen making excuses to meet their lovers, and courtesans attempt to claim citizenship and legitimacy for their offspring.[19] As with most ideals, a large number of people failed to live up to them or perhaps did not aspire to them in the first place.

In the Roman world, a wife's place in the family evolved over time, as was discussed earlier in this chapter. The property of husband and wife was kept separate throughout a marriage, which gave an affluent Roman wife considerable economic, and thus social, power. For women, marriage and motherhood granted status; not to marry was regarded as both odd and unfortunate. Some wives may not have been directly involved in child care, but they were expected to be able to run a household. The standard epithets for a good wife included having children, working wool, and being thrifty, chaste, and loyal.[20] Nearly five centuries after Xenophon offered advice in the persona of Isomachus, Pliny the Younger (ca. 62–ca. 113 C.E.) wrote to his young wife's aunt about her exemplary behavior in a similar vein. He praises the thriftiness of Calpurnia, his wife, and claims her love for him is a sign of her virtue and that it has driven her to take an interest in literature—particularly his own writings, which she memorizes. She worries about his success in the courts and sits modestly behind a curtain to hear the praise he receives when reciting his works; she even spontaneously sets some of his poems to music.[21] This letter is a compliment to Calpurnia's aunt, who raised her niece to such an excellent standard as evidenced by her perfect wifely attitudes; it also says much about Pliny and what he expects as a husband. His letters give the impression of genuine affection for his wife, but they fail to tell us anything about Calpurnia's own feelings: has she internalized these values and is she happy to behave like a model wife or would she have preferred a husband a little younger and slightly less opinionated? Her opinion, like that of most wives in the ancient world, is lost to us.[22]

Segregation was not a part of Roman life, and wives accompanied their husbands to social gatherings, both private and public. A wife's social circle would not be as wide as her husband's, perhaps, but her life was not as constrained as that of her Athenian counterpart. Joint decision making over the lives of their mutual children was one aspect of the *concordia* (marital harmony) hoped for between husband and wife. The letters of Cicero to his wife, Terentia, demonstrate a partnership that offered emotional, social, and financial support. Those written during his exile (58–57 B.C.E.) mention how much he misses her and his children and how he worries about the "most faithful and best of wives."[23] The relationship between Cicero and Terentia also demonstrates a wife's ability to run her husband's affairs while he is absent, organize her children's lives and arrange a marriage (overriding her husband's favored candidate), and use her own finances to maintain the family.[24] Such independence in wives did not subvert cultural ideals so long as their actions were considered in the best interests of the family; this also demonstrates that society was not constrained by its own ideals and that these ideals adapted over time to suit changed social practices. Cicero's family history also offers a dose of reality in that, despite the affectionate letters of the 50s B.C.E., Terentia and Cicero divorced after thirty years of marriage.

Parent-child relations in antiquity were framed by the assumed social hierarchy of control and power on the part of the parents and respect and obedience from the child. The presumption of affection is harder to ascertain, but certain evidence suggests that affection between parents and children, however culturally constructed, was considered a part of human nature. A child was not an automatic member of the family; instead, the child had to be acknowledged and accepted by the father before he or she was given the right to be raised within the family. There has long been a debate about parental affection in the historiography of the ancient family.[25] One side argues that parents did not invest emotionally in their offspring until they were of an age likely to survive given the high rate of infant death. Two ancient practices are often used to support this argument: one is the practice of exposing or abandoning newborn infants, the other is the common use of wet nurses. There is an extensive discussion of exposure in modern scholarship; here, it is enough to say that it was often simply a pragmatic decision in the ancient world and to stress that abandoning a child was not equivalent to infanticide, as many babies were picked up and raised by others. Infants could be abandoned if they were considered less than physically perfect (this was particularly so in Sparta), if the family simply did not have the resources to feed an extra mouth, or if there were questions over legitimacy. It is unlikely a firstborn child would be exposed unless seriously deformed and perhaps girls were more likely abandoned than boys—however, the evidence for both of these assumptions is scanty. This is not to say that exposure was universally approved. There was a presumption that abandoned children were likely to end up as slaves or prostitutes, but laws to prevent the practice were not enacted until the fourth century C.E.[26] The practice of wet-nursing has also been used in the affection debate. It has been read as a form of institutionalized neglect by some modern authors, and even ancient commentators were a little worried about it: In Athens, poor Athenians rather than slaves or outsiders were preferred as nurses. Tacitus (first century C.E.) expressed concern that children were imbibing servile manners with a nurse's milk and criticized mothers who wished to spend their time doing things other than caring for their children.[27] Wet-nursing, however, was common and recommended by some doctors (see chapter 9). Both these practices, it can also be argued, support the existence of parental affection: the abandonment of one child might favor the survival of other children already in the family; wet-nursing was considered by tradition to be best practice for both child and mother, and, thus, parents were given guidance on how to choose the best woman for the job. Indeed, nurses often had long and, it seems, affectionate relationships with their charges. Pliny the Younger bought a farm to provide for his nurse in her old age, and Augustine, writing in the early fifth century C.E., talks about the elderly nurse who had been his grandfather's wet nurse, had looked after his own mother during her childhood, and, coming with Monica on her marriage to her new home, had ended her days looking after Augustine and his brother and sister.[28]

Alternative evidence can be read as showing deep affection for children: parents indulge childish manners and desires, educate their children themselves, and mourn their early deaths.[29] Representations of children in the visual media of Greece and Rome emphasize their physical childish qualities and the activities of childhood. Chubby children are depicted pushing trolleys or animal carts and playing games or with tiny birds, animals, and an assortment of toys.[30] The cultural construction of affective bonds between parents and children must be acknowledged. Suzanne Dixon has made the point, for instance, that modern historians should beware of oversentimentalizing motherhood; however, mothers (or female figures) are more closely associated with small children than fathers. On Attic vase paintings, for instance, mothers appear with children in domestic scenes far more frequently than fathers (or male figures), and some fifth century B.C.E. Tanagra figures show women cooking meals and feeding and bathing a baby. The Roman mother was also associated with young children and is portrayed in some images as interacting with small infants, but she was equally as likely as her husband to be a figure of authority in her own home, rather than an indulgent intercessor.[31] The cultural understanding of family structure, especially the need for legitimate children to maintain the family and look after aging parents, framed parental affection in a way no longer common in the modern urban West.

The power of the Roman father is a case in point. By law, the father (or the oldest living male of a family) had, in theory, the right of life and death over all his children until his own death. The clearest expression of the power of life

FIGURE 1.2: *Tanagra figure of woman cooking, watched by girl, 500–475* B.C.E. *from Boiotia, Greece*. Museum of Fine Arts, Boston. Museum purchase with funds donated by contribution. Photograph © Museum of Fine Arts, Boston.

FIGURE 1.3: *Attic red figure* chous *showing small girl, bird.* Worcester Art Museum, Worcester, Massachusetts, bequest of Sarah C. Garver (Mrs. Austin S. Garver). 1931.56.

and death was the decision to raise or reject a child. Roman children, however old (and even if married themselves), were dependent on their father for all resources.[32] In reality, paternal power was very rarely taken to its extremes and was militated against by a number of factors—not least demographics. Saller has shown that even with an optimistic assessment, fifty percent of men over thirty would be lucky to have a living father.[33] After the death of the father, all his children—daughters as well as sons—became legally independent (*sui iuris*). If they were underage, they would be provided with a guardian who would deal with all business matters.[34] Paternal power was also balanced by the virtue of *pietas,* a key element of Roman identity: on a civic level it meant duty to the gods and the state; on a private level it meant a duty of mutual care and respect between parents and children. Children owed a duty of respect and honor to their parents and were expected to return the care given to their upbringing by looking after their parents in their old age. In Athens, the care of parents was a legal obligation. Parents were expected to raise and educate their children, arrange suitable marriages for them, and name them in their wills.[35] This makes parent-child relationships in antiquity sound like a contract—the social reality was different, of course, but the underlying assumptions are important to bear in mind.

SIBLINGS

Sibling relationships are likely to be the longest close family relationships in an individual's life course. There is very little information from antiquity on sibling relationships during early childhood, but the closeness exhibited between adult siblings presumably was grounded in a shared experience at a young age. There is some visual evidence from classical Greece that may show siblings. Small boys and girls are shown sharing childish activities on miniature *choes* (vases presented to boys at the Anthesteria festival): playing with dogs, tortoises, birds, and other pets; shaking rattles; riding on miniature chariots; and holding hoops for dogs to jump through. There are over a thousand of these vases extant today, and they demonstrate the full range of childish activities.[36] Even if not demonstrating sibling behavior, they offer a rare insight into a child's life (figure 1.3). There are also several grave stele that show boys and girls together, but again their relationship is often ambiguous. One famous example does make the relationship explicit. This image shows a naked youth holding an *aryballos* (a small flask for oil associated with gymnasium activities). The youth drapes his arm in a protective manner over a smaller female figure standing by his side.[37] The difference in height may represent a difference

FIGURE 1.4: *Marble stele (grave marker) of a youth and a little girl from Attica, Greece, ca. 530 B.C.E.* On the base is the inscription: "To dead Me[gakles], on his death, his father and dear mother set [me] up as a monument." Metropolitan Museum of Art, Frederick C. Hewitt Fund, 1911, Rogers Fund 1921, Anonymous Gift, 1951 (11.185a-c, f, g). Image © Metropolitan Museum of Art.

in age but may also signify the relative importance of sons and daughters (figure 1.4). Several inscriptions suggest that a close relationship between Athenian brothers and sisters continued into adult life. The notion of attachment between brothers—with each other and their half siblings—is a regular theme in Greek rhetoric: brothers are meant to support each other in court cases.[38] Love between siblings was framed by the prevailing age and gender attitudes; older siblings deserved respect by virtue of age and were also expected to take responsibility for their younger brothers and sisters. When brothers did fall out, it was often caused by disagreements over status (older brothers not being given enough respect) or inheritance.

In Rome, siblings of a similar age were expected to share an early childhood within the house. The work of Richard Saller, however, does suggest that large families were rare and that there might have been large age gaps between siblings.[39] Again from Rome, Cicero offers the most intimate insight. The letters of Cicero and his younger brother Quintus indicate close interest in each other's private lives, especially the moods of their wives and the upbringing of their children. They manage each other's affairs in event of a brother's absence; Cicero has no qualms about interfering in his brother's failing marriage and cares about his nephew, taking him with his own son, Marcus, to Cilicia in 51 B.C.E. He also arranges Quintus's *toga virilis* ceremony.[40] It appears from the letters that Cicero's and Quintus's sons grew up together and were a rare example of close cousins, born about eighteen months apart. They were closer in age than Cicero's own son and daughter: Tullia was of marriageable age when her brother Marcus was born.[41] Interestingly, perhaps as a consequence of marriage traditions in the late Roman republic (where wives did not legally enter their husband's *familia*), it seems that wives often favored the interests of their brothers and sisters rather than their husbands.[42]

FAMILY ABUSE AND VIOLENCE

The ancient world was a slave-owning society. With a recognized inferior and subordinate class in the household, most children would have grown up well aware of implicit levels of potential violence and an innate understanding of their own status.[43] Abuse of wives and freeborn children within the household is not commonly documented as it reflected badly on the husband/father, but it was clearly not unknown: Caligula, a notoriously tyrannical emperor, killed his wife, and even Constantine, known to history as the first Christian emperor, was rumored to have had his wife murdered.[44] Augustine praised his own mother for understanding that violence from a husband was to be expected but could be alleviated or avoided by behaving in subservient ways. His assumption that wives were regularly beaten suggests that spousal violence outside the imperial family was not uncommon.[45] The acceptance of a certain level of domestic violence is also evidenced in Justinian's repeal of an earlier law of Theodosius, which had made it possible for a wife to divorce her husband for abuse, replacing the punishment with a fine.[46]

Although in both Athens and Rome the physical punishment of pupils was an expected part of education—with school masters having a reputation for beating their charges—it was not considered good form for fathers to beat their sons. A correct *paterfamilias* differentiated the treatment of his children from that of his slaves: physical abuse in the form of beatings and kicking should be aimed at slaves, not sons. The very act of whipping demeaned both the son and the father: it put the son on par with a slave and demonstrated a father who could control neither himself, nor his sons. It humiliated them both.[47] Philosophers encouraged parents to tread a middle path where children should be coerced into right behavior: they should be praised and encouraged, they should not be spoilt and should not be put in a position where they might have to act in a servile way, and they should be reasoned with.[48] However, in a sense this is an academic nicety. Greek and Roman fathers (and mothers) had the right to beat their children, and faced with a recalcitrant son or daughter, would philosophical reasoning have restrained them? Perhaps, but equally this might not have been the case.

The role of the child in the family was somewhat redefined by Christian teachings, but to what extent this might have changed actual behavior is debatable—a concern for souls did not necessarily translate to a general concern for physical care.[49] Some canon and imperial laws suggest that practices such as exposure or selling of children came to face both moral censure and legal penalties. In the fourth century, parents who sold their children into slavery faced excommunication, and imperial legislation ruled that children who were abandoned by their parents could not later be reclaimed.[50] Churches became places where abandoned or unwanted infants could be brought, and children unreclaimed by their parents became the property of the finders. It is hard to claim these laws were concerned with the actual welfare of the children rather than their loss of status; some were more concerned that abandoned children might be forced into prostitution and in the future a father might unknowingly commit incest. Exposure was finally outlawed by Justinian in 541 C.E.,[51] although any perusal of modern newspapers demonstrates that legislation will not affect the behavior of desperate parents even today.

CHILDREN IN MARGINALIZED FAMILIES

In antiquity, legitimate marriage was narrowly defined, and to a certain extent any quasi-marital relationship outside of this privileged group could be defined as marginal—slave marriage is a case in point. A slave's body was entirely the property of his or her master or mistress, and both could find themselves subject to sexual advances. If allowed, slaves could form unions and have children of their own, but these relationships were entirely at the master's whim. In Athens and Rome, children of slaves were one way of keeping up the supply of servants. Slave children could have very hard and short lives. They could be sold as infants or simply enter the slave ranks of the household, where their treatment depended entirely on their master's tendency to tolerance or cruelty. Slaves were always at a disadvantage; even as children the potential for abuse was high. In Rome, some young slaves were kept for their cuteness qualities as attractive accessories. The position of these *deliciae* was ambiguous, but some were certainly used as sexual playthings by their masters and discarded once they reached puberty.[52] Some lucky young slaves might be raised by their owners as quasi-offspring. In Rome, these children, known as *vernae*, appear to have held a privileged position. They could be playmates for the master's own children (indeed, they could be one of his own children by a slave mother) and were allowed to stay close to their parents. Roman families might also have included children known as *alumni*. This is often translated as "foster children," but their status is ambiguous and hard to define; they appear not to be sons or daughters or slaves but could take on all these roles. Inscriptional evidence suggests they could be freed at an early age in recognition of bonds of affection and, once freed, could inherit from their foster parents.[53] Rome was rare among slave-owning societies in that manumission was a real hope for some slaves, particularly those in urban households. This was not due entirely to altruism on the masters' part: slaves often bought their freedom, thus in effect replacing themselves in the system. However, freedmen and women, whose children had free status, formed a large social group in Roman society, and their desire to create legitimate families of their own and advertise the fact forms a very influential part of the visual imagery of Roman families. The social mobility within the Roman Empire allowed many sons of freedmen to make very successful lives.[54]

Groups that were socially marginalized by poverty or lack of family support suffered in antiquity unless they were lucky enough to find a patron to provide for them (see chapters 2 and 7 on state support offered in classical antiquity). In late antiquity, the establishment of Christianity had positive effects for some of the more vulnerable groups in society: widows, orphans, and the elderly. This support was not uniform and was often hard to provide or maintain, but a rhetoric of charitable almsgiving was developed that identified widows, including young mothers and their children, and orphans as within a bishop's duty of care, and a tradition of *xenodochia* (guest houses) developed. These provided the basic necessities of food and shelter for the needy. Houses expressly for children were established by the fifth century.[55]

The evidence for childhood and the family is fragmentary throughout the period covered by this volume, and it is not consistent in its fragmentary nature. A different picture appears from law codes than from personal letters, histories, inscriptions, or material culture. While it is tempting to try and create a normalizing image of the family across time, it must be remembered that the ideals and rhetoric that frame family life in the classical and early medieval period are in some ways very alien to any modern understanding of the family. That said, couples came together and shared the upbringing of their children even if their aspirations for and expectations of family life were vastly different across time and cultures.

CHAPTER TWO

Community

RAY LAURENCE

At the very center of the study of antiquity lies the ancient city, or *polis* (a sociopolitical form reproduced across the Mediterranean and adapted and reproduced across northwest Europe by Rome), governed by adult males within which citizen women had a set of rights but not equality with men. The extensive literature on the city reveals much about the nature of ancient communities, but the place of children and the family within the city has been neglected.[1] It is worth noting at the outset that it is the community's interaction with children that we can recover in antiquity. The family was a concern of the community, but most of the evidence for this comes from legal systems developed by the state and forms the subject matter of chapter 6. The focus of this chapter is on the child in the community and, specifically, two intertwined themes: the first deals with mapping the social and spatial aspects of the community as the location of childhood; the second focuses on how the community regulates and imposes order on the lives of children. Most of our evidence for children in the community, or the community's attempts to control children in antiquity, is derived from two cities: Athens and Rome. Our discussion oscillates between these locations, but it ends with a consideration of the survival of family and community structures after the disintegration of the Roman Empire in the West from the fifth century C.E.

CHILDREN AND THE ANCIENT CITY

The *polis* was defined in antiquity by two aspects of its existence: as an urban center and its hinterland and as a political community. The latter has taken on a dominant role due to numerous texts referring to offices held by men as often recorded in inscriptions. This slants our vision of the city toward the male elite with infrequent references to women. This view can be justified by the fact that in antiquity the city was conceived as made up of a community of households (Athens was composed of more than ten thousand of these) and a series of public spaces that included temples, a market place (*agora* or *forum*), roads, the gymnasium (*palaestra*), theaters (and later amphitheatres and circuses), buildings and spaces for government and decision making, city walls, and harbors.[2] Quite a number of a city's institutions were exclusive to its adult male citizens and might exclude outsiders such as the young and women. Also, we need to remember that for commentators like Aristotle the size of the city was not dependent on total population but instead on the number of citizens, which equaled the number of free males of military age. The preconceptions in our sources—which view a city as made up of an adult male group (citizens) and constructed from houses and households in which these adult males act as head of the household—cause freeborn women as well as freeborn children (let alone slaves and foreigners) to disappear from the relevant literature.[3] Yet the *polis*, with its focus on its own internal logic as a political community, was reproduced over many generations and survived as an idea from 500 B.C.E. to at least 300 C.E. As institutions, ancient cities produced generation after generation of adult citizens, and when new cities were founded in the lands of former barbarians, the construction of the physical city—with its temples, marketplaces, and houses—was accompanied by the training of the sons of the leading local men.[4] With these positive developments of the city came the negative aspects: colonnades, baths, and lavish dinners—aspects of the city that were seen as threatening, not least to the young. This is, of course, an adult viewpoint, but it expresses a concern for the production of future citizens—the ancient city's amenities were both a benefit and a threat to the process of creating adult males for the future.

The ancient city was not really concerned with regulating the lives of children within their families or household. Children were, for the most part, private beings subject to the authority of a father. It was, however, the duty of the city or community to ensure a substitute father in the form of a guardian was appointed to care for orphans.[5] Of course, children were subject to the community's surveillance of their lives within their homes and at a neighborhood level, but the city itself did not need to intervene or create opportunities with children in mind until they were much older. Often, when a child was understood to be in the process of becoming an adult, intervention was seen to be necessary and a matter of public, as opposed to purely private, concern.[6] Typically, the concerns of city authorities in antiquity were directed toward the regulation of the lives of young men over the age of fourteen and young women approaching marriage. This represents a period of time in which these individuals had technically ceased to be children but had not reached the age of majority. They were, to use Aristotle's words, citizens "by presumption," or incomplete citizens lacking the competence of adults.[7]

CORRUPTING THE YOUNG: A CIVIC CRIME?

There is a certain irony in the fact that what many people today see as the freest city in antiquity, democratic Athens (508–322 B.C.E.), was the location for the persecution and death of its freest thinker—Socrates—on a charge of corrupting the young. However, this crime was not unique to democratic Athens. In republican Rome, we find Catiline corrupting young supporters through the provision of favors, bribes, sex, and other means. Philosophers seem to have been the culprits in the discourse of corrupting the young in Rome, as well as in Athens: the reforming tribune Tiberius Gracchus (133 B.C.E.) was seen to gain some of his more radical plans for land reform and poor relief from a philosopher, Blossius of Cumae. In the Roman Empire, the general Agricola managed in his youth to avoid straying too deeply into philosophy— thanks to his mother's intervention.[8] Underlying these cases strewn across the history of antiquity is a fear that an adult from outside the family might gain a hold over the young and lead them astray from the right path. The community in crisis and the actions taken to remedy a crisis are seldom directed at older children or young adults but at the older men, often considered intellectuals or philosophers, who led them astray. In contrast, the young were seen as malleable victims who needed to be set back onto the correct path.[9] This reveals an anxiety about the place of children and young adults in the cities of the ancient world, a fear of what they might become and a need to regulate their thinking and behavior. This fear was perhaps reinforced by the demographic fact that there were more young adult males than there were men at any other adult stage of life.[10] Moreover, these young adults, as we have seen, were regarded as unstable. As a consequence, it was thought that young men tended to support conspiracies and thus needed to be regulated and advised by older men. For example, the pontifex maximus (head priest)

Publius Cornelius Scipio Nasica Corculum, in his midforties, felt the need to control the reforming zeal of his younger cousin, Tiberius Gracchus, by leading senators in an attack that resulted in Tiberius's murder.[11] Lacking the legal niceties of the case against Socrates in Athens, Scipio Nasica's removal of Tiberius Gracchus is a case of community action underwritten by a perceived need to regulate the actions of its younger members. These are extreme cases, as we see the regulation of young men and children for the most part taking place in the actions of fathers and mothers cajoling their offspring.[12] However, these accounts of community crisis make clear that the young, whether in democratic Athens or imperial Rome, were regarded with suspicion, and their training was a matter of public concern as well as something to be dealt with by their parents or guardian.

THE CITY AND ITS CHILDREN

At the heart of the establishment of the Greek *polis* was collective action. The experience of this aspect of the city occurred in middle to late childhood—sometimes in schools, but often in the forms of clubs or messes where young men gathered. Aristotle saw these institutions as the breeding ground of independence and self-confidence and at the heart of the production of the culture of the city.[13] These institutions were widespread and can be charted across the Greek world in the presence of the *Ephebia;* in pre-Roman Italy, there is evidence of a similar set of associations defined by the word *Vereia* in the Oscan language; and in the Roman Empire, we can locate a similar institution in the *Collegium* of *Iuvenes*.[14] Membership in these institutions occurred in late childhood or young adulthood and can be regarded as part of the training to become a citizen and participate in civic life. Such institutions moved the individual into a wider social and civic world from that associated with their kin and neighbors and seem to have been established for the wider development of a conception of citizenship and a sense of belonging to a city.[15]

These institutions revolved around a gymnasium, a basic open court with a running track developed in the fourth century B.C.E. in Greece. The pre-Roman *Vereia* at Pompeii was centered around a number of *palaestrae*, or colonnaded rectangular spaces located close to the triangular forum that enclosed the running track and a temple dedicated to the city's founding deity, Hercules. It is clear that in the Greek East, some cities possessed three gymnasia: one for boys, one for *ephebes*, and another for young men.[16] Bathing facilities were often located close by, and later, under the emperor Augustus, new spaces were built to include large swimming pools—as can be seen in the large *palaestra* in

Pompeii adjacent to the amphitheatre or in Agrippa's *stagnum* in Rome, adjacent to the training ground of the Campus Martius. These were public spaces for the training of the young and subject to the scrutiny of the city authorities. Not surprisingly, it was here, under the gaze of the city magistrates, that teaching was carried out by grammarians and rhetoricians, whose salaries may have been paid by the city.[17] There is evidence for language learning in private, but what we see in the gymnasia of Greece and the *palaestrae* or *porticus* of the Roman world are public spaces in which physical and mental exercise were combined under the gaze of other citizens.

YOUNG MEN AND THE COMMUNITY

Stories of young Spartans lying in ambush all night to commit daring thefts were famous both in antiquity and today. The veracity of these tales of daring need not concern us, but instead we must heed their importance as repeated hundreds of years later in the Roman Empire; these stories portray the respect of a culture that did not punish a daring deed carried out by a young man, however illegal, and instead chose to punish the man for his inability to accomplish the task without discovery.[18] Young men were also reputed to have roamed the cities of the Roman Empire at night, attacking others. The emperor Nero famously went about the city of Rome at night in disguise with his young associates, attacking, robbing, and committing burglaries as well as sexually assaulting both women and men. His only real crime was his discovery when a senator fought back only to recognize his assailant and apologize—the story spread prior to the senator's suicide.[19] Within years of this event, a bloodbath occurred at the games held in the amphitheater at Pompeii. Visitors from the neighboring town of Nuceria were attacked by the *iuvenes* (youths) of Pompeii. This event was celebrated as a great victory in a number of houses in Pompeii; in the house of Actius Anicetus the events were captured in a wall painting that dominated the peristyle (rear courtyard). The Nucerians sought redress in Rome, and a ban on games was imposed on Pompeii by the senate.[20] The cities of the ancient world had no institutional structure to police violence. Rome, a city of over a million inhabitants, only gained a police force in the form of urban cohorts with the accession of the emperor Augustus (31 B.C.E.–14 C.E.). Even in Rome, where there were soldiers to police the city, violence was a persistent feature of urban living, and the soldiers also had a reputation for handing out beatings; seldom, however, did the emperor send troops against his own people.[21]

Youthful violence, however, does not destroy the community and appears to have been embedded within the structure of urban society; it was policed

FIGURE 2.1: *The Forum of Pompeii destroyed in 79* C.E. The forum was the central space in which the community met and was a place over which the gods presided, as seen here in relation to the Capitolium temple (photo: Ray Laurence).

not by armed soldiers (policemen) but rather by rumor, discussion, and court action. In 415 B.C.E., the Athenian assembly made the decision to send an expedition of sixty ships to Sicily and was led in that decision by a youthful thirty-five-year-old (Alcibiades) in debate with a man in his fifties (Nicias). Behind the younger man were the youths of the city and the rashness associated in antiquity with young men. This is classic ancient thinking in action—wrong decisions lay in the hands of young men and children. Alcibiades's popularity rested on him providing, at his own expense, choruses at the plays held at festivals—an action guaranteed to appeal to the young.[22] A key factor in the decision of the assembly, we are told, was its composition by age: the older generation had been decimated by plague (430–29 B.C.E.), and the population was only just recovering; as a consequence, there were a far greater number of younger men voting in the assembly than formerly. In this debate over the wisdom of going to war, the nocturnal activities of some older children or youths caused a great stir. Hermes set up throughout the city in front of houses and in sacred places were mutilated at night.[23] Resident aliens in the city (*metics*) stated that drunken young men had previously mutilated other statues, and blame focused on Alcibiades and his young friends. He was accused of attempting to overthrow the democracy of Athens as well as sacrilege. A witch hunt followed, and stories tell of young aristocrats taking part and secret meetings in the theater with up to three hundred attending. The law against torture was suspended. However, a confession came from another source: the members of a single dining club, a *heteira,* were responsible for the mutilation of the herms, and the original tale of a conspiracy was exactly that. The culprits were hunted down and brought to trial—those who fled could be legitimately killed. The expedition to Sicily failed, and Alcibiades was duly brought to book; the actions of a group of drunken youths formed a significant part of the accusation that he wished to overthrow democracy, and he fled into exile.[24] This entire episode of Athenian history is full of rumor and hearsay about the actions of young men to the point where it was the young, as opposed to the citizen body, who were blamed for the decision to send ships to Sicily. This perception of the predominance of young men in the assembly depends on taking the sources at face value and believing that the city's population had actually recovered. However, this would seem unlikely given that the assembly occurred only fifteen years after the plague.[25] This demonstrates the ability of the community to police the actions of its younger members by acting on rumors and hearsay and to attribute disastrous collective decisions to one group in the community—young adults. The decree of impeachment against Alcibiades mentions actions taking place in his home, the form of dress he wore, and the words he used in private.[26] Verbal accusations of extravagance, the breeding of horses, debts, sex with prostitutes, and sex with older men can be found elsewhere with reference to Alcibiades; similar elements can be found in Rome in Cicero's defense of the young Caelius Rufus some three hundred and fifty years later. Cicero's defense was based on the understanding that good-looking, rich young men attract all sorts of rumors—many of Rome's leading statesmen had less-than-savory reputations in their youth. Rumor and hearsay in the ancient city created a mechanism by which the actions of youths were placed under scrutiny, discussed in public and, in extreme cases, policed via the courts.[27]

BOYS AND THE POLITICAL COMMUNITY

At the age of six, the child Numerius Popidius Celsinus was nominated onto the town council of Pompeii. The reason for this extraordinary action was that he had rebuilt, at his own expense, the city's temple of Isis, which had been destroyed in an earthquake. At the heart of these actions was that the child's father was a former slave and, hence, excluded from joining the town council. Other examples of children serving on the town council at Pompeii are known, so Numerius Popidius should not be regarded as unique. From another Italian town, Canusium, we have a list of town councilors from 223 C.E.[28] Alongside one hundred adult members of the town council are listed twenty-five *praetextati,* or those who wear the childhood toga. It is unclear what this group did, as they certainly did not vote on decisions—but they might have been entitled to other privileges derived from being *decurions*—members of the local ruling classes. It was not impossible for young men to hold their first office prior to the age of majority, and magistrates as young as seventeen have been identified.[29] All these young men had to do to gain office was be elected to a magistracy for a single year.

The unique evidence from Pompeii of notices (*programmata*) set up by residents supporting a candidate provide us with an insight into the social networks from which these men drew their support. The supporters' notices also allow us to see into the social world of males who had just transitioned into the adult world. Interestingly, there is a great variety in the number and types of supporters, and there is no generic pattern to permit modern scholars to identify the factors important in elections.[30] The language of these notices defines the candidate as a fine or upright young man—he has no political record, and, reading the evidence, the social world the notices evoke is that of a boy needing the support of those who know him: his neighbors, the innkeeper across the street, fellow candidates, clients, groups of craft workers, and even more dubious groups such as late drinkers. The fact that these supporters do not map directly onto the results of elections is confirmed by the presence of notices of support on the part of women (none of whom were voters).[31] Here we have evidence of the social world of young men within Pompeii, structured quite differently depending on the individual involved, with men accounting for a far greater proportion of a young man's social world than women by about ten times.[32] This factor points to a community that was not totally divided by gender; however, gender was a fundamental factor in the construction of a person's social world within the city. Also, the distribution of these notices tends to cluster within the vicinity of a candidate's place of residence, underlining the fact that such young men had not completed the transition from the social world of childhood, centered on their home and its neighborhood, to that of a citizen known throughout the city. They are almost there, but only after their first magistracy (the *aedileship*) would the transition have been completed.[33]

FROM GIRLS TO VIRGINS: CATEGORIZING THE FEMALE CHILD

Gender distinctions were established at birth with the first pronouncement of the midwife: whether the child was male or female. There is evidence that the poor regarded boys as preferable to girls with the result that there may have been a greater frequency of exposure of girls than boys, which may have produced an unequal sex ratio.[34] We should also consider the possibility that male children might have received more nourishment than female children; perhaps it is significant that a marriage contract from Judaea stipulates that daughters were to be "nourished and clothed." Indeed, there is evidence that in Greece (with the exception of Sparta), male children were given more food than female children.[35] The frequency of exposure and the level of differential nourishment are impossible to establish (see chapter 6), but what the evidence does tell us is that the experience of childhood was distinguished according to whether you were a boy or a girl.

The effect of being a girl rather than a boy affected the individual's interaction with the city. Girls may have learned to read (on education see chapter 5), but physical exercise in a gymnasium seems to have been a male affair. Interestingly, the literate female was represented rather differently from the literate male in carved images found on late Roman sarcophagi, and we may conclude that learning in childhood produced a different intellectualized adult according to gender; we may also assume that the nature of education was different in childhood according to gender. At home, at least in the ideal upper-class house in classical Athens, women were segregated from males and were considered better off staying indoors.[36] This phenomenon might have a wider application than appreciated by modern writers on the subject and might be evidenced in the Roman context: female bodies in Pompeian wall painting feature pale skin tones, whereas male bodies were characteristically bronzed.[37] The door of the house was a boundary that separated a world outside from the domestic realm that was the expected *habitus* of a girl or young woman and segregated her from men. What we can see, though, at least in the Roman context, is that the home was inhabited by women, children, and slaves—even if its decoration and spatial structure highlighted the presence of a male head of the household— and there is good evidence from Greece that women managed the household. However, our source material highlights the surveillance and critique of females, particularly in drama, who talked to men, asked passersby for information, and even opened the main door to the house themselves. Women, including girls and young adults, helped their friends when pregnant, borrowed provisions from neighbors, and visited the houses of friends, but they did not have the same spatial range across the city as their male equivalents.[38] The *oikos* or the *domus* was their locale, whereas, at least in Rome, the male elite would have spent seven hours of the day outside the house in the forum or the agora, frequently intersecting with the wider community. When girls ventured out, their dress was indicative of their status—freeborn citizens walked through the city and expected not to be subject to verbal and sexual abuse from men.[39] Not everything was provided for them within their home or those of their neighbors; bathing took place outside the house and was likely to have occurred either in separate baths from those of men or at different hours of the day. There are, of course, periods of time in the ancient world—notably the first century C.E.—from which we do have evidence for mixed bathing.[40] What perhaps needs to be remembered is that the act of bathing was undertaken with a view to its medical benefits to the body, which were perceived to be quite different according to gender, and the information we have for boys suggests variation according to age as well.[41]

The appearance of girls in religious rituals associated with festivals offers a public recognition of their existence within the wider community than that of their family, kin, and neighbors. Girls at festivals seem to have been differentiated from adult women and younger children—they were defined as virgins.[42] The most revealing example of age-related service in rituals comes from the remote Athenian sanctuary of the goddess Artemis at Brauron. Athenian girls between the ages of five and ten served as "bears" at the sanctuary during the year of the festival, which was held every five years. Their variation in ages was due to the fact that all girls had the opportunity to serve as bears, and we can expect a fair amount of age mixing with the oldest bear entering service to the goddess at nine and the youngest aged five. Obviously, those turning ten would have had a higher prominence than younger girls during the year of service at the sanctuary. The age of ten for Athenian girls marked a point transition from child to potential marriage partner and coincided with Roman preferences for the age of betrothal of girls. Service as a bear also can be seen as a premenarche rite of passage that resulted in the recategorization of these girls as entering the phase of puberty, also signified physically by the appearance of pubic hair or the development of breasts. The fact that service to Artemis was a public action advertised these girls as future marriage partners and ensured their transition to puberty was recognized, both by the participant as a bear and by the community as onlookers. This could be described as a way for the community to control the unpredictable phase of the female life course that led up to menarche.[43] This example demonstrates that the community sought to control the transition from female child to pubescent or marriageable woman via the public performance of service to Artemis. In so doing, ritual performance aligns or shapes the future of marriageability attained after menarche while recognizing their premarital status as virgins rather than girls.[44]

THE COMMUNITY AND THE SUPPORT OF CHILDREN

Wherever we look in antiquity, we can identify a concern with what we now call demographic decline. For most communities, its citizens were its soldiers, and young adults in their late teens undertook military training.[45] What concerned the ancients was the possibility of not having enough soldiers in the future, which was seen as a consequence of their fellow citizens' unwillingness to have children.[46] This is not just rhetoric; the foundation of the colony of Cosa in 273 B.C.E.—a new community made up of 3,500 families—provides both archaeological and textual evidence that allows us to begin to understand the phenomenon. Seventy-five years later, the colony was asking for additional colonists to be sent, as were other cities in Italy. Dominic Rathbone has suggested that colonies such as Cosa would experience a "natural" decline in their population at a rate of a half percent per annum simply because these communities had no way of creating new citizens via immigration—these were closed communities subject to depletion through warfare.[47] The ancient explanation of this phenomenon was rather different: due to poverty, citizens ceased to be willing to take part in military service and were equally unwilling to bring up children, who would have served in the army in the future. The exposure of unwanted children was linked to a desire not to bring up children in poverty. Cities could be wiped out through the action of migration, ineffectual biological reproduction, or poverty. At about the same time these ideas were expressed in the Roman republic there was a virtual cessation of the founding of colonies.[48]

Not surprisingly, men and women who produced large numbers of children gained greater respect from neighbors and from the community of the city as a whole.[49] There was a desire on the part of these cities, or the state authority in the shape of Roman imperial patronage, to ensure communities survived into the future. When faced with a food shortage in the third century B.C.E., the city of Samos appointed corn commissioners—one of whom, Boulagoras son of Alexis, had been a strict controller of the gymnasium. This man chose to provide, from his own funds, money for the purchase of food at no return from the community. Afterward, Boulagoras was crowned with a golden crown when the tragedies were performed as part of the festival of Dionysius.[50] This form of charity, in which an individual made a gift to the community (rather than to an individual via patronage or testamentary procedures) and as a result received a position of honor, has been systematically investigated by scholars of antiquity and is described by the term *euergetism*. Banquets associated with festivals were the most frequent benefactions to a community, often stipulating that not just adults but also freeborn children and even the children of slaves could dine.[51] One scheme, known as the *alimenta* and set up originally under the emperors Nerva and Trajan, looks as though it was intended to resuscitate Italian agriculture via a system of loans. From the interest on these loans, children were

FIGURE 2.2: *The Arch of Benevento constructed in 114* C.E. This scene represents the establishment of the Alimenta represented by the goddess carrying the (now fragmentary) plough (photo: Ray Laurence).

paid a monthly allowance. However, it is clear that at the time these sums were not paid to the neediest but instead were distributed to those who were of the greatest importance or highest status—significantly, in most of these schemes, boys received rather more than girls.[52] It is only later in the fifth century, when the Christian ideals of helping a needy poor had developed, that the *alimenta* was regarded as relieving poverty. By that time, Christian emperors had issued edicts that newborn children should be provided for in an attempt to prevent the sale of children and limit infanticide.[53] The pre-Christian distributions emphasized and reinforced the structure of the community by providing more for those of higher status and somewhat more for males than females rather than ensuring the demographic survival of the needy.[54] However, this should not cause us to dismiss these communities as not concerned with the support of children and the continued survival of their community. The provision of money was directed at those best able to bring up additional children—those who already had the most money.

CHILDREN IN A WORLD OF FEWER AND QUITE DIFFERENT CITIES

By the end of antiquity, the city had become something quite different from the *polis* with which this chapter began. Children, it can be argued, were born into a different form of urbanism—where the physical environment and its associated material culture were quite different from the earlier classical period. Whereas previously the city had been at the heart of the community serving a hinterland, it had now become increasingly irrelevant to those residing in the countryside. Ausonius (fourth century C.E.), Sidonius (fifth century C.E.), and their associates seem to have spent much more time outside the cities of their region in their villas. This was not an entirely new phenomenon as the villas of the wealthy had always acted as a community with the potential to rival that of the city.[55] In 527 C.E., King Athalaric urged the governor of Bruttium (in Southern Italy) to ensure that the *curiales* (town councilors) and *possessores* (land owners) return to their cities. The takeover of whole regions by barbarian kings may have aided this process, but we should note that Alaric, the Visigothic king of Spain, published a law code, *Lex Romana Visigotorum,* that adjusted the laws found in the *Codex Theodosianus* for the new situation.[56] Roman social practices do seem to survive, even with the appearance of a barbarian king, as is revealed in the published works of Cassiodorus; it is as though the Goths became the preservers of Roman culture.[57] Interestingly,

Christianity did not alter the definition of the ages of childhood—the age when a young person could be married was maintained (legally twelve for girls and fourteen for boys), and the age of first marriage has been found to map onto the point at which individuals entered the church.[58] What is significantly different, particularly in the West, is the gradual disappearance of teachers in the *gymnasia* or *palaestrae* of the cities. There is a concomitant expansion of religious schools run by the church, training not just the future clergy but also educating others within the community.[59] The role of teaching in the conversion of pagans to Christianity is noted in a number of sources and perhaps should not be underestimated in the establishment of a role for the church in the cities of the later Roman Empire.[60] Strangely, it was seen as a necessity of education for boys to read and learn from pagan authors—including, for example, Cicero—but regarded as a sin for adults to read the same authors for pleasure.[61] As adults, many found the Latin translations of biblical texts lacking the literate niceties of the pagan classics they had read at school. The classical values of virtue and modesty found in such texts were supplemented with another one—faith in God.[62] Authority over the lives of the young continued, but the source of that authority had shifted away from the community to the church within the community. The intriguing reinvention of and reverence for the Roman past created an illusion of childhood remaining unchanged. The structure of childhood had a consistency or a convergence with childhood two, three, or even five hundred years earlier. What had changed was the nature of the community into which children were born and lived their lives. In this new world order, family, kin, and church appeared to have greater resonance in the structure of childhood than the reinvented notions of *communitas* from the classical past.

CHAPTER THREE

Economy

LENA LARSSON LOVÉN AND
AGNETA STRÖMBERG

The ancient Greco-Roman economy had two distinct and contiguous characteristics: agriculture and the use of slave labor. These two features characterized
the economy in general throughout antiquity in both urban and rural contexts.
These characteristics were also fundamental for the economy of many households and the financial well-being of the family, and both adults and children
were dependent on these elements for their continued existence.

The material comfort of the life of a child in antiquity was naturally closely
linked to the family's prosperity or poverty. The economy was a vital element
in determining how many children a family could raise—if they had a choice.
This chapter focuses primarily on how the family economy affected the life of a
child and his or her family and also highlights other factors relevant to discussion of the economy, such as the social and legal status of the family, gender
structures, and social practices. These factors all shaped the lives of children
and their families in the ancient world. Much of our evidence for this topic
comes from Athens in the fifth century B.C.E. and in Rome from the late republican period and in imperial times until about 200 C.E. The discussion and
examples from the Greco-Roman world concentrate on these cities and these
periods, but this chapter also embraces a longer period of time by bringing
the discussion into the early Middle Ages. In late antiquity and the medieval
period, Athens and Rome were no longer leading financial centers, and during
these periods the evidence concerning children and the family economy comes

mainly from other regions, reflecting the changing political landscape of the time and also the changing nature of the sources.

CHILDREN AND THE FAMILY ECONOMY

Children, particularly sons, were necessary for the continuity of the family line. The importance of children is demonstrated, for instance, by childlessness being an accepted reason for divorce in ancient Rome. Childless marriages were always considered the fault of the wife, and a man could divorce his allegedly sterile partner in order to remarry and have children with the intention of saving his family lineage for the future. According to Aulus Gellius (second century c.e.), the first divorce in Rome for this reason occurred around 230 b.c.e. when Spurius Carvilius Ruga divorced his wife because of her sterility.[1]

The actual birth of a child, even if freeborn, did not automatically make the infant a member of the family of his or her parents. The final acceptance of a new child was made by the male head of the family—in Athenian society by the *kyrios* and in Rome by the *paterfamilias*. His decision would have been based on a number of factors such as gender of the child, the absence of any visible defects, and the size of the family.[2] However, at the birth of a new child, the crucial concern must often have been if the household possessed the economic means to bring up another child. A child who survived the first critical years of life could at a later stage in the life course become an economic asset to the family. Thus, the economic well-being of the family would have depended on the number of children it could maintain.

Poorer parents might not have had the economic means to raise all children born to them, which may explain why exposure may have been used as a method of birth control. Child exposure and abandonment were practiced by the Greeks as well as the Romans. Exposure is a much-debated issue and is often believed to have been practiced more often on baby girls than newborn boys. It is clear from the ancient sources that abandoning children was not considered a criminal act and that it was not an uncommon practice, but it is impossible to determine precisely how frequently it occurred, both before and after the abandonment of children was prohibited by law in the late fourth century c.e. A poor family who could not afford to keep a new child might have been forced to have their children adopted by others or to sell a child, perhaps even into slavery.[3]

A child who lived to be a teenager or young adult drew on the economic resources of the family in a number of ways. The costs involved were different and differently paced according to the gender of the child. There were costs connected to the upbringing of sons in terms of school education and socio-ritual events that, like many other ritual acts, involved the sacrifice of animals and large feasts. Thus, it is likely to have been something of an economic relief for a family when a son became financially self-supporting.[4] Children living in a town or an urban center had more and probably better opportunities for education and training than children in the country. There was a greater stress on a boy's education than a girl's in both Greek and Roman society. Sparta was the only ancient state that prescribed a general education for girls. In light of the greater emphasis on male education, it has been questioned whether Greek girls and women in general could read and write.[5] However, with the absence of a general school system, all children could neither hope for nor claim education as a right. A family's social status and, probably most of all, its financial situation must have been decisive in the matter of formal aca-demic education. Wealthy Roman families had their own educational system whereby both sons and daughters were often taught by a learned slave. The education of the young males of the family was likely to imply larger costs than for daughters, since a son's education was more extensive, often includ-ing time abroad and preparing for a public career. A daughter in a wealthy Roman family was provided some years of education, thus making her a liter-ate and educated person—a factor in her high status in adulthood.[6]

A girl's life in general was much more focused on a future of marriage and family life, and if she had any education, her school days were probably over by the time she approached marriageable age (normally the age of twelve). An important part of bringing up a daughter, as well as a son, was training for adult life. For a daughter, such training implied preparation for her future role as wife in her husband's household. For this role she would probably have been trained by older females, either family members or slaves. Thus, the part con-sidered most essential in a girl's training for life as an adult (i.e., as a wife ca-pable of running a household) mostly took place in her own home. Financially, this training would have involved hardly any major cost for the family and did not incur the expense of engaging a teacher. If a girl's education involved lower costs for the family than educating a son, marrying off a daughter was likely to have been more expensive. The preparations for the girl's marriage may have begun several years before the wedding by looking for an appropriate husband, preferably of an equal, or perhaps higher, social and economic status to the daughter. The choice of husband could be followed by a betrothal.[7] For a first marriage, the girl was probably still living in the house where she had grown up, and when the day of the wedding had been set, preparations for the wedding ceremony, her bridal outfit, and the dowry began. The jewelry a bride wore at her wedding represented part of the wealth of the household, but the largest cost for her parents was her dowry.

In contrast to a daughter, a son was normally older at the time of his first marriage and by that time was likely to have already established a household of this own.[8] In the capacity of master of his own home, a man in his early or midtwenties would, at least on a daily basis, have been economically less dependent on the older generation than a daughter living with her parents or other adults or relatives until the day she married.

DAUGHTERS, DOWRIES, AND FAMILY STATUS

From an economic point of view, a daughter may not have contributed much to a family's financial well-being. Instead, she may have been seen as a burden to the household because a dowry would strain the family economy. In most European preindustrial societies, a dowry was the means for a daughter to claim a share of the father's estate, but the size as well as the legal and practical arrangements concerning dowries varied considerably over time. In classical Greece, the legal system and practices on dowry varied from *polis* to *polis* as is demonstrated from those states where evidence survives. In the law code from Gortyn in Crete (fifth century B.C.E.), a daughter had the right to one-half of the share of a son, and it could be used either as a dowry by the time of her marriage or inherited at the death of her father. Had a daughter's share been used for a dowry in a marriage that ended by divorce, the woman could keep what she had brought to the marriage.[9] Contemporary with the law code from Gortyn, in classical Athens, a dowry was essential for a girl's marriage since the marriage could be considered illegal without it. The importance of a dowry was demonstrated by the fact that if a father could not by economic means provide a dowry for his daughters, it would have to be produced by relatives or even by the city of Athens itself. The size of an Athenian dowry was related to the prosperity of the girl's father. Thus, a man would perhaps not have the option of raising more daughters than he could afford to furnish with dowries. In Rome, however, there were no legal obligations of a dowry to grant validity to a marriage, but it was a widespread practice. A substantial dowry could increase a girl's status as a marriage partner, and vice versa—the lack of a dowry might ruin her chances of marriage. The dowry could be composed of money and/or actual property that immediately became the full legal property of the husband, or his *paterfamilias*, once it was handed over to him.

There was also some variation in the size of dowries in antiquity. Most of our information from both Greek and Roman contexts concerns dowries for daughters of elite families, but a broad pattern can be discerned. Dowries in Athens were in general moderate compared to those in Rome. This is especially true from the second century B.C.E., when the Roman aristocracy allowed very substantial dowries to become important economic tools. The more generous dowries coincide in time with a general increase in wealth among aristocratic Roman families, partly through republican warfare that resulted in war booty that made already wealthy elite families even richer. Even an Athenian dowry could occasionally represent a substantial share of the patrimony, taking up to about twenty-five percent of the whole estate. But still, even the most substantial dowries in the ancient Greco-Roman world were much lower than dowries in the wealthy families of early modern Europe.[10]

Regardless of whether a dowry consisted of money, as was customary in classical Athens, or if it involved actual property, as it often did in wealthy Roman families, its overall purpose was to contribute to the maintenance of the wife during marriage. The size of the dowry and its composition was a reflection of the economic means of the bride's family. In Rome, the dowry could be reclaimed by her family in case of the death of the woman or the husband or in the case of divorce. If the dowry was reclaimed, it was often with the intention of using it again in the formation of another marriage. Roman law of the early imperial period included a relatively liberal divorce policy, and children from a marriage ending in divorce remained with their father and were still under his control. However, a mother might have had some financial responsibility for the children after a divorce.

The liberal view of divorce changed in later Roman law, from the fourth century C.E., when divorce, as well as the possibility of remarriage, was more restricted than in earlier periods. During the reign of the emperor Constantine (305–337 C.E.), laws were enacted to restrict divorce, especially for a wife who wanted to divorce her husband. In general, Christian leaders opposed divorce except if a wife was involved in adultery. It is difficult to know to what extent the laws of late antiquity in combination with the diffusion of Christian ideology may have affected popular opinion on divorce, but it seems that at least among the Roman aristocracy, Christian or pagan, divorce was extremely rare by the fifth century C.E.[11]

FAMILY PROPERTY AND RIGHTS OF INHERITANCE

In many ways, an ancient marriage was an alliance between two families—that of the bride and that of the groom—but it was not primarily an economic pact. In the interest of both families, the properties of a Roman husband and his wife were legally kept apart by restrictions in relation to gifts, inheritance, and financial commitments. During the period of betrothal, gifts between the partners were allowed, but gifts between husband and wife once married were not permitted in Roman law. The intention of these marital restrictions was to secure and keep separate the property of the family of the husband from that of the wife and to prevent any reduction in economic value in either *familia*. Consequently, inheritance between spouses was not allowed unless it was the type of marriage where the husband had been appointed guardian of the wife (i.e. a marriage *cum manu*, rare after 100 B.C.E.). From the first century C.E., the protection of separate property was taken a step further by the *senatus consultum Vellenaium*—husband and wife could no longer stand surety for each other's debts. In late antiquity, the legal view of property within a marriage changed radically. The laws of the fifth century C.E. were less interested in keeping property between spouses apart, and, as a consequence, husband and wife could now inherit from each other and were even looked upon as each other's natural heirs if there were no children.[12]

All families, rich or poor, might have had an interest in limiting the number of children—either due to the costs of maintaining a child or with the intention of maintaining the inherited wealth of the *familia*. Sons and daughters tended not to inherit equal shares of an estate. In the laws of Gortyn, discussed earlier, a daughter inherited half the share of a son; in classical Athens, a daughter did not inherit anything while all sons inherited equally, although the eldest son might have had some privileges in relation to his brother(s), such as claiming the family name as well as having first choice when landed property was divided between brothers. The division of land, of course, could cause problems if the original estate was very small because very small plots of land were insufficient to support several new families. This problem is well attested in ancient sources. The inheritance laws of Athens reflect the importance of having a son because only males could inherit; thus, the economic value of a child was clearly related to gender. Even in the context of high child mortality and the potential problems caused by multiple heirs, many families still raised more than one son for insurance against another's death.

If there were no sons, or if a man was unmarried, the adoption of a male could be the solution to perpetuate the *oikos*. Because girls could not inherit property or wealth from their father, they were rarely adopted. The purpose of adoption was not to care for an orphan or to provide childless couples with children. Instead, the intention was primarily to perpetuate the *oikos* and the family line through a male heir. An adopted son became the heir to his adoptive father's estate and was known by the patronymic of his father by adoption.

Because of this, small children were very seldom adopted; instead, an adult relative was preferred. Logically, the adopted son lost his right to inherit his natural father.[13] In classical Athens, a daughter would gain her share of her family's estate mainly through her dowry, and normally she would not inherit on the death of her parents. In certain circumstances a daughter could, however, technically become an heiress. She would then be an *epikleros*—"attached to the family property" (see chapters 1 and 7).

Roman law presents a different perspective on male and female rights of inheritance since both legitimate sons and daughters inherited from the father. Yet female inheritance in Rome was, by tradition, much more restricted than male inheritance, and a son was more likely to be the primary heir. In 169 B.C.E., the *Lex Voconia* limited the rights of inheritance for Roman females. From then on, a man could no longer make a daughter heir to more than half of his property.[14] Roman sons and daughters could inherit through a mother's will, and, from the second century C.E., intestate inheritance was also possible from a mother. A child of either sex in a well-to-do Roman family who lost one or both parents early in life could, thus, be wealthy at a very young age. Such a child would normally be under the guardianship of a *tutor*, an adult responsible for the child's economic assets and transactions. An example that may illustrate a Roman daughter's right of inheritance from a father is the case of Antonia Minor (36 B.C.E.–37 C.E.), the youngest daughter of Mark Antony (83–30 B.C.E.). At his death in 30 B.C.E., all his children inherited from his estate. Antonia was Antony's last legitimate child and only six years old when her father died. She probably never even met her father, but, nevertheless, she inherited a share of his estate, including large estates in the eastern Roman provinces, and became very wealthy by age six.[15] In such a situation—the death of a father—a guardian would normally be appointed for the younger children to protect the property left to the children; a mother, if still alive, would be responsible for the upbringing and welfare of her children. In the late fourth century C.E., a widowed mother who declared she would not remarry could herself be the guardian of her own children. In the later Roman Empire, the idea of marriage shifted from a general civic duty to a more personal choice or a choice of the family. Within marriage, inheritance remained a vital aspect, and parents were prohibited from disinheriting their children. The shift in attitude and law on marriage also affected unmarried persons. In Augustan legislation, unmarried men and women experienced restrictions on inheritance rights, but changes in late antiquity implied improved rights for unmarried persons to inherit and leave property not only to family members but also to unrelated persons. For example, unmarried Christians may have preferred to give some or all of their property to the church.[16]

WORK, THE FAMILY ECONOMY, AND SOCIAL STATUS

The financial well-being of a family depended on its social status and wealth, which could derive from work, marriage, and/or inheritance. The head of the family (a *kyrios* or *paterfamilias*) had overall responsibility for the household and its economy. In an ideal world, the male citizen would have been the owner of productive land that made him financially independent and also enabled him to devote his time to the public duties of a citizen. However, few could match this ideal.[17] Family finances, however, were not solely a male preserve; a husband's wife was also an important partner in the household economy. Once married, the woman was expected to run the household in a responsible way and oversee the work of slaves, duties for which she was trained prior to marriage. The family economy was partly dependent on how well the housewife ran the household. Some insight into what was expected from a housewife can be found in Xenophon's book *Oeconomica* from the fourth century B.C.E. It is clear from this book and other sources that female work, by free women or slaves, was mostly confined to indoor activities, while it was more common to expect men to work outdoors.

Some of a girl's premarital training, whatever her social status, would have been devoted to wool working. The homespun bridal dress was a very public proof of a girl's aptitude in textile production. Throughout her life, from cradle to grave, a girl was associated with symbols derived from the working of wool. In the restricted lives of Athenian women, textile production was part of their daily routine, and from the early Roman republic (fifth century B.C.E.), textiles were produced by the women of the family as important contributions to the household economy. In addition to its economic value, textile work was a strong and persistent symbol of female moral virtue from antiquity into the early Middle Ages. The symbolic value of wool working in the Roman period is illustrated by the story of the emperor Augustus wearing clothes made by the women of his household—this was of little economic consequence but said much about the moral values associated with the emperor's household. The symbolic values attached to wool working do not rule out the possibility that many households economically benefited from textile work undertaken by the women in the household. The intermingling of two sets of values—one economic and the other symbolic—associated with domestic wool production presents difficulties of interpretation. It is possible from the same set

FIGURE 3.1: *Terra-cotta* lekythos *(oil flask) showing women weaving.* Attributed to the Amasis painter, Attica, Greece, ca. 550–530 B.C.E. Metropolitan Museum of Art Fletcher Fund, 1931 (31.11.10). Image © Metropolitan Museum of Art.

of evidence to conclude, on the one hand, that wool-working women were a cliché and that upper-class Roman women did not do wool work at all and, on the other hand, that even women of the nobility continued to produce clothes worn by members of their families.

Ideally, the Roman household was a self-sufficient economic unit whose needs were supplied from its own produce and by its own labor force. However, with the sophisticated monetary economy of the Hellenistic and Roman world, few households maintained this ideal of self-sufficiency. Several household products seem, in fact, to have been cheaper to buy at the marketplace than if they were produced within the household.[18] An example of how household production may have become outdated within the changing economic conditions of the early second century B.C.E. is reflected in the writings of Cato the Elder, renowned for his parsimonious nature. Among his advice to wealthy landowners is a recommendation to *buy* clothing for slaves at the market instead of producing it on their estates. It was simply cheaper to buy some ready-made products, and there was also a thriving secondhand market in Rome.[19] As demonstrated by the advice of Cato, textiles continued to be part of the basics of life and maintained their economic importance even if some textile items could be bought more cheaply outside the household. The ideology of the landowning, economically self-sufficient Roman citizen comprised the ideal of *otium* (learned scholarship)—a wealthy man who would at times withdraw from public duties and politics. However, in reality, *otium* and business were closely linked, and, from late republican times, *otium* was sometimes used as an excuse to withdraw from public duties in the city to go the country estates and see to business. However, the same ideology caused many to distance themselves in public from any sort of occupation considered unworthy. This is most forcefully expressed by Cicero in his work on occupations and duties, *De Officiis* (*On Duties*). Cicero, consciously echoing Aristotle, considered physical work and many occupations to be of low social standing and unworthy of a Roman gentleman. However, ideals and reality are often divergent, and it is well-known that many aristocratic Roman families were involved in a wide variety of trades and businesses deemed by Cicero as unworthy of their status. In order not to appear as businessmen of low social standing, they often engaged their freed slaves as front men or managers while they as proprietors of the business enjoyed a profit.[20]

A characteristic feature of the ancient economy was slave labor. Warfare and piracy were the major sources of slaves, and slave trade was an established form of commerce in antiquity. Work in the ancient Greco-Roman world was frequently pursued by slaves of almost any age, and slaves worked in nearly all

FIGURE 3.2: *Monument set up outside the Herculaneum Gate at Pompeii by Naevoleia Tyche to commemorate her dead husband, Gaius Munatius Faustus (buried elsewhere).* He was a freed slave whose standing was recognized by the town council and was also a priest of Augustus. The scene here shows a distribution of food or money. Above the inscription is an image of Naevoleia Tyche. *Corpus Inscriptionum Latinarum* 10.1026 (photo Ray Laurence).

economic sectors. Many families, even those of modest wealth, had slaves who were an essential feature of the household economy. The price of a slave bought from a slave market was based on age, gender, ethnicity, and skills. Information on prices paid for individual slaves are rare, but it appears that prices varied in the ancient Greco-Roman world. Walter Scheidel has concluded that in relation to daily wages slave prices were low in classical Athens. This was probably also the case in Italy during the Roman republic. However, in the Roman Empire of the first two centuries C.E., the cost of slaves seems to have been fairly high.[21] For the individual purchaser of a slave, the outlay was an investment expected to render the owner future income through work. Slaves had no legal right to marriage or families of their own, but it was an established custom among slave owners to encourage them to have families. The children of slaves were thought to provide stability in a household and were the property of the owner of their parents (i.e., slave children could be acquired without having to buy new ones). Such children could be developed as an economic resource by their owner: they could be sold at any age, or they could be trained for a job that would result in future income for the family. Slaves could also be hired out to work for someone else and still create income for the family.

It was not only slaves who worked but also male and female adults and children in many families of freeborn and freed slaves. With the exception of the elite families, it seems plausible that work of all sorts must have constituted an important part of the everyday lives of all members of the family, regardless of age or gender. In antiquity and the early Middle Ages, agriculture formed the economic basis of society. With agrarian production such a pervasive element in the economy, the financial well-being and living conditions of many families were closely related to agricultural production and animal husbandry. Many people worked in agriculture or related areas, especially those living in the countryside or agro-towns as land owners, slaves, or hired workers. The number and status of people involved in agricultural work is a matter of some controversy, but obviously it embraced both adults and children of both sexes. According to Varro, writing in the first century B.C.E., many poor Roman families relied on their children for agricultural work. Other Roman writers express similar views: children were capable of helping with farm work, especially unskilled tasks that needed little or no training and could be undertaken from a very early age.[22] A parallel to this practice can be found in modern developing countries, where many owners of small farms rely on the work of the whole family, including their children.

Over the course of the Hellenistic and Roman periods, a higher degree of specialization in production was developed. Very specific job titles attest to this development. Job titles were used primarily by Roman slaves and freedmen and appear in the epigraphic evidence for the first time in the third century B.C.E. In this period, a monetary economy was being established in Rome. The occurrence of job titles is particularly noticeable in urban contexts of Roman Italy, especially in the city of Rome itself. The evidence for job specialization increases over time and involves a variety of occupations including the production of various kinds of goods, tradesmen and shopkeepers, jobs in the service sector, and so forth by the first and second centuries C.E. Roman occupations are best known to us from inscriptions, often found on tombstones, and they mirror a wide spectrum of work and occupations pursued in the Roman world. Adults of both sexes as well as children appear in inscriptions with job titles, although male workers occur in greater numbers and in a greater variety of jobs than both women and children.[23]

In spite of the disdainful attitude toward physical work displayed by the upper classes, for other social groups all kinds of work played a central role in their lives and in the family economy. Funerary inscriptions and visual images of work, especially on funerary monuments, reflect this view. Success in the field of work was the basis for many families' economic status, and it probably also provided social and financial advancements for members of these families. Both men and women worked, but it is not clear if Roman women pursued the same kind of occupations as men and to the same extent. In public, women's primary roles as mothers and housewives were more essential than their occupation or work, and wifely virtues are recurrently stressed in inscriptions while men are more often presented as family breadwinners. But, in reality, husbands and wives seem to have been involved in family businesses where children could also have a place.

In a rich family, children would have experienced material wealth and would not have worked. All other families were dependent on their children to work in order to make a living, both in rural and urban settings. Children were looked upon as the private possessions of the household and contributed to the household economy by working in the fields, in workshops, or caring for younger siblings. In this way, childhood as a stage of life involving preparation for adulthood functioned in a different way from that of the upper class. Among working families, children were part of the labor force in the ancient world, either involved in household work or participating in or learning a professional trade with a craftsman from outside the family. Evidence for apprenticeship contracts has been found among the surviving papyri in Egypt and dated to the Roman period. These contracts are concerned mostly with jobs in textile production, including several examples of weavers and some who specialized in weaving linen; there is evidence for other jobs as well, such as training for builders, musicians, and other crafts. Training for a profession normally began at an early age—probably younger than fourteen—although the exact age when a child's training started is unclear from the contracts that survive. Training could, however, last from a couple of months or a year to several years with a maximum of between five or six years.

Funerary inscriptions provide further evidence of children's work and display a variety of occupations pursued by children, especially boys. The documentation of girl's jobs is more scant and usually involved domestic tasks—probably reflecting gender roles in Roman society. The same pattern can be seen in jobs performed by adult men and women, where female occupations are fewer in number and relate more to the domestic sphere. Some children worked as entertainers and could apparently start their careers early in life. Entertainers were, according to Cicero, among the lowest of the low in the Roman social hierarchy. Children working as entertainers were most likely to have been slaves or slave descendents, working for either private owners or theater companies. It would mean hard work, even for small children, and the prospect of a short life. There is evidence for child labor in antiquity that reveals the brevity of children's lives; among examples are dancers who died between the ages of ten and twelve and a mime artist who died at the age of twelve. But there are many examples of children in other occupations who also died young, such as the gold spinner, Viccentia, who died at age nine.[24]

The evidence of widespread child labor in antiquity has formed part of the now-controversial argument for an absence of the concept of childhood in antiquity. In his now classic work on childhood, Philippe Ariès argued that childhood as a separate stage in life was invented in the Middle Ages.[25] However, most now recognize that childhood was seen in the ancient world as a distinct period in the life course, at least for the Roman period, although for many children it implied work, sometimes very hard work.

CHILDREN AND THE FAMILY ECONOMY
IN THE POST-ROMAN WORLD

The political crisis in the fourth and fifth centuries C.E. led to the fall of the western Roman Empire, while in the east a more stable political system remained in place for several more centuries. In the Latin west, many novelties appeared: a new political structure with groups from outside the Roman world holding power and new economic conditions for people living in the former western provinces. New social structures were created, but some continuity from Roman times remained.

Marriage was still important for individuals and for the family to transfer family property. Unmarried and married women were still subject to fathers and husbands, and children continued to inherit from their parents. The inheritance rights of both sons and daughters that characterized Roman legislation continued into later periods in some regions of the post-Roman world but in some parts with a more restricted inheritance for females.

The later Roman Empire saw a decline of large cities that continued into the Middle Ages. Many people, in economic sectors other than farming, became more tied to their work in the late- and post-Roman period since sons were forced to follow in the footsteps of their fathers in a wide range of occupations. Thus, a job in this period may be seen as part of the family inheritance, especially for sons. In the fragmented society of the post-Roman world, the documentation of work is generally less frequent both for adults and children than for the high Roman Empire. Both iconographic work scenes and job titles in inscriptions gradually became fewer until they finally vanish from our sources, but for most people work must have continued more or less uninterrupted throughout these periods as it was still fundamental to the economic standard of most families.

The gendered view of male and female work that is significant in Roman society continued in this later period. Women were still mainly supposed to engage in traditional indoor female occupations—*opera muliebra*, such as running the household and textile work—while men worked outdoors.[26]

In the post-Roman world, the economic situation as a whole was very complex. However, farming and animal husbandry continued to form the economic basis of society, and many families were still engaged in and dependent on this kind of work as their financial platform. Nuclear families seem to have been normative both in late antiquity and in the early Middle Ages. The fall of the former political organization also affected the economic system and led to the collapse of the system of long-distance trade offered by the Roman Empire.[27] In the countryside, economic power was concentrated in large farming estates—*latifundiae*. These were economic centers owned by wealthy families who also formed a strong political group and whose counterparts in earlier periods were the senatorial aristocracy for whom *otium* had been a hallmark. In the west, the former secular elite disappeared, and in the circle of *latifundiae* owners a new, more utilitarian ideology was created to replace the ideal of *otium*. The constantly increasing inflation of the period put a heavy financial pressure on many small landowning farming families who could be forced into serfdom and, thus, tied to their farming lots. Peasants who lived close to the frontiers had to produce food for the legions, and mighty landowners could force the sons of peasants to serve in the Roman army, which would affect the family economy negatively if one or several sons had to leave the farm for a longer period of time, especially during harvest. If peasant farmers could not supply the required goods or pay taxes, they became *coloni*—peasant farmers who in practice were serfs of the rich and powerful landowners and had to work on the *latifundiae*. However, the proportions of slave labor, free wage labor, and tenants on rural estates is somewhat unclear during this period, partly due to regional differences with variations from one region to another.[28]

To conclude, in the post-Roman world the family remained the basic social and economic unit, and children were still important to the family, whose economy shaped the life of the child. As social structures in both ancient and medieval times mostly favored patrilinear systems, a family normally depended on a son for its continuity. A child was proof of the fulfillment of a marriage, and a son would give hope for the future and family continuity. Throughout this period there is scant material—both written and archaeological—connecting economic conditions to the lives of ordinary people, not least in the Roman west. This situation causes problems for the interpretation of the relationship between economic conditions and the lives of families and children during the fifth to the eighth centuries C.E., but it is still possible to conclude that marriage, family life, and work continued to be vital agents in shaping the lives and economy of both adults and children.

CHAPTER FOUR

Geography and the Environment

LOUISE REVELL

Children grow into their sense of self through their daily activities, which have a necessary spatial element. Activities of play, learning, eating, and sleeping are carried out within a particular place, and these places help inform a sense of who the child is and how he or she relates to other people. There are two elements to this geographical variability.[1] The first is the specific places where children carry out these daily activities as children sometimes have to carve out spaces for themselves in an adult-dominated world. The second of these is the regional context: childhood is culturally variable, spatially as well as temporally, and so the environmental and cultural characteristics of the specific area will affect the experience of the child and the construction of childhood within that society. Therefore, this chapter addresses these two elements. The first is the nature of the household into which the child was born, and the second is the geographical variability between different areas.

HOUSEHOLD SPACES IN ANTIQUITY

The house is an important environment for learning social norms. Here the child learns not only how to interact with immediate family members but also about the relationship between the family and wider society. The ancient household differed from the modern nuclear family. The household, as a unit, consisted of a married couple and their children. The husband was the head of this household, and he had legal responsibility for the women and children within the family. This need for a male guardian meant that more distant female relatives within the house, such as unmarried sisters or widowed aunts, may also have been legally dependant upon him. There may also have been elderly relatives, and if one of the spouses had been married previously, there may have been children from the former marriage. In addition, many households had one or more slaves. The household was therefore a mix of generations, and events such as marriages or deaths would have altered this mix, disturbing the stability of the family relationships (see chapter 1).

Within the Greek world, a key concept was the *oikos,* which refers as much to the people within the household as the physical structures of the house itself. The layout of the house developed from very simple, single-roomed structures into multi-roomed buildings arranged around a courtyard.[2] Although precise layouts differ between so-called *prostas, pastas,* and peristyle houses, by the fifth and fourth centuries B.C.E. they had the same principle elements.[3] The inside of the house was cut off from the rest of the community: the high walls and lack of windows made it difficult to see in, and there was usually only a single door to enter the house. This entrance led into an open courtyard, which may have had some form of adjoining portico. Grouped around the courtyard were a number of rooms—two or three in the most basic houses, more in houses of some status. More complex houses might have a bathroom, a room with a hearth, and the *andron,* a room marked out as a particularly important space by its pebble mosaic floor, raised area for benches, and possible antechamber.

If this is the basic layout of the classical Greek house, what can it tell us about the organization of the household? Textual and archaeological evidence can be used together to argue for specifically gendered areas.[4] A number of Greek texts refer to men's and women's quarters (*andronitis* and *gunaikonitis*), such as the description by Xenophon (ca. 430–ca. 350 B.C.E.) of male and female quarters divided by a lockable door. However, the situation is more nuanced. The best examples of domestic housing were excavated at the site of Olynthos, which mainly dates from the first half of the fourth century B.C.E. and was destroyed in 348 B.C.E. Research into these buildings, which has integrated the layout of the house with the everyday objects found within specific rooms, has pointed to a much more flexible use of space.[5] The distribution of material such as pottery or loom weights shows that rooms were used for multiple activities rather than a single function. The courtyard, for example, seems to have been used for chores, storage, and the household cult. These activities may have shifted to the rooms surrounding the courtyard during the winter months. This picture of flexible space is reinforced by texts such as the speech by Lysias (459/458–ca. 380 B.C.E.), which recounts how a wife's bedroom was moved from the upstairs to the ground floor.[6]

The one exception to this flexibility was the *andron*. Although there is some evidence that it might have been used for domestic activities during the day, the preferential decoration and presence of the antechamber mark it out as a space of more importance. This was the venue for the male-dominated *symposia*, or drinking parties, when the man of the household entertained his male friends. The only women present were slaves, musicians, and possibly prostitutes; respectable women were excluded. This might lead to the assumption that the *andron* was physically separated from the rest of the house and its inhabitants, but this does not seem to be the case. Spatially, it was located deep within the house and had to be accessed through the central courtyard, although the antechamber distanced it from more mundane activities. This further muddies the picture of strict gender segregation between men and women: the activities within the *andron* were separated from the rest of the house, but male guests may have encountered female members of the household.

A second key element was the relationship between the household and the rest of the community: the relationship between the *oikos* and the *polis*. The picture presented by the textual sources is that of the *oikos* as a private area in contrast to the public sphere of the *polis*. This was a shifting relationship, and it has been argued that the private, domestic sphere became increasingly important from the fifth century into the fourth century B.C.E.[7] The courtyard with its porticoes was the key space within the house: the entranceway led to it, and the other rooms were reached from it. Yet, in most cases, the courtyard could not be seen from the street, thus separating the inside of the house from the outside world. The passageway from the street to the courtyard might be off center, or the view might be obscured by a screen. This emphasized the seclusion of the household and the separation of public and private. Female activities were focused on the house and removed from the public sphere, possibly a reflection of the concern with inheritance and the legitimacy of children as expressed in textual sources. In contrast, men's activities were carried out in public outside the house; these activities included taking part in politics or agricultural work in the fields. Children would be part of the domestic sphere, but boys, unlike their sisters, would have an expectation of entering the public world.

This strict division between public and private is missing in Roman housing. As in the Greek world, the house itself was considered to be associated with the *familia*. Roman housing took a number of forms, but the archetype was the atrium house. The layout of the house was organized on a visual axis from the street into the depths of the house.[8] This gave it a physical permeability that echoed the intermingling of public and private space. If we look at examples from Pompeii and Herculaneum, we see the main elements repeated again and again. The entrance was set directly on the street and possibly accentuated by columns and pilasters. The entrance led down a straight passageway (the *fauces*) into the atrium, a partially covered room that functioned as a quasi-public space. The atrium was visible from the street, and the head of the household received his clients and political supporters within this space. On the same axis was his office, the *tablinum,* and behind might be the vista of a garden or peristyle. These were more private spaces, and often they were associated with dining rooms for entertaining friends and political allies. These quasi-public spaces were opulently decorated with mosaics, wall paintings, and statues, turning the house into an extension of the owner's political persona.[9] Even spaces that we think of as private, such as bedrooms, could be used for receiving particularly close friends.

However, as in Greece, the rooms of the Roman house were also used in a flexible way. The atrium, peristyles, and dining rooms took on different functions at specific times during the day.[10] The atrium, for example, was used during the ritual of the *salutatio,* in which clients assembled at their patron's house at dawn; for the next two hours, the atrium was filled with the male head of the family carrying out his political business. However, he and his attendants then left for the forum, leaving the rest of the family behind. At this point, the atrium was used by the women and household slaves for activities such as weaving or washing pots and by children for play. The peristyle seems to have had a similar multifunctional use. Chairs, tables, couches, looms, and storage chests tended to be portable, and the presence of household slaves made it relatively easy to change a room from one use to another. In this sense, we should look for Roman children throughout the house, although only in certain spaces at specific times.

We see a shift in housing and housing style from the fourth century onward.[11] The declining importance of towns as a focus for politics, pagan religion, and elite display led the house to be used for many of these roles. This produced an increased emphasis on rooms for receiving guests, particularly ornate reception rooms and large dining rooms. The key rooms were the audience chambers and the dining rooms. The former tended to be large rooms, often with an apse and located very close to the main entrance of the house. Dining rooms became larger with the development of large dining rooms for very formal, ceremonial banquets and existed alongside smaller, more private rooms for entertaining family and close friends. The larger ones were again

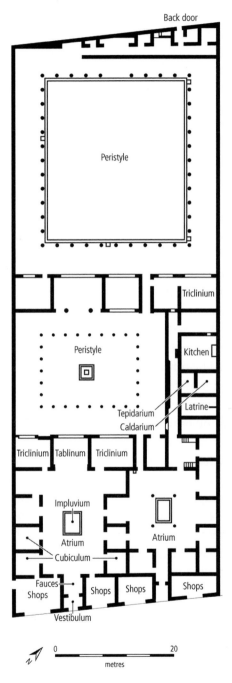

FIGURE 4.1: *Plan of the House of the Faun.* This is the largest house from Pompeii established in this format by the second century B.C.E. The basic layout was replicated in many houses in Pompeii although the double atrium & peristyle are unusual (illustration: Harry Buglass).

situated near the entrance of the house. While these elements were present in the houses of previous centuries, the difference is in their emphasis and the way they absorbed the functions of the town buildings into the house itself as the relationship between the elite and their dependents became more formal. In contrast to these very public areas, the rest of the house became increasingly private and reserved for the family itself. In particular, areas such as the peristyle and the main dining room were closed to clients, thus ending the overlapping public and private spaces that characterized earlier Roman houses.

REGIONAL VARIABILITY

The second area where spatial geographies had an impact on family life was in the differences produced by environmental and cultural variability. We tend to treat the Mediterranean region as a homogenous unit when it is a very diverse geographical area. In 600 B.C.E., the Mediterranean was a patchwork of groups with considerable variability in social and cultural structures. In the eastern Mediterranean were a series of powerful states, while the Greek world was dominated by small independent cities and islands. The Iberian Peninsula and northern Europe were mainly inhabited by tribal groups governed by a martial ideology. None of these cultures existed in isolation, and from the second millennium B.C.E. this complex cultural environment produced a series of interactions—sometimes through conquest, at other times through colonization, and at others through more informal ties of influence and cultural borrowing.[12] Even restricting ourselves to Greece and Rome, the Greek city-states were influenced by Phoenicia and other cultures in the eastern Mediterranean. They in turn sent out colonies so that Greek culture spread from the northeastern coast of Spain to the Black Sea. Greek influence continued through the Hellenistic kingdoms formed after the death of Alexander and spread as far as Ai Khanum in Afghanistan. The later conquests of the Romans brought a new wave of cultural transformations broadly covered by the catch-all term "Romanization" but that was, in fact, a complex interaction with Hellenistic and indigenous cultures.[13] From 400 C.E. onward, internal changes and external pressures on the Roman Empire through migrations and warfare produced a split between the eastern and western empires and increased cultural divergence.[14] This cultural mix undermines the idea of the antique world as a geographical unity and problematizes the notion of a fixed and single experience of family relations across the area.

There are problems with the various forms of evidence related to how this regional diversity might have affected childhood and the family. Whether

FIGURE 4.2: *Through the Roman house.* Looking from the peristyle through the atrium to the main door into the street in the House of the Menander at Pompeii (photo Ray Laurence).

archaeological or textual, none gives a problem-free glimpse into the lives of children and the family. As one scholar concludes, "There is too little evidence and no reliable means have been found of extrapolating general truths from the few cases we can document" when examining the evidence for the family in the northwest provinces of the Roman Empire.[15] We lack direct accounts of the lives of women and children in the first person and instead have caricatures of family roles, whether in a positive or negative light. Most relate to Athens or Rome and central Italy but are often taken as typical of all classical Greece or for the Roman Empire as a whole. The writers discussing these societies are outsiders, often not contemporary, and as such subject to their own biases and assumptions. Inscriptions, and more particularly epitaphs, have a much wider distribution but, again, are subject to their own biases, with certain people and ages more likely to be commemorated than others. While this has led to a certain amount of pessimism about their usefulness for the reconstruction of demographic realities, it has also led to the development of an understanding of patterns of commemoration with a view to relating these to a wider under-standing of the family across the Roman Empire.

The archaeological record has revealed children in places we did not expect them, such as the milk tooth found in the legionary baths at Caerleon in Britain indicating the presence of children inside the fortress.[16] However, can we go beyond this and use the material evidence to understand the nature and daily experiences of family life? Identifying the material culture of specific family members can be based on uncritical assumptions about which artifacts might be associated with each role. The material culture of modern children is primarily categorized as toys. These are often smaller, brightly colored versions of adult material used to socialize children into cultural norms and gender stereotypes, such as dolls and miniature kitchens for girls and spacemen outfits and cars for boys. There are other kinds of material culture we do not expect to be associated with children, particularly tools and weapons.[17] Concepts of play and toys are products of a specific idea of childhood as a time of economic nonproductivity possibly idealized as a carefree time of innocence. Evidence of children involved in economic activity should caution us against assuming we are looking for a distinctive material culture. Similarly, gender roles within the household can be difficult to assign. We may be able to identify activities such as cooking, weaving, or grinding grain, but it is more difficult to assign these to specific members of the family. We may assume that the production of ceramic vessels was a male activity, but ethnographic parallels suggest that women could just as easily have been responsible. Moreover, in late antiquity, there is some evidence for the preparation of bread by men in some areas and in other areas by women.[18]

A lack of systematic research means it is impossible to reconstruct regional pictures of childhood in antiquity in detail. However, we are able to identify broad patterns of variability and so extrapolate a geography of homogeneity and difference. This is particularly true for the Roman Empire and the first three centuries of the first millennium C.E. The Roman conquest of both the eastern and western Mediterranean and much of temperate Europe brought them into contact with many different cultures, and the process of Romanization did not eradicate these differences. While there was broad-based cultural homogeneity, recent work has pointed to the coexistence of regional variability.[19] There are two aspects we can focus on: firstly, how these regional differences affected the world of the child; and secondly, whether the makeup of the family and the roles assigned to individuals varied between the different cultural traditions of the Roman world.

THE WORLD OF THE CHILD

Recent archaeological research has pointed to variability in the material world within which Roman families lived. When we conceptualize these material worlds, we usually populate them with adult men, rendering invisible other types of people (women, children, slaves, the disabled, and so forth). However, these material worlds were those in which families lived their daily lives: the different structures they inhabited, the food they ate, or the clothes they wore. As these were the environments within which children were born and raised, they would have had a fundamental impact upon the cultural norms and routines they learned. This is not just applicable to childhood as a theoretical construct; instead, it provides a starting point for understanding the impact of geography on children's experiences.[20] Environmental variability is likely to have produced different daily experiences and activities for children. However, we are left with a certain level of speculation: How did differences in climate affect daily routine? What was the difference between areas with high levels of rainfall and areas with periods of drought? Or where there was a higher average temperature and more hours of sunlight? In part, any answer is conditioned by our assumptions about what kinds of activities children carried out. If we assume the child's day was mainly filled with play and learning, then being able to spend more hours outside would have led to different kinds of games and different spaces in which to play them. In contrast, if we assume most children were expected to contribute to the smooth running of the household—through fetching water, for example—then average rainfall and easily accessible water resources would have affected how much time each day a child would have spent on such chores.

Variation in mineral resources becomes important if we accept that some children would have been economically active. At the Roman imperial stone quarries at Mons Porphyrites in Egypt there are burials of young children and juveniles and shoes whose sizes suggest they were worn by those not yet fully grown. These children may have formed part of the labor force, and Diodorus Siculus (first century B.C.E.) describes prepubescent boys working in the goldmines of Egypt, collecting the ore and carrying it from the galleries to the open air[21]—quite different childhood experiences to those we imagine when viewing a Roman house in Pompeii. We should not underestimate or isolate these experiences in the quarries of Egypt. Scientists analyzing Greenland ice cores have discovered that the period from approximately 500 B.C.E. to 300 C.E. shows high concentrations of lead and copper pollution that were not matched until the Industrial Revolution.[22] This was due to a marked increase in metal production caused in part by the demand for coinage. One of the centers of copper mining and production was the Wadi Faynam in southern Jordan, and the analysis of human skeletal data from the fourth to seventh centuries C.E. shows clearly the effects of metal pollution on the industrial workers.[23] The skeletons show high levels of lead and copper poisoning either due to working the material, living in close proximity to the works, or a combination. This would have made them more susceptible to a range of illnesses, including gastric and renal problems and cancer. The exposure to lead could also have had a dangerous effect on fetuses and nursing children. Children living and working in these metal-working areas would have contrasting daily routines and experiences from those in regions dominated by different forms of economy, such as agriculture or ceramic production.

Another aspect of daily existence that demonstrates marked variations is that of diet, which reflects not just regional availability of resources but also different cultural norms. A study that compared the composition of the evidence for animal remains from Roman sites across Western Europe found marked variations.[24] In west-central Italy (including Etruria, Campania, Rome, and Ostia), the diet was high in pork from the first century B.C.E. through to the third/fourth centuries C.E. In Spain, pork again was prominent, but it was secondary to cattle. Southern Gaul shows a very different pattern, with the dominance of sheep and goat (it is difficult to distinguish between them osteologically). Further north in the other Gallic provinces (Aquitania, Lugdunensis, and Belgica), the diet was dominated by cattle and pork, and the Rhine provinces show a similar pattern but with cattle outnumbering pork. In Britain, there was a change from predominantly sheep and goat consumption to incorporate large proportions of cattle and pig while still retaining a considerable proportion of sheep and goat. This regional variability in diet extends to cooking techniques. Studies of ceramic cooking pots have demonstrated that in North Africa, food was cooked over a fired clay brazier, whereas in Britain, it was cooked in ash at the base of an oven.[25] When legionaries recruited in North Africa were stationed in Britain, they took this regional form of cooking with them. This raises questions about how these different cooking techniques were incorporated into family routines and whether the techniques had an impact on the facilities within the house or family roles.

The archaeological record reveals answers to other questions of regional variation, including differences in urban density and facilities. In a densely urbanized area such as Italy or southern Spain, many families would have lived either in or within easy reach of a town or city. Their daily routines would have contrasted with those of northern Gaul or Britain, where there were fewer, more dispersed towns. The lives of these families would have been based in the countryside, possibly centered around villages, with a trip to the political center of the chartered towns a much rarer event. It is possible that the economic basis of the family differed and consequently, the contribution of each family member to economic production. This presents us with the possibility of different routines and family roles dependent upon the local context. By putting children and the family center stage when exploring the consequence of such regional diversity, we may not be able to fully reconstruct the effect on the family unit, but we can break apart the homogenous picture that has in the past been constructed from the textual sources in isolation.

THE FAMILY IN ITS GEOGRAPHICAL CONTEXT

While we can detect difference in the material context of childhood and family life, a more problematic question is whether there were similar regional differences in the idea of the family—the way in which the family was constructed and how the relationships between individual family members were structured. Much ink has been spilled over two central questions: whether the family was nuclear or extended and whether it was matriarchal or patriarchal. Although this debate goes back to the nineteenth century, more recently a geographical perspective has been developed within which two different modes of family structure have been proposed in the Mediterranean: European and non-European patterns characterized by traits in opposition to one another.[26]

Although this dichotomy was primarily concerned with the early modern period, there have been suggestions that this model can also be applied to antiquity. However, in view of the cultural complexity and diversity of antiquity, it is perhaps unsurprising that it is not easy to map this binary model straight onto the past. Instead, the evidence seems to suggest a mosaic of regional differences in family structures that resists such a simplistic mapping. The far-reaching influence of cultural groups such as the Phoenicians, the Greeks, and the Romans interacting with different indigenous traditions had the potential to produce distinctive family structures between areas.

Table 4.1: Hajnal's modes of family structure.

Non-European	European
young age of marriage for women	delayed marriages for both sexes
strict patrilineality and agnatic preference	bilineality
endogamy	exogamy
segregation of the sexes	less segregation
exclusion of women from the public sphere	less exclusion of women from the public sphere

One factor is age at first marriage and age differences between husband
and wife. Working with data from epitaphs, estimates have varied according
to the sampling method adopted and the sample used. An early but influential
study concluded that the average age of marriage in Rome was twenty-four and
twenty-six for women and men respectively. More than a century later, we have
come to appreciate regional variations in both age at first marriage and family
structure. A series of studies based on the epitaphs of the western provinces of
the Roman Empire from the first to the third centuries c.e. has produced patterns of commemoration that show considerable variability.[27] These are based
upon the premise that the average age at which a tombstone commemoration
of a young adult switches from the stated responsibility of parents to a spouse
reflects the average age of first marriage. In northern Italy, parents commemorated their daughters until their early twenties and their sons into their early
thirties, whereas in southern Italy parents only ceased to be the primary commemorator for their sons when these men reached their late thirties, suggesting
a later age for their first marriage. In the Danube provinces, women were most
frequently commemorated by their husbands from their mid-twenties whereas
men were commemorated by wives from their early thirties. These variations
become more acute in the case of Spain, where husbands do not become the
dominant commemorators until the women are in their late twenties and early
thirties, and for men the transition is even later, in their early forties. Here,
there is a notable difference between the Iberian Peninsula and the other western provinces. The way in which a married couple detached themselves from
the parental family unit and formed their own separate family unit may have
been different and possibly occurred sometime after the marriage itself. There
is a comparatively high frequency of women as commemorators: there are almost as many wives commemorating their husbands as vice versa, and far more
mothers commemorating children than fathers.[28] Ethnographic writers of the
period, such as Strabo (ca. 64 B.C.E.–ca. 20 C.E.) and Posidonius (135–51 B.C.E.),
commented on the prominent role women played within Iberian societies, and
while not a matriarchal society, evidence does suggest the mother had a more
prominent role within the family in this area in this period.[29]

Staying with the Roman period, the clearest distinction in family structures is between the civilian and military spheres. The civilian pattern shows
the majority of epitaphs recording commemoration by the nuclear family
(spouse, parents, children, and siblings). This is in contrast to military commemoration, which displays two distinct patterns: one of high levels of commemoration by the nuclear family and a second of lower levels of familial
commemoration. In Britain and Germany, seventy-five to ninety percent of

civilian men were commemorated by their immediate family, in contrast to thirty to forty percent of soldiers. Whether these differences in commemoration reflected different patterns of local or nonlocal recruitment is a matter of some debate.[30] Alternative explanations for the lack of commemoration by the nuclear family in the armies of antiquity revolve around the legal status of these attachments. The law relating to the marriage of soldiers is complex, and the sample sizes have caused some researchers to group legionary and auxiliary troops together.[31] This is relatively unproblematic in Africa and Spain, where the majority of the troops were legionary and therefore Roman citizens. In contrast, a substantial proportion of troops stationed in Britain and Germany were auxiliary soldiers who only gained citizenship on discharge and whose families had little standing within Roman law. Nevertheless, this does not mean the soldiers of Britain were living monastic lives, devoid of women and children. The archaeological evidence from Hadrian's Wall points to a very mixed community: the sizes of leather shoes and the presence of other personal items points to women and children in and around the forts.[32] This suggests the soldiers were forming family units based in the forts and their environs but that, for whatever reason, the strength and social pull of these relationships was weaker than the soldiers' relationships with their fellow soldiers. It is possible that because the soldiers were recruited from outside the immediate area, these families were left behind on retirement or, alternatively, that the designated commemorator, to a certain extent a legal relationship, was chosen from outside the family unit.

Another side to the possible disruption caused by army recruitment was the effect on the family structures of those left behind. By the first three centuries C.E., the majority of soldiers were being recruited from the provinces and increasingly from those further from Rome.[33] Two regions that provided a substantial proportion of young men to serve in the legions and auxiliary units were northwestern Iberia and Batavia. In the case of the latter, it has been suggested that in Batavia each household must have contributed at least one man to military service. This must have had an impact on family relationships, possibly giving women a more prominent role in the family.[34] When their menfolk were discharged from the army, their weapons were hung in the house as symbolic decorations of honor, promoting a martial ideology within the family and possibly giving rise to military families supplying troops to the Roman army for a number of generations.[35] This level of recruitment can also be seen in northwestern Iberia. It has been estimated that at least 15,180 men were recruited as auxiliary soldiers, and more were recruited into the legions and the Praetorian Cohorts.[36] In contrast to Batavia, there is a strong likelihood these men never returned home once discharged. This raises the issue of the impact on family relations of a sizeable proportion of young men leaving the area. Again, this may have given women a more prominent role within the family. If discharged soldiers settled elsewhere, it probably produced an imbalance between the numbers of men and women available for marriage. A sizeable number of unmarried women may have led to different roles and influence for them within their families and the wider society. Although we cannot answer these questions, the demands of Roman military recruitment had the potential to disrupt family relationships and produce localized family structures.

Another suggestion of different family structures comes from the layout of domestic houses. We are used to broadly equating the *domus* with the *familia,* but in some areas the pattern of housing differed from the single-family atrium or peristyle house that dominated Italy and North Africa. This was the case in Galilee in the first century B.C.E., for example.[37] Although the majority were single houses adjoining a courtyard, approximately ten percent were multiple houses of two or three rooms sharing a courtyard with a single entrance. This would have allowed an element of privacy but with a communal courtyard for domestic tasks such as grinding, cooking, or spinning. These houses may have been occupied by related families who were able to provide support and assistance to each other, whether in child care, household duties, or food resources in times of shortage. Similarly, it has been argued that in Britain and northwestern Europe, the layout of rural villas points toward a continuation of extended family structures.[38] Prior to conquest (43 C.E.), so the argument goes, land was owned by kin groups, although not all constituent families were necessarily of the same status. This organization continued after conquest and is reflected in the design of the area's villas, which can be divided into individual sections for each family; these villas contain one part larger than the others, suggesting that one family was considered senior. Many of these villas seem to contain two sets of living quarters, with reduplicated rooms and entrances, which alongside their size points to occupation by more than one family.

A similar form of close family groups may be seen in Egypt. Here the evidence is for endogamous marriages, with instances of marriage between siblings.[39] This difference in incest taboos was the result of a different family structure—with an inner core, between whom marriage was prohibited, and an outer group, with whom the inner core could marry. For sibling marriages to be acceptable, one sibling had to be regarded as part of the inner core and the other as part of the outer core, pointing to a different family organization from societies where sibling marriages were considered taboo. Furthermore, the close relationship between family members also seems to be echoed in the customs of property ownership, where although the nuclear family unit might occupy a single house, the extended family often owned a series of adjoining properties, and the combined family had a stake in all the houses.

Although the significance of this has been downplayed, these differences in family structure had an impact on the upbringing of the child. The age at first marriage is one of the primary factors in family structure and fertility rates for the population as a whole, and so differences in the age of marriage would have had an impact on the overall demography of the provinces. In addition, in areas where the father married later in life (in his late twenties or thirties), there would have been less chance of his children knowing their paternal grandparents, particularly their grandfathers. In many rural societies, the rearing of children is considered a communal activity that involved the entire family, particularly grandparents and elder siblings. While Roman texts give the impression of nurses drawn from slaves or freedwomen, below the level of the elite, nuclear and extended families played a part.[40] Children brought up within extended families or multiple family units would have had access to a wider circle of people: there might have been aunts, uncles, and cousins nearby, possibly sharing cooking or courtyard areas.

This picture of different family structures becomes even clearer during late antiquity, where there is evidence for three regional legal codes.[41] In the Mediterranean, there was the continuity of Roman law, while areas settled by Germanic groups retained their legal customs, although sometimes incorporating elements of Roman law. Finally, on the Atlantic fringe, we see a different Celtic custom, possibly but not necessarily, a continuity of pre-Roman social customs. These different codes altered patterns of marriage and inheritance: in the Roman Mediterranean there was a strict delineation between a single form of legally sanctioned marriage and concubinage, whereas within the other two customs there were multiple forms of official marriages, which allowed for a single lead wife but other simultaneous wives of lesser status. Similarly, there were different laws stipulating who could inherit dependent upon both the gender of the child and the status of the union between the parents. There were also differences in what constituted an incestuous union, which, at the most extreme, included godparents, co-parents, and in-laws. All these elements come together to suggest different family setups and the concept that who was seen as a child's sibling, and the relative status between them as denoted by inheritance, could also be variable between different cultural areas of the world of late antiquity.

THE REGIONALITY OF THE LIFE COURSE

A third area where we can detect regional variability is the way age was understood, in particular the transitions between the age stages of the life course and the way they were valued. Age identities are not cultural universals but vary depending on social context and cultural influences. The age at which a person progresses from childhood to adulthood may be judged by different social norms. It may be marked by a biological transition, such as the first shaving for a boy or menarche for a girl; or it might be a social transition, such as marriage or apprenticeship; or it may be legally sanctioned, such as the ability to vote or own property. The way in which these were valued and marked might also vary and correspond to the wider ideologies of the society. These differences can be seen in Latin epitaphs.[42] Age statements are included in a variable proportion of the total number of epitaphs and do not follow the expected patterns of mortality. Instead, certain ages are more likely to be mentioned when they take on particular significance.

The cultural variability in the meaning of age and age stages can be seen clearly within Italy itself, where there is evidence for the continuation of social norms from the period prior to the Roman conquest. For example, epitaphs from Samnium, Picenum, and Umbria (*regiones* 4–6) in central Italy show a marked emphasis on children and young adults, with over eighty percent of age statements recording the age thirty or under. In contrast, in Etruria (*regio* 7), and specifically at the city of Tarquinia, the figures are sixty-three percent and thirty-two percent, respectively. The profile from Samnium, Picenum, and Umbria reflects an ideology of age that sees the transition to adulthood as marked by taking up the roles of wife for women and citizen/magistrate for men.[43] Death is seen as more poignant when the deceased has not yet made this transition. This underpins the pathos behind the epitaph to thirteen-year-old Coelia from the town of Forum Novum in central Italy, which reads: "Traveler, halt a moment and look upon my tomb, for you do not know the brief span of my life."[44] Age statements for those whose deaths occurred in childhood up to the early twenties are included because they point to this unfulfilled promise of the deceased.

In contrast, evidence from other areas, particularly Tarquinia, shows less focus on the commemoration of children and a more pronounced concentration on those in their forties to seventies. This echoes the pattern in the inscriptions in the Etruscan language found in south Etruria and Volterra dating from the fourth to the first centuries B.C.E. Here there is a similar concentration on those who died in early adulthood or old age. This could indicate

Table 4.2: Cumulative percentages of inclusion of age statements from samples in Italy.

Age in years	Regiones 4–6	Regio 7	Tarquinia
0–10	19.40%	19.25%	6.25%
11–20	56.62%	36.34%	16.07%
21–30	83.12%	62.73%	32.14%
31–40	90.38%	77.33%	42.86%
41–50	93.06%	86.02%	55.36%
51–60	95.43%	90.37%	73.21%
61–70	97.63%	95.34%	88.39%
71–80	99.21%	98.45%	96.43%
81–90	100.00%	99.07%	99.11%
91–100	100.00%	100.00%	100.00%

a respect for the older generations and grandparents in particular, a pattern that continues to a degree into the Roman period and accounts for the variation between this region and other parts of central Italy (Samnium, Picenum, and Umbria), leading us to conclude that childhood was also conceptualized in a different manner. This regional variability can also be identified outside Italy—at Cordoba in Spain and the province of Britain. Even more marked is the pattern found at Thugga in North Africa, where continued commemoration of those from fifty to one hundred shows it was considered a significant stage within the life course.

Such regional patterns are not attributable to demographic variability but demonstrate marked differences in the ideologies of aging and which stages are considered more important to commemorate. It shows that the categories of infant, child, youth, adult, old adult, and elderly were culturally variable within the Roman world as Roman norms interacted with preconquest traditions. The picture from the textual sources—of childhood marked by specific ceremonies in the teens and a period of adolescence for men until their mid-twenties—can be seen in certain areas in Italy, but in other places (e.g., Tarquinia) it was less pronounced. In Italy, there was ambivalence toward the elderly and little use for age statements on epitaphs after the age of thirty. This does not mean that those over thirty were not afforded written memorials but rather that age statements were not included as they no longer carried the same significance. When we look at other areas (Etruria, southern Spain, and North

Africa), we see a very different construction of the life course and a greater commemoration of those over the age of thirty. There is a clear commemoration of the elderly in Thugga, and this may also be the case for men in southern Spain. This was a product of a different attitude toward the elderly and older members of the family and raises the possibility that relationships between various family members may have differed. Grandparents, for example, may have played a more active and authoritative role in family decisions and family activities. It certainly reinforces the arguments already made that family relations and childhood within antiquity need to be seen as culturally variable.

Looking for children in antiquity first seems something of a mirage. We have an image of their experiences from a range of texts. However, these have a limited outlook (Athens or Rome, elite families, public life), and when we look outside of these areas, children and the family rapidly vanish. This is not solely the fault of the evidence, although it does play a part. Instead, it is caused by the way we approach the past and the nature of the questions we ask. There is a tendency to look at the past as the product of great men or political and economic processes, and there is a concentration on the material evidence as the end in itself, depopulated of the people who once produced and interacted with it. However, as we have seen in this chapter, it is possible to repopulate antiquity with a view to establishing the geographical and cultural patterning of the experience of childhood in antiquity.

CHAPTER FIVE

Education

CHRISTIAN LAES

The modern imagination of scholars and the general public alike latches onto a series of idealized images to create a normalizing picture of education in antiquity: young boys all dressed in chitons (tunics) diffidently looking at their master, who taught writing skills, playing the flute, or bodily exercises; or an austere grammarian reciting verses and literary wisdom to an audience of obedient pupils; or a toga-clad adolescent boy proudly showing off his rhetorical skill at his first public performance. The modern mind will not spontaneously link education in antiquity with Jewish boys being taught the Torah in synagogues spread throughout the Roman Empire or with young Celts acquiring arcane knowledge from the Druids and almost certainly not with the images of children being taught the catechism, young initiates in monasteries, or lessons in the Islamic kuttabs.

There are many reasons for these firmly rooted assumptions. Firstly, they reflect the opinions that Greek and Roman writers, who focus almost exclusively on upper-class Athens and Rome, want us to follow. For Greek history, our knowledge is for the most part confined to what Athenian writers of the golden age of Greek literature (the fifth and fourth centuries B.C.E.) bring to our attention. It is hazardous to extrapolate to the hundreds of other city-states. Admittedly, Sparta is often brought to our attention, but it is usually mentioned as the exception to the rule, and a degree of utopian projection certainly plays a major role in the representation of Sparta.[1] If one wants to know about practicalities of school life in the plethora of cities in the west or east of the Roman Empire, it is inscriptional evidence (Latin for the west, Greek for the east) one needs to consult, not the writers of Latin literature.

Secondly, our assumptions reflect the outstanding success of the Greco-Roman schooling system in antiquity. Though schools were not organized by governing authorities, the entirely private approach to teaching resulted in a concept of encyclical studies, a program involving a number of subjects to be taken in a particular sequence: reading and writing, grammar, study of literature, some knowledge of geometry, mathematics, music and astronomy, and rhetoric. While state intervention was largely absent and deliberate plans of colonization and Hellenization were virtually nonexistent, Greek schools and gymnasia spread to the borders of modern Afghanistan, creating a *lingua franca* and a shared lifestyle of Greekness over an enormous territory ranging from Egypt through Greece to the center of Asia. Later, Roman conquerors were eager to take over the Greek education system and take advantage of it while also emphasizing their own identity. A pure Roman culture never existed at any time in antiquity; from the very beginning of our source material, schooling and education were Greco-Roman, and these schools spread all over the Roman Empire.[2]

Thirdly, throughout several cultural revivals of which the Renaissance is the most famous, Greco-Roman educational ideals have been adapted; these ideals continue to have a tangible resonance in the twenty-first century. Unlike modern systems of education, the antique system did not have a uniform pattern, yet a three-grade system (in some ways comparable to our pattern of elementary, secondary, and higher education) was frequently followed.[3] Moreover, deeply rooted scholarly fashions and beliefs in the perennial value of our classical heritage have reinforced the focus on Athens, Rome, and the education of the upper class. Perhaps this aspect has resulted in the claim that a multicultural overview—taking into account Egyptian, Jewish, Persian, Celtic, and other traditions of education in antiquity—would result in a superficial work, a claim that has been clearly refuted by studies that have emphasized the wider context and the *longue durée* of ancient education.[4] Finally, Greco-Roman antiquity is often thought to end at roughly the third century C.E., but Peter Brown has convincingly argued that the process of continuity and change was far more gradual and that the end of antiquity should rather be fixed around 800 C.E., when the Mediterranean was culturally separated from the eastern part (the Arab Umayyad dynasty lost to the Persian Abbasid dynasty, which turned toward India and the Far East) as well as from the western part (Rome and Italy were cut off from the West by the end of the sixth century C.E.).[5]

This chapter follows the educational path of children in antiquity along lines by and large drawn by ancient writers themselves. Each stage includes evidence chronologically drawn from classical Greece, the Hellenistic world, the Roman Empire, and late antiquity, and factors of continuity or change are indicated wherever possible. The concluding paragraphs look at the broader context, taking into account evidence from other cultures around the Mediterranean and searching for phenomena of the *longue durée,* which characterizes the way children were educated and socialized in the period from 500 B.C.E. to 800 C.E. The focus of the chapter is on education rather than the upbringing of children. In reality, both socialization and education are everyday processes that need to be studied in the wider context of the family and community, housing and environment, and religious practices and cults. These are subjects of other chapters in this volume.

EARLY CHILDHOOD: EDUCATION WITHOUT KINDERGARTEN

Ancient authors have a lot to tell us about the early childhood years—roughly up to the age of seven. Much information comes from medical writers, but philosophers, rhetoricians, and theologians have contributed to the discussion of education. At first sight, this may seem strange. Greco-Roman culture valued rhetorical skills and the display of literary knowledge. As a consequence, the age of *logos* or *ratio* (reason) was thought to occur after rather than before the age of seven. Yet because ancient philosophers were convinced young babies were almost as irrational as animals, education in these early years focused on an infant's adaptation to society and its norms. This might be described as a battle between nature and nurture, with a child's innate characteristics from nature only being overcome by scrupulous attention to their moral education. Young children were as weak as wax, and their infant tenderness had to be molded from an early age in order for them to become full-fledged adults. The image of the molding of children can be found in ancient philosophers as well as in early Christian patristic authors.[6] Rhetoricians believed the formation of the ideal orator was a continuing process that needed to start almost from the cradle. So when Cicero writes about little toddlers being curious to learn—showing the behavior one may expect of adults, lying on the ground helpless or soulless at the beginning of their lives but afterward rising to their feet; learning to use their hands and senses; recognizing friends and educators; finding joy in play, competition, and being with others their age; hearing stories and exchanging gifts; and hardly bearing their loss in games—he speaks to us as a philosopher in the tradition of his Greek predecessors (e.g., Plato and Aristotle), not as a psychologist with educational views on the kindergarten phase.

The same applies to Quintilian's (ca. 35–ca. 95 C.E.) observations on children's first linguistic and moral performances or to Augustine's (354–430 C.E.) description of early childhood, which fits into the discourse of original sin and human greed as observable from the earliest years.[7]

According to Plato, the formation of human character starts with motions in the mother's womb as well as with the gymnastics of midwives rocking a little child. A fourth-century Roman grammarian, Nonius Marcellus, mentions midwives in the series of successive educators of a child.[8] It would hardly be an exaggeration to state that midwives occupied a vital role in the education of children. Indeed, they decided whether an infant had any chance of survival. The newborn child was placed on the ground, and his or her viability was assessed. Only after this assessment was it decided to cut the umbilical cord. Throughout antiquity, midwives were viewed with ambivalence. Connections between midwives and witches or old women of inferior social status frequently occur (lower status and often servile descent is also attested in inscriptions). In comedy, the midwife is sometimes introduced as an old, drunken slut. But in Soranus's *Gynaecology*, the ideal midwife appears as a perfect doctor: trained and discerning, equipped with a good memory and a manly drive, decent and discrete, sober minded and level headed, and not at all superstitious.[9] Soranus does not actually promote these women to physicians *tout court;* however, he does give them a role as the first educators of the babies of wealthy Roman aristocrats (Soranus's clientele). This upgrading of midwives testifies to the great value attached to children in Greco-Roman society. Soranus's idealized picture was taken up by late antique medical compilers, and this positive image of midwives was incorporated into Arabic medicine. In antiquity we see a folk tradition in which the working methods of midwives hardly changed over centuries. Their secret knowledge was passed on from woman to woman.[10]

Immediately after birth, the infant was entrusted to the care of a nurse. The wet nurse was entrusted with the task of breast-feeding whereas the Latin term *nutrix assa* refers to the dry nurse who took care of the child without actually sharing her milk.[11] These nurses had many tasks: swaddling the little baby; feeding; bathing; taking care of its health; helping it to sit, crawl, and walk; and storytelling (an important feature of early moral education, as ancient writers were well aware). It should be noted that Sparta acted as the exception to the rule throughout classical tradition: Spartan nurses were said not to swaddle little children in order to secure the free movement of future brave warriors.[12] Undoubtedly, the little child spent most of his early years with the nurse, who acted as a kind of surrogate mother. There is every reason to believe that the phenomenon of nursing was relatively widespread in Greek and

Roman antiquity and not only confined to upper-class and wealthy women who disregarded breast-feeding for fashionable reasons. Wet-nursing contracts from Hellenistic and Roman Egypt refer to people of relatively meager standing who hired wet nurses; cross-cultural evidence demonstrates it was often economically more profitable to hire a nurse, thereby granting the biological mother the opportunity to carry on with her work; asides in letters or fables testify to the frequency of the phenomenon. The majority of wet nurses were undoubtedly poor women or slaves who were obliged to share their milk with a stranger's or the master's child (the latter situation being amply attested in inscriptions).[13] The connection with social inferiority appears first in Athens, from where it crossed over into Hellenistic epigrammatic tradition and sculpture (the drunken nurse) and was finally incorporated into the repertoire of Roman traditionalists of the second century C.E.[14]

Nursing was by no means a form of institutionalized abandonment, not least because most nurses spent their days with the nursling in the biological parents' house. It needs to be stressed that large orphanages were unknown in Greco-Roman antiquity and only came into being in the third century C.E. and became established in the early Byzantine Empire. Some nurses were valued and appreciated by their former charges and were sometimes taken into their employers' houses when they had reached old age or were cherished as persons of trust through donations.[15] Ancient writers were well aware that the close proximity between a nurse and her charge could create bonds closer than the parent-child relationship. Since many nurses were outsiders in aristocratic society, some authors were deeply bothered by this fact. Both Cicero and Seneca explicitly acknowledged the profound influence and possible intimacy in later life between nurses and their charges. Hence, some moralists (e.g., Favorinus of Arles, second century C.E.) opposed the institution, an opposition enforced by the belief that character traits were actually transmitted through breast milk. This seems to have been a minority viewpoint, and nurses, like midwives, were upgraded into a key educational position: nurses can be identified as the first teachers of eloquence, as authoritative figures with imperial airs, or as perfect physicians or medical tools—again, an image elaborated upon by Soranus that found its way into late antique compilations.[16]

Pedagogues were introduced into the lives of young children when they were about to attend school. Though their tasks somewhat overlapped with nurses, who attended their young masters for several years, pedagogues were linked with education and the school phase of a child's life. They guarded their young masters on the way to school and offered private instruction, both moral and intellectual. Like nurses, they were mostly drawn from the lower classes or were slaves. Once again, we only get a glimpse of the socialization of young children and the practicalities of their daily life through information about their educators. We read about strong alliances between pupils and pedagogues as the origin of attempts to overthrow the rule of the aristocracy in Athens in the fifth century B.C.E. and, in another age, the deep affective bond between the future emperor Julian the Apostate and his pedagogue-eunuch Mardonius (mid-fourth century C.E.). On the other hand, there is evidence of pedagogues enforcing their will on young and pampered aristocrats who despise them for their low social status.[17]

The emphasis on midwives, nurses, and pedagogues may create the impression that parents in antiquity were not involved with the education of their children. Historians have interpreted this distant attitude as a defense mechanism securing parents against the grief of premature death—a possibility explicitly acknowledged by Greek and Roman authors. In the Greek comic tradition, fathers taking care of young children were ridiculed.[18] However, one should not be misled by literary sources that emphasize rhetorical skills and education. Iconographic evidence, both Greek and Roman; explicit literary statements; and ample epigraphic evidence in the form of thousands of funerary inscriptions for deceased children point to parents being concerned and involved with the welfare and education of their toddlers. "One can hardly believe it, he was already able to recognize his parents" reads a metrical inscription for a child who died when he was six months old, and a beautiful poem from Cologne mentions a mother who is reminded of the childish play and sweet laughter of her young Catulus, who died after only thirteen months.[19] Other factors contributing to education are hardly mentioned in the sources but must have been important. Early education up to the age of four was entrusted to the mother or other women of the household. Interaction and play between young children was another significant factor of socialization (images of children playing in groups and pulling each others' hair are found on sarcophagi, and there is a famous apocryphal story about the child Jesus becoming angry and killing a boy who interfered with the pools of water Jesus had formed at the brook to make clay). Children played with dolls: Plutarch sadly remembered how his young infant daughter used to ask her nurse to give milk to her little toys.[20] On the darker side, the high mortality rates must have caused every single child to be confronted in his or her young life with the experience of playmates, siblings, parents, or other relatives dying.

PRIMARY EDUCATION WITH THE SCHOOLMASTER

Ancient schools lacked two features we consider self-evident in our schooling system: there was hardly any state intervention or control, and attendance was a private matter of choice. This implies teachers being privately paid, no official certificates or degrees, plus a very limited possibility of social promotion through schooling for the less affluent in society. In addition, it is worth pointing out that chronological age was not an important factor in determining the nature of the training given (the system of classes as connected with ages is a Jesuit invention from the late sixteenth century). According to our evidence, schools emerged in Athens from the beginning of the fifth century B.C.E., which seems to be linked with the development of democracy. Conservative aristocrats had opposed the institution, emphasizing the value of innate virtue, or *kalokagathia*, and despising those who had reached knowledge "only because they have learnt it."[21] It is traditionally acknowledged that Athenian boys attended school from the age of seven or so and that their schooling was divided into three areas: reading, writing, and some arithmetic with the *didaskalos*; physical training with the *paidotribès*; and music and poetry with the *kitharistès*. While some have argued this may even have been a traditional pattern in the Greek world, this is a pet theory of philosophers. In fact, we hardly know anything about the institution and practicalities of the day-to-day activities in schools in classical Athens.[22] It is preferable to see Athenian schools as neighborhood schools bringing together boys of different social class and economic status, with badly paid schoolteachers teaching different subjects to a too-large group of pupils in very primitive material circumstances deprived of any pedagogical comfort. Wealthier children may have profited from private education or may have attended school for a longer period, while the learning of *mousikè* (poetry sung to music) by the poor was regarded as an unnecessary luxury. Gymnastics were taught at a different location with space and facilities for physical exercise.[23]

Ample evidence sheds interesting light on the daily practices of schoolmasters in Hellenistic and Roman Egypt as well as in different provinces of the Roman Empire, and conditions were undoubtedly not very different from earlier periods. Contrary to other teachers, schoolmasters were hardly ever exempted from taxes or municipal duties, and elementary education was never freely provided by the state in order to ensure the literacy of a large part of the population.[24] Teaching was provided in a room that was hardly separated from busy outside life, pupils lacked the comfort of handbooks or a blackboard, and didactic methods were completely based on imitation, rattling off lessons, and drill. Authority was often enforced by physical means. Firstly, the alphabet was learned by heart and recited, from beginning to end and the other way around, then all possible combinations of syllables. Only after this strenuous task of memorizing without having seen a letter did pupils proceed to writing, which was learned by endlessly copying words (often not common vocabulary but archaic or literary language) or little moralizing fables. One of the latter was a popular story about the murderer who fled to the Nile, climbed into a tree when he was chased by a wolf, jumped into the water when he was confronted with a snake in the tree, and finally was torn to pieces by a crocodile in the river.[25] The schoolmaster or his assistant held the pupil's hand, guiding it over the letter shapes. Inevitably, the learning process was slow, and pupils stayed for many years until parents believed they had acquired sufficient skill to stop or to proceed with another teacher. Most of the children who attended the schoolmaster possessed only very basic reading and writing skills. As a consequence of *scriptura continua*, or continuous writing, reading was always a difficult and oral affair that involved trying to recognize word or word groups by laboriously reading aloud. Hence, most people were proud to be able to spell their proper name or show off some basic literacy. Counting was also an oral matter, often taught by numbering on the fingers.[26]

Not surprisingly, there is an elaborate discourse on schoolteachers stressing their humble descent and task. "One is either dead or teaching elementary skills" was proverbial for contempt throughout antiquity. As with other educational figures, schoolteachers sometimes made the best of it, as we know from inscriptions proudly erected by teachers in small or remote villages. They enjoyed certain esteem in their environments as disseminators of culture—the only people able to read and write properly or even able to teach some higher forms of education such as Greek or Roman authors since grammarians were not available in the wider region.[27]

Despite the concerns of Christian writers about classical education being entirely centered around pagan mythology and religion, Christians certainly committed themselves to the task of elementary teaching (Hippolytus's *Apostolic Tradition* from the early third century C.E. allowed Christians to continue in the teaching profession if they could not earn their living in another way). The short-lived legislation of the emperor Julian the Apostate (361–363 C.E.) that forbade Christians to teach in schools did not change this situation and indicates that by that time many Christians were in the teaching profession. When the emperor Theodosius declared Christianity the only legally permitted religion in 391 C.E., it may safely be assumed it became the mainstream religion in elementary schools, too. We know of Christian schoolteachers in the fifth and sixth centuries, again proof that this form of education lasted well into late antiquity only to collapse altogether with the fall of the Greco-Roman educational system. Christianity did not significantly change the contents of education. Christian teachers continued to teach classical mythology and the classical authors, though we may safely assume they criticized the contents of pagan literature or interpreted it allegorically, and Christian children learned to read and write together with their pagan peers.[28] Christianity did bring some changes: catechetical teaching involved people of both sexes and of mixed social status and age, including children, but was kept outside the normal school curriculum. It was probably in this context that young children learned to recite the sacred liturgy, as the lector Vitalis had by the time he died at age five. The daily calendar of the week with the free Sunday was another Christian innovation from the reign of the emperor Constantine. It replaced the former school calendars, which had relied on the numerous pagan holidays of the city of Rome or on local custom. Some radicals advocated sending children to monasteries for their education,[29] but these forms of education did not become mainstream in late antiquity. Finally, in the context of Christian charity, there is evidence from the third century of a sort of Christian boarding school for orphans, paid for by the Christian community and presided over by the bishop, but we do not know about the content of the education provided except that the orphan boys learned a craft. Generally speaking, Christians understood how encyclical studies made it possible to acquire status and positions in society, and they accepted the system and used their knowledge to study and assimilate Christian writings into that system.[30]

As to the presence of girls in elementary schools in antiquity, there is no unambiguous evidence that they attended them in Athens in the fifth and fourth century B.C.E. (a fact that might be linked to the seclusion of Athenian women), but they certainly were present in Hellenistic schools as well as during Roman times until late antiquity. The poet Martial explicitly mentions a schoolmaster terrifying both girls and boys attending his classes. These girls sat together with lower class boys and sometimes even slaves; however, the more well-to-do received private elementary instruction rather than attend the classes of a schoolmaster.[31]

SECONDARY EDUCATION WITH THE GRAMMARIAN, HIGHER FORMS OF EDUCATION

By the end of the fourth century B.C.E., a pattern emerged in which the teacher who came after the elementary educational phase, commonly known as a grammarian, took up the task of teaching literature.[32] Their audiences consisted of boys from roughly twelve to fifteen years of age (though age boundaries were not at all strict) of higher social class. Grammarians are undoubtedly the best-known instructors of Greco-Roman antiquity. Dozens of school texts preserved on papyri survive (word lists, gnomic texts, scholia, authors, grammars) as penned by students or teachers from Hellenistic Egypt to the Byzantine age; these self-conscious educators even produced hundreds of pages recording their instruction, proudly displaying their ability to unravel every single sentence or grammatical construction found in their favorite school authors: Homer was the basic classic, while other important Greek authors were Hesiod, Euripides, Menander, Isocrates, and Demosthenes and, for the Latin, Cicero, Virgil, Terence, and Sallust.[33] However, some basic features of the role of teachers are frequently misunderstood. Though there is plenty of evidence of Hellenistic city-states or towns of the Roman Empire granting privileges or immunity to grammarians, providing space to teach and sometimes public salaries, their instruction always implied a considerable sum of money being paid by the parents. There was never any state intervention: even in late antiquity, when the Roman state was desperate to find skilled administrators, the idea of paying grammarians from the treasury never occurred.[34]

While there is plenty of evidence of learned women from the Greco-Roman world, there is not a single unambiguous reference to girls sitting together with boys in the grammarians' classes: private home instruction, possibly involving a small group of girls, might have been the way in which upper-class women acquired literacy and culture.[35] The pretentious, unworldly, and pedantic grammarians' approach was often ridiculed even in their own time, but their instruction was in fact very practical and perfectly fitting to the needs and mentality of their elite audience.[36] Their pupils understood that the path to knowledge was a harsh and tiresome one and that learning could only be attained by great effort and obedience to an authoritative instructor who held the keys to a difficult and well-defined system of knowledge. When they left the grammarian, they were endowed with a layer of varnish—enough to proudly present themselves as literate persons, able to bring up some quotes of ancient authors and perform on public occasions, giving speeches or taking part in lawsuits.[37]

There were many ways for the rich to refine this knowledge: education with a rhetorician was their most frequent option. The system of rhetorical instruction involved endlessly polishing one's style in various exercises and public performances. It is a well-documented feature ranging from the fifth-century sophists in Athens and Isocrates's school in the fourth century B.C.E. to the intellectual superstars of the second sophist movement of the second century C.E. to late antique orators such as Ausonius in the west or Libanius and Themistius in the east.[38] Of course, there were plenty of other possibilities for those who could afford it. The gymnasia of Hellenized towns invited public speakers and *ephebes* (young men) to listen them. At a local level, wealthy youngsters could perfect their knowledge in libraries, which were sometimes donated by rich benefactors, or they could learn a politician's job through tuition from a senior politician.

FIGURES 5.1–5.2: *Attic red figure kylix showing school scenes of boys and teachers, signed by Douris, ca. 490–80* B.C.E. *Berlin, Staatliche Museen, Antikensammlung.* Images © Bildarchiv Preußischer Kulturbesitz.

Some cities evolved into what have been anachronistically called university towns: Athens, Rhodes, Antioch, Alexandria, and Constantinople (the latter three in late antiquity), while others such as the law school of Beyrouth and the famous medical school of Pergamum offered specialized opportunities. Hellenistic papyri, letters by Marcus Tullius Cicero, and late antique testimonies by church fathers offer unique insight the tumultuous life in these university towns, with noisy and rebellious gangs of students with their own initiation rites and friendships as well as rhetoricians struggling to make the best out of it or being cherished as intellectual superstars and acquiring considerable wealth. Those students who came as foreigners from about fifteen years of age (although younger students are known) entered a new life: separated from their parents and family (sometimes guarded by a pedagogue), they lived in a new environment with its own codes—quite often students' bad behavior was tolerated whereas the very same acts perpetrated by others were punished. This is as close as one comes to a youthful subculture in antiquity, a phenomenon of a very restricted class who had time and leisure to indulge in intellectual activities and peer group behavior. In the year 370 C.E., the emperor Valentinian I tried to restrict students' activities in the cities of Rome and Constantinople by imposing a maximum age of twenty—creating for the first time an end point for a person's education.[39]

However, to a Roman gentleman the rhetorician was by no means the end of his education. The *artes liberales,* initially taught at school, occupied a central place in the lives of civilized Romans. In the first century C.E., *bildung* gradually became synonymous with *schulbildung.* Hence a specific vocabulary for pupils and adults was lacking: both were depicted as proud participants in Roman rhetorical culture. Education was very much a continuing process. Moral philosophers wrote for adult learners wishing to develop their self-restraint and moderation. Keeping up the appearance of manliness and culture was vital to members of the higher classes.[40]

FIGURE 5.3: *Relief depicting school scene from Neumagen.* Second century C.E. Rheinisches Landesmuseum, Trier. Image: Bridgeman Art Library.

THE WORLD CONTEXT: OTHER FORMS OF EDUCATION

The Spartan educational system has become well-known because it was to-tally regulated by the state and because of its brutality and stress on mili-tary skill. At the age of seven, boys of true Spartan provenance were taken from the family home to training schools. Gymnastic exercises and the art of fighting were the primary subjects. In structured age groups (eight to eleven, twelve to fifteen, and sixteen to twenty years of age) they lived in "Spartan" conditions supervised by a special magistrate; lightly clothed and barefooted even in winter, they slept on straw mattresses without covers and were poorly fed. No formal lessons in literacy were given (though Plutarch stresses that Spartan aristocrats were not illiterate), but music was encouraged in the form of patriotic songs and poetry. To toughen body and spirit, beatings and whip-pings were handed out, and pupils were not allowed to express pain. From the age of twenty, young men lived in barracks. Girls were subjected to an education in which dance and music were the main subjects due to eugenic concern—the aim was to shape strong bodies to give birth to new Spartan warriors. From the second half of the fourth century B.C.E., the number of Spartan hoplites steadily declined, and the Spartan state shrunk to a little folkloristic village: in Roman times, tourists flocked to a specially built the-ater to watch the bloody floggings of Spartan boys. The idealized image of a state-controlled militaristic upbringing was cherished by supporters of Sparta in other city-states. Xenophon pointed out that Sparta was one of those exceptional states in which pederastic relationships were pure educational friendships, not sexual debauchery.[41]

The Greco-Roman world came into contact with other cultures with long-established traditions on education and schooling. Egyptian educational prac-tice and ideals were remarkably persistent for more than two thousand five hundred years. They were permeated with ideas on harmony and justice (Egyp-tian Ma'at) and obedience toward elders and parents. Due to the nature of hieroglyphic writing, reading and writing skills were a highly technical and specialized matter: sons of courtiers, and later also talented boys from the middle class, went to palace schools in order to become scribes, civil servants, priests, courtiers, ministers, and diplomats. Endless drill and repetitive exer-cises were the main features of Egyptian teaching: we know of schoolbooks containing glossaries, proper names, moralizing rules, and wisdom literature. Discipline was harsh: "a boy's ear is situated on his back; he listens when he is beaten" is a stock phrase of Egyptian education. Schooling of those boys (we hardly know anything about girls, though some were literate) began as early as age six and continued until age twenty. Egyptian schools persisted well into Greco-Roman times, and Demotic was still taught in Roman Egypt.[42] Little is known about the educational system of ancient Persia, on the border of the Greco-Roman world. Herodotus, who also refers to ages five to twenty, mentions ethical guidance and the desire to produce efficient soldiers as the main purposes of Achaemenid education; so does Xenophon in his idealized *Cyropaedia,* as well as Plutarch, who mentions the wisdom of the magi in connection with Cyrus the Younger. Most Persian nobles were literate, and the Persians also used professional scribes for the state chancery. There is no concrete information on schools in Parthian times, but Pahlavi treatises do inform us about the schools of noble boys in Sassanian times. A child would begin attending school between age five and seven and would complete his general training at age fifteen. Reading and writing were linked with religious instruction (memorizing the sacred texts and listening to the Zand, the Pahlavi translation of the Avesta). Astrology, physical education, and training in courtly arts (such as playing musical instruments or playing chess) were part of the curriculum. While some girls probably attended school for religious reasons, the main part of their training was in domestic skills. Again, the sources provide evidence on administering physical punishment.[43]

The best established foreign schooling tradition in the Greco-Roman world was undoubtedly the Jewish system, with its synagogues spread all over the empire, and conversions to the Jewish religion were increasing in the third and fourth centuries C.E. The Jewish school system was already well established in the second century B.C.E. when we hear of tensions between Jewish schools and Hellenistic gymnasia. According to the Talmud, there were 480 synagogues in Jerusalem in the beginning of the Christian era, each equipped with a *bet-sefer,* for elementary schooling and reading holy scripture, and a *bet-talmud,* for teaching the Misjna. The high priest Jozua ben Gamala (63–65 C.E.) decreed that each synagogue should appoint a teacher to instruct children from age six or seven. Both in purpose and practice, these schools were very similar to later Islamic kuttabs: instruction was focused on religion and sacred texts, the teacher sat in the forecourt on a bench and recited knowledge amidst a group of pupils of mixed ages (a maximum of twenty-five according to rabbinic tradition), and students sat on the bare ground and held writing tablets. Teaching methods were dully repetitive, and corporal punishment was frequently handed out. While everything was centered around holy scripture, skills such as counting and geographic knowledge were taught to help the understanding of biblical passages. Even the alphabet offered the possibility of teaching moralizing sentences from the Torah. Besides schools, religious instruction was always considered a home affair and the parents' duty: the young Jesus not only learned the carpenter's craft with his father but was also instructed in holy scripture.[44]

We have little information on other indigenous teaching traditions. The Oscan language survived in Italy well into the first century B.C.E., but we do not know whether there were Oscan schools in Campania during the late republic.[45] Some Celtic nobles continued to send their sons to Druids, where they learned sacred lore, religious tasks and duties, and sacred texts, which were transmitted orally without reference to an alphabet during an apprenticeship of twenty years. The emperors Tiberius (14–37 C.E.) and Claudius (41–54 C.E.) found Druidic instruction a threat to the Roman state, a clear indication of its continuing success in the first century despite the fact that the geographer Strabo mentions that aristocratic Celts were sending their sons to Greco-Roman schools in Marseille in the first century B.C.E.[46]

EPILOGUE: CHANGE AND CONTINUITY, THE *LONGUE DURÉE*

By the fifth century C.E., Greco-Roman schools withdrew from the stage of public life since they had lost their breeding ground—the ancient cities. The western part of the empire was the first to succumb: in the period from 450–600 C.E., people sought refuge from foreign invaders in the shelter of warlords' domains or walled and protected monasteries. The age of the forum, with orators declaiming and competing in public for municipal glory, was past, and in the early medieval world learned and cultivated people were almost invariably monks and clergymen. In the shelter of their monasteries, they cherished a sophisticated Latin while reverting to a basic form of the language in their sermons or hagiographic stories for ordinary folk. It was in many ways a closed (contacts and traveling became less frequent and more difficult) and middlebrow culture. In the sixth century, the eastern part of the empire suffered from invasions and endemic plagues. When the enterprising emperor Justinian (527–565 C.E.) passed away, he left an empire in which the Greek city-states and their rhetorical culture had been replaced by gangsterism and theology: bishoprics, located in city centers and monasteries, became flourishing hiding places in a totally Christian society. The sharp boundaries between aristocratic culture, cherishing the idea of *otium* (leisure), and the popular culture of men in the street faded away. Parents continued to care about the instruction of their children, and some sent them to monasteries as oblates (see chapter 8). As apprentices they could learn a trade or reading and writing (contrary to pagans, Christians, as believers of the book, valued reading much more than writing). As stated in the Pachomian rule (fourth century C.E.), teaching methods remained very traditional: a monk firstly spelled out letters, followed by syllables, verbs, and pronouns. Novices were obliged to learn the psalms by heart. In the same way, Benedictine monasteries in the west cared for the literate instruction of young monks: monks up to age fifteen learned to recite the liturgical material of the daily services.[47] When Arab Muslim culture later entered the Mediterranean, the teaching methods of Islamic kuttabs were very much in line with Jewish synagogue schools and Byzantine primary schools in monasteries: connected with the mosque, a badly paid schoolmaster taught young children (from age four, mostly separated by gender) for a period of between two and five years. The teaching involved reciting, endless repetition and memorization, and a completely Koran-based form of instruction, also utilized for reading and writing, with all other subjects subordinate. Physical punishment and rather primitive material conditions were common elements of everyday school life as they had been centuries before.[48]

Of course, the change from an open Greco-Roman culture to a closed society was slow, and some patterns did not change at all. Firstly, child beating remained a constant feature of educational practice. There are changes in the discourse on the matter (dissuading advice on the ideal moderate and self-restrained aristocratic father's behavior toward his children versus a strong emphasis on corporal chastising in a Christian discourse of the punishing God), but in daily life, education was a tough process for the great majority of children throughout antiquity.[49] Secondly, it was invariably expected that children would follow their parents' professional path. Child labor was the ancient response to a schooling system utterly unable to serve the needs of the majority of the population. Children gradually learned a trade by watching their parents perform it. Some were sent out as apprentices. Our modern viewpoint tends to condemn the institution of child labor as it excluded children from the possibility of acquiring literacy and schooling. However, the educational figure of the master was much closer to his apprentice than a schoolteacher or a grammarian: they lived close to each other for longer periods (sometimes apprentices stayed with their masters overnight), and the master embodied what the apprentice wanted to become. Apprenticeship also accustomed young boys to working with slaves: from Egyptian papyri we know of both freeborn boys and slave girls or boys working as apprentices. So, besides the economic aspect, the phenomenon of child labor was eminently a matter of upbringing and socialization.[50] Finally, throughout antiquity up to 800 C.E., the approach to children and education was characterized by a discourse aptly summarized in the Ciceronian saying on childhood: "The thing itself cannot be praised, only its potential."[51] Children had to be turned into full-fledged adults, and there was little particular appreciation for the life stage of childhood per se. Hence, children were immediately faced with adult literature and adult morality. The world of the grown-ups was the phase they had to reach, without lingering too long in the peculiarities of childish life. In the end, this should not surprise us too much as developmental psychology was, after all, an invention of the nineteenth century. The fact that childhood was not appreciated in the same way as it is today does not exclude children being welcome or valued. Parents invested high hopes in their offspring and their education, even though educational practice throughout antiquity never reached what we might consider suitable for children.

CHAPTER SIX

Life Cycle

TIM PARKIN

In considering the ancient life course, the first question one may consider is the way in which different age classes were defined. What did the Greeks and Romans mean when they called someone a child? The literary and philosophical *topos* of the ages of humankind (*gradus aetatum* or *aetates hominum*) are of obvious relevance here, at least one might assume, and have a long history from Solon to Shakespeare and beyond. Often these systems—whether the number of life stages are three or ten and whatever their relative individual length—give precise chronological breakdowns of the ages considered. Solon, for example, gave a description of human life divided into ten successive seven-year periods up to the age of seventy years; each stage is marked by physical (and the focus is on the male) and/or mental developments:

1. birth–7 years   growth of teeth
2. 7–14 years   capacity to emit seed
3. 14–21 years   growth of beard
4. 21–28 years   increase of strength
5. 28–35 years   ripeness for marriage
6. 35–42 years   understanding reaches full bloom
7. 42–49 years   improvement of mind and reasoning
8. 49–56 years   perfection of mind and reasoning
9. 56–63 years   emergence of moderateness and gentleness
10. 63–70 years   beginning of deterioration

The tenth and final age, that of decline, ends with death at three score years and ten, just as the Psalmist would have it.[1]

Solon's is the first system for which there is evidence, but it is by no means the only of its type. One that is similar, attributed to Plato in the manuscript in which it survives (though Plato has no such item in his extant works), breaks down as follows (the Greek terms for each stage and a plausible English equivalent are appended)[2]:

1. 0–4 years   *brephos*, infant
2. 4–10 years   *pais*, child
3. 10–18 years   *boupais*, teenager
4. 18–25 years   *meirakion*, youth
5. 25–35 years   *akmazon*, adult (at the prime)
6. 35–45 years   *kathestekos*, adult ("settled")
7. 45–55 years   *omogeron*, older adult
8. 55–65 years   *geron*, old person
9. 65+ years   *bougeron*, very old person

In this case, nine ages are described (nine, like seven, was a number routinely accorded special significance). The age ranges are ten years in length and not unlike those employed by modern demographers in age breakdowns of populations. In one work in the Hippocratic corpus, however, the doctrine of the seven ages, familiar today from Jaques's description in Shakespeare's *As You Like It*, seems to have become first established; in this instance, each age itself consists of seven years, or a multiple of seven. Here is the Hippocratic system as described by Philo[3]:

1. 0–7 years   *paidion*, small child
2. 7–14 years   *pais*, child
3. 14–21 years   *meirakion*, youth
4. 21–28 years   *neaniskos*, young adult
5. 28–49 years   *aner*, adult
6. 49–56 years   *presbutes*, older person
7. 56+ years   *geron*, old person

As with the Solonian system, and perhaps not surprisingly in the context of the system's alleged creator, each age is described in terms of physical development. But the mathematical significance of the number seven here is clearly the most important feature. It is very important to note, moreover, that in the various accounts of the Hippocratic system, while the basic seven ages remain the same, the year divisions vary.[4] The first two stages are consistently described as ages birth to seven and seven to fourteen years (which for our purposes is striking), but the third stage, that of the youth, can extend up to the age of twenty-eight years (i.e., two periods of seven years instead of one), and, indeed, the seventh stage—old age—begins from the age of forty-two, fifty-six, or sixty-three years.

Very similar to and clearly influenced by the Hippocratic system is the description written in the second century C.E. by Claudius Ptolemy where the seven stages were further linked to astrology, and each stage of life (as well as its length in years) was depicted as being under the sway of one of the seven planets.[5]

1. 0–4 years	*brephos*, infant	Moon
2. 4–14 years	*pais*, child	Mercury
3. 14–22 years	*meirakion*, youth	Venus
4. 22–41 years	*neaniskos*, young adult	Sun
5. 41–56 years	*aner*, adult	Mars
6. 56–68 years	*presbutes*, older person	Jupiter
7. 68+ years	*geron*, old person	Saturn

While there are seven ages in Ptolemy's system, the length of each stage in years is not itself a multiple of seven. Significantly, Ptolemy precedes his description of the seven ages with a comment on the wide variety of earlier treatments of the *topos* and notes one must be careful to assign the correct features to each age. But it is clear at least that fourteen years was regularly regarded as a significant division in these age systems. It is worth remarking that the mathematical neatness of the number usefully coincides, approximately, with the age of puberty for males as described by medical and legal writers from ancient times.[6] In fact, Aristotle went so far as to state that there was much to be said for the hebdomad, or group of seven, system, in accord with nature as it was.[7]

To continue our exploration of the various extant systems of age grades: Censorinus, writing in the third century C.E., recorded a simpler system of five ages, each of fifteen years' duration, described by Varro in the first century B.C.E. in the context of the (four) ages of Rome (with age terms, of course, in Latin)[8]:

1. 0–15 years	*puer*, child
2. 15–30 years	*adulescens*, young adult

3. 30–45 years	*iuvenis*, adult	
4. 45–60 years	*senior*, older person	
5. 60+ years	*senex*, old person	

Because the age of (to take one example) sixty years is in line with some modern conceptions of the onset of old age in ancient times, Varro's system is regularly adopted by modern scholars as definitive of Roman (and Greek) reality. But there is no good reason for this since Varro's figures are only one set in a long tradition, and it is explicitly stated by Censorinus (as well as by Servius) that the system described is Varro's, not Rome's. One might also compare the earlier Pythagorean system of four ages (preserved by Diogenes Laertius), each of twenty years' duration and with each age linked to a season.[9]

1. 0–20 years	*pais*, child	Spring
2. 20–40 years	*neaniskos*, young adult	Summer
3. 40–60 years	*aner*, adult	Autumn
4. 60–80 years	*geron*, older person	Winter

More than a millennium after the time of Solon there was clearly still no universally established allotment of years to any particular stage of life. Isidore of Seville, writing in the early seventh century C.E., states that "there are six stages of life: infancy, childhood, adolescence, adulthood, maturity, and old age."[10] In his work *Origines*, Isidore divides up these six ages as follows:

1. 0–7 years	*infantia*
2. 7–14 years	*pueritia*
3. 14–28 years	*adolescentia*
4. 28–49 years	*iuventus*
5. 49–70 years	*gravitas*
6. 70+ years	*senectus*

And yet earlier and later in the same text[11] Isidore speaks of three ages (*infantia*, *iuventus*, and *senectus*), and in other works[12] he changes his description of the system of six ages, as follows:

1. 0–7 years	*infantia*
2. 7–14 years	*pueritia*
3. 14–28 years	*adolescentia*
4. 28–49 years	*iuventus*

5. 49–77 years   *senectus*
6. 77+ years   *senium*, extreme old age

This is only a very brief sketch of the complexity of descriptions of age, of interest in their own right and, as noted earlier, with a very long history. The *topos* was also extended to anthropomorphizing the life course of a city, a people (typically Rome and the Romans, as was mentioned in relation to Varro), or history. Rome was said to be in childhood under the kings, who brought her under the authority of individuals who acted as educators and trainers until she broke free in *adolescentia* and became a republic.[13]

Two important points about these systems of age divisions emerge: firstly, the variety of treatments; and secondly, the artificial nature of the divisions. What the tradition of the ages of man represents is not, it is important to realize, a realistic, everyday, or universal categorization of age classes from antiquity; rather, it is a poetical and philosophical convention influenced by mathematics, astrology, and superstition and dominated by a desire for numerical symmetry. Censorinus and Isidore both specifically say that *philosophers* describe the lifespan in this way. While the numbers for the various ages change almost by individual whim, the basic method and mathematical structure are constant. Yet one cannot envisage such systems being used on a general daily basis, even unconsciously, as a means of defining the age class of every individual. As Isidore's three general age categories suggest, more general and less specific descriptors of age classes certainly existed—just as, *mutatis mutandis*, they exist today—and perhaps better reflect contemporary, general reality without the imposition of definitive chronological age boundaries. In other words, *pais* or *puer* means "a child," not "a person of x number of years," and thus is as general as the English term in such contexts. In special circumstances, age terms might convey a more specific meaning, just as, for example, *pensioner* may today. In military contexts, terms like *ephebe* (in Athens, eighteen to nineteen years of age, as outlined in the following) or *iunior* (in Rome, seventeen to forty-five years) were more specifically linked to age limits, but in more general contexts these terms did not entail such set figures.

A passage from Aeschines is also quite instructive for comparative purposes, displaying as it does an awareness of the fact that people of the same age may look and feel considerably different. Aeschines's point is to stress that Misgolas, who took in Timarchus as his lover, is much older than he looks:

There are some people who by nature differ a great deal from the rest of us with respect to their age. For some who are young (*neoi*) seem mature and older than they are; others, who have lived a good number of years, seem to be mere youngsters. Misgolas is such a man. For he happens to be the same age as me, and was an ephebe with me; we are now in our forty-fifth year. I am quite grey, as you see, but he is not.[14]

In short, it is clear that different ages and the impressions and images associated with them never were (just as they still are not) thought of simply in terms of the number of years lived. Physical appearance, mental attitude, circumstances, and intention also affect the way a person thinks of him- or herself and is regarded by others. One rather touching example of this is provided in the fourth century c.e. by Ausonius; early in their marriage, he urges his wife to ignore the arrival of old age when it eventually comes and for them to always call one another *iuvenis* and *puella*: "Let us refuse to know the meaning of ripe old age. Better to know Time's worth, than count his years." In fact, she was fated to die when she was only twenty-seven years old.[15] The realities of high mortality shall be discussed presently.

Even in the context of Roman law, there were very few circumstances in which specific ages were applied to individual terms. The jurist Ulpius Marcellus, for example, writing in the second half of the second century c.e., notes a (hypothetical) case in which a man in his will bequeathed all the *iuvenes* in his service to another individual. The question is asked, by what upper and lower limits of age are *iuvenes* to be defined?[16] Marcellus concludes that in the case of wills people may write without precision (*abusive*), and each case must be judged by its own circumstances; no strict age limits can be imposed in such contexts in regard to particular terms describing general age categories. But then he adds that it could be thought that a *iuvenis* is someone between the ages of the *adulescens* and the *senior*—note that there is no Latin term here for middle-aged; one progresses directly from *iuvenis* to *senior*. And, clearly, legal definitions of age classes overlap with general conventions; nothing more precise is required, even by the lawyer.

It is likely that most people in everyday life considered the life course in such general terms (if and when they considered it at all) and, if asked to be explicit, would have thought of life as having three or four stages, just as Isidore (see the aforementioned discussion) can talk of three ages while also describing systems of six ages. Just as the day may be divided into morning, afternoon, and evening, and the year can be divided into four seasons, so the life course allowed for flexibility, according to stereotypical stages of development and decline, of life's duties and expectations. As Servius wrote in his commentary on Vergil's *Aeneid*, the lot of childhood is play (*ludus*), of *adulescentia* is love (*amor*), of adulthood (*iuvenalis aetas*) is ambition (*ambitio*), and of old age is peace and quiet (*quies et otium*). A millennium earlier, Hesiod attributed deeds to the young, advice to the middle-aged, and prayers to the elderly. This triple or quadruple division is very common. In Sparta, according to Plutarch, there were three choirs at festivals corresponding to the three ages, with the choir of old men singing that they were once the warriors, the adult men responding that they are now the warriors, and the young boys thirdly retorting that in time they will be mightier warriors than both older groups. This division between old, adult, and young is made very explicit in Aristotle's *Rhetoric* and Horace's *Art of Poetry*, where the characteristics of each stage are outlined, the middle ("those in their prime") being the ideal.[17]

TRANSITIONS IN LIFE

In all this it is tempting to see distinct parallels with our own twenty-first-century conceptions of age groups, and of course there is much that rings true over the millennia, nor is this coincidental: not only is much in the human experience timeless, but the influence of the Greeks and Romans on our Western systems of thought is also strong. This influence may also be seen to an extent in another means of conceptualizing divisions of the life course—namely in so-called rites of passage, stages of the life course that relate not only to the individual but also to the family as a whole. These stages occur as new members enter the household grouping, as existing members age and their roles change over time, and as existing members—whatever their age—leave the household to enter another group, perhaps to found their own family or as they leave life itself. Birth rituals, including naming and baptism; rites marking and safeguarding the transition from childhood into early adulthood (marked in various cultures by ceremonies, some gender specific, such as circumcision and confirmation); the change in both status and role brought by marriage and entry into adult public roles (again often gender specific)—all these are common to most societies despite the diversity of the details.

The transition from adulthood into old age—marked in most modern societies by systems of retirement and financial arrangements such as pensions and superannuation—is typically much less evident in the ancient world. But for earlier life stages there are some very clear signposts. Discussion shall presently return to the first weeks of life; at the other end of childhood, in the transition to adulthood, the emphasis of rites is frequently placed on the emerging new roles—social, political, and religious—of the individual, be it as soldier, active citizen, spouse, and/or parent. The symbolism of this transition typically involves a process of separation, exclusion, and then reincorporation.[18] In Athens, for example, a young male, from the age of about sixteen to twenty years, undergoes the process of emerging from the private to the public, from childhood to the position of active male citizen within the democracy; his hair is cut and his name is entered on the local (*deme*) register after his eligibility is scrutinized. He also undergoes a two-year period of military training as an *ephebe*. For females, on the other hand, it would appear from our sketchy evidence that some girls at least participated in religious rites as they approached womanhood.[19] In Roman society, pagan and Christian, the physical transition from early childhood to puberty was one marked both socially and legally, particularly if the postpubescent child had lost his or her *paterfamilias*, a not unusual reality given the high mortality levels and relative late marriage ages for males (see the following). In every age, to different degrees, the transition to marriage, especially for females, typically indicated a decisive step from childhood to adulthood and also marked a significant event in the life course of the family.

THE DANGERS OF LIFE

It is also worth emphasizing that for all the perceived similarities between antiquity and the modern age in the stages of life and the family, the differences are fundamental. Although it is now recognized that the nuclear family was the typical basic unit of obligations and affection in the ancient world, at least as far as the evidence allows us to surmise for certain times and places,[20] the underlying demographic realities, in terms of mortality and fertility, meant that the household and family life cycle of the ancient world would typically have had a more temporary or transitory feel to it than the cycle familiar to modern children. The ancient world was a young world; high levels of infant and early childhood mortality, balanced to varying degrees by comparatively high levels of fertility, meant that early rites of passage constituted a very real record of emerging survival, as will be examined presently. It was a world in which death cast its shadow widely and visibly. Marcus Aurelius and his wife Faustina had at least twelve children, of whom only one son, Commodus, survived to adulthood; in his *Meditations*,[21] Marcus quotes the chilling words of Epictetus: "When you kiss your child at night, whisper in your heart: 'Perhaps it will be dead in the morning.'" This demographic reality and its relationship to rites of passage needs to be explored. For no history of childhood or the family, incorporating a discussion of the images and emotions attached with childhood or any stage of life, can ignore demography: the effects of fertility

and mortality are closely connected with, for example, the emotional relationship between parents and children. Demography, the study of the structure and
dynamics of human populations, is not a cold, heartless science; it is intimately
linked to social and cultural realities. Demographers look at age of marriage,
levels of fertility and mortality, age spacing of children, ages at which children
leave home, and so on, and then map these factors onto economic and social
histories of childhood. Demographic realities would have shaped every aspect
of childhood and the family in the ancient world.

Ancient demography concerns itself not only with the size of populations
but also with their structure.[22] Three factors are crucial: mortality, fertility,
and migration. Ancient evidence is sparse and problematic; the ancient de-
mographer has very little in the way of census material or records of births,
deaths, and marriages with which to work. Most ancient evidence—such as
tombstone inscriptions and skeletons—is, unfortunately, of very little value.
Over three hundred copies of census returns from Roman Egypt have survived
and with sophisticated interpretation can yield important clues.[23] But this discussion is very much reliant on comparative evidence, especially model life
tables, to clarify what is plausible or probable in terms of ancient populations.
There is every reason to believe that many demographic variables differed little
between the Greek and Roman worlds (despite the difference in population
sizes). The most striking feature regarding the mortality rate is how high it
was from an early age. In general terms, average life expectancy at birth was
between twenty and thirty years. In this regard, the ancient world is more
comparable to third-world countries today than to developed nations. This
low life expectancy is mainly reflective of very harsh levels of infant mortality,
the result particularly of gastrointestinal illnesses. It may be estimated, as a
generalization, that one in three children died in their first year of life—a great
proportion within the first few weeks, depending to some extent upon whether
or not infants were breastfed immediately. One in two children probably did
not survive beyond the age of ten. After that life looks a little brighter. A ten-
year-old might expect on average to live another thirty-five to forty years, a
forty-year-old at least another twenty years. So some people in the ancient
world did survive into old age, however defined, though not as significant a
proportion as do today. But most older adults would not have parents alive
and would quite likely have lost children.[24] The chances of children having a
full set of grandparents to help cater to their needs are minimal; given the difference in age of marriage between men and women, paternal grandfathers—
the very epitome of conservative patriarchal authority, especially in the Roman
world—would have been particularly rare. Mortality differences due to gender

cannot be asserted with any certainty. It is highly probable that women did not generally live as long as men (maternal mortality is one relevant factor, though its level should not be exaggerated) and that males very slightly outnumbered females in the population; this is in large part the result, it would appear, of the benign neglect of female children in many households, the consequence of economic realities more than anything else.

Such high infant and early childhood mortality may be attributed to a combination of low levels of hygiene and sanitation (particularly in urbanized areas) and low standards of medical care, as well as poor nutrition for poorer people. Ancient sources frequently mention food shortages, epidemics (infectious diseases must have taken a severe toll), and war—Malthus's positive checks.[25] Modern demographic methods also allow us to glimpse the nature of the living population in terms of age structure, and here another notable difference from our own experience occurs. Ancient populations would have been very young; something like half the population would have been under the age of twenty-five at any one time, and only about seven to eight percent, at most, over the age of sixty. The following table, though simplistic, approximate, and generalizing, serves to highlight these similarities and differences: while the proportion of adults in ancient and modern populations is comparable, the differences lie in those one might class as "the young" and "the old."

	<15 years	15–59 years	>59 years
Ancient population	33%	60%	7%
Modern population	19%	60%	21%

To counteract such high mortality, fertility levels also needed to be high. A woman in the ancient world on average gave birth five or six times (and knew that a number of these births would not survive). Some women produced many more; the (alleged) record was thirty births, while one woman in Roman Egypt was said to have given birth to quintuplets on four separate occasions. Other women, especially due to quite high levels of infertility, never gave birth at all—this was a constant complaint of upper-class men in antiquity (as women tended to get the blame). On the other hand, there is evidence in a fair number of texts for contraception (a mixture of magic and medicine), abortion, and exposure and/or infanticide. Poorer families, and even richer families who did not want to spread their wealth too widely, limited their family size by such means. But even with such relatively high fertility levels, mortality rates ensured that average family size was small.

Low fertility levels, at least among the elite classes, were regarded as such a problem that, for example, the Roman emperor Augustus introduced legislation to benefit those married with children and penalize those who were married without children or who never even married in the first place (18 B.C.E. and 9 C.E.).[26] But never-married adults would have been rare: Greeks and Romans married routinely, at least until later Christian times: females in their mid- to late teens, males some ten years later. Again, however, mortality would have taken its toll. Either husband or wife on average would have died within some eighteen years of married life. And it would seem divorce rates were high as well in many periods in antiquity.

In order to calculate levels of population growth or decline, one needs to be able to measure rates of mortality, fertility, and migration. Evidence for the variables for these calculations does not exist for antiquity. But it is reasonable to assume that at most periods in ancient history levels of growth were close to zero (there are some major probable exceptions—for example, eighth-century B.C.E. Greece). High mortality rates were balanced by high levels of fertility. As recent scholarship has discussed, a society with such a high rate of infant and childhood mortality might view the death of small children quite differently and perhaps with less grief or concern than today. This is one of many aspects of life in ancient society where judging actions or situations by our own moral or ethical criteria would be unjustified and misleading. There are many indications that, at least in theory, parents were able to deal philosophically with the death of an infant son or daughter, but at the same time there are indications of parents whose grief was very powerful and presumably very real.[27] That infants were not regularly accorded full burial or commemoration, as noted earlier, should not be interpreted simply as parental indifference. It is also worth considering, in terms of the life course of the family, that there would have been greater spacing of children over a lengthy reproductive career given the effects of early childhood mortality. It was certainly not routine to grow up with a large number of siblings close in age; age differences would have been marked, and stepsiblings would have been likely given the high mortality and often relatively high divorce rates. The ancient world had a high percentage of young people in the population; this meant, in economic terms, that there would typically have been an expectation, at least among the less affluent, that children would contribute to the family economy at an early age: children could not remain totally dependent.[28]

What effect did demography have on the very perception of childhood in antiquity? It is an inevitable conclusion that our assumption of childhood as a period of relative security, at least for children not born into abject poverty or war zones, is not applicable to the ancient world. Certainly Cicero, writing in 44 B.C.E. about old age, associated childhood with *infirmitas*, or vulnerability[29]:

> The course of life [*cursus aetatis*] is fixed, and nature admits of its being run but in one way, and only once; and to each part of our life there is something specially seasonable; so that the vulnerability of children, as well as the high spirits [*ferocitas*] of youth, the *gravitas* of maturer years, and the *maturitas* of old age—all have a certain natural quality which should be secured in its proper season.

This is a reflection not only of the troubled times in which Cicero was writing, following the Ides of March, but more fundamentally of the overall reality of high infant and childhood mortality in the ancient world and the reality of the life course for both individuals and families. This generalized picture may be made more tangible, perhaps, by considering the following tombstone—that of Veturia, the wife of a centurion, buried in Aquincum in the province of Pannonia Inferior[30]:

> Here do I lie at rest, a married woman, Veturia by name and descent, the wife of Fortunatus, the daughter of Veturius. I lived for thrice nine years, poor me, and I was married for twice eight. I slept with one man, I was married to one man. After having borne six children, one of whom survives me, I died. Titus Julius Fortunatus, centurion of the Second Legion Adiutrix Pia Fidelis, set this up for his wife: she was incomparable and notably respectful to him.

What is revealed here is a glimpse of the omnipresence of death in the life course of the family and in the lives of parents and children; it is an image vividly and pathetically brought to the fore also through iconographic evidence, such as the Attic white-ground *lekythos* (ca. 430 B.C.E.) of a small boy with his toy roller, waving farewell to his mother to his left and about to move on to meet Charon to his right (figure 6.1).[31]

One can point to isolated instances from literary sources where high mortality rates (though not necessarily infant deaths) are recorded. The case of Marcus Aurelius has already received mention. Perhaps the most famous and most frequently quoted example in this context is that of Cornelia, mother of the brothers Gracchi, who had twelve children and who was to become a symbol and an ideal of maternal fertility and discipline. Apparently all twelve

FIGURE 6.1: *Terracotta* lekythos *(oil flask) showing dead child waving farewell to his mother.* Attributed to the Painter of Munich, Attica, Greece, ca. 430 B.C.E. Metropolitan Museum of Art Rogers Fund, 1909 (09.221.44). Image © Metropolitan Museum of Art, New York.

children were born between 163 B.C.E. and the death of their father, Tiberius senior, around 152 B.C.E.; of these twelve, all survived their father, but only three (the two famous boys and one sister) survived childhood, and—so it is alleged—none survived their mother.[32] Similar cases of high fertility and high mortality can be found, particularly from the Roman world, but they tell us nothing of the general demographic realities of the time.

It is also possible to detect, not surprisingly, an awareness in some of our written sources of the mortality risks for the very young in antiquity: Aristotle noted that most child deaths happen in the first year and most of those in the first week after birth—what today is called early neonatal mortality. Hence, adds Aristotle, the fact that one waits a week before naming the child. Macrobius reaches the same conclusion about Roman naming practice: on the *dies lustricus*, the Romans named their children—girls on the eighth day, boys on the ninth—and on this day the child received the *bulla*, the insignia of childhood. Plutarch, half a millennium after Aristotle, adds to his account: seven days after birth, he relates, occurs the loss of the umbilical cord; until then, the newborn child is more like a plant than a human being. Plutarch also wonders about the difference in days according to gender: perhaps, he says, it is because the number nine is suitable for boys, being three (Roman men have three names) squared—perfect and complete; whereas eight is two (Roman women typically have two names) cubed—a cube, he says, is stable, domestic, and difficult to move, like a woman.[33]

It is one thing to realize that the infant mortality rate in the ancient world was high and to suggest an order of magnitude based on comparative evidence; it is quite another to try to measure the rate by reference to literary or inscriptional evidence. Records of infant burials are drastically underrepresented in the extant funerary inscriptions. The infant mortality rate (IMR) as a demographic measure is the number of deaths per thousand births of those under one year of age. Infant mortality was and is due to a combination of endogenous and exogenous mortality. Immediately following birth, when the newborn infant is particularly vulnerable and may suffer from birth trauma, the risk of mortality is the highest even today, and such severe mortality risk must have been far more prevalent in ancient times, with exogenous mortality (due particularly to infections) much more common than today. The list of infectious diseases is long: prominent for ancient children would have been typhoid, cholera, diarrhea, dysentery, influenza, pneumonia, and tuberculosis.[34] Skeletal evidence has provided us with valuable evidence in recent years regarding the prevalence of malaria in ancient societies, and it is important to take this into account when considering both fetal and infant mortality.[35]

An IMR of 250–300 per 1,000 is what may be expected from comparative preindustrial history, though much higher rates are possible, especially among populations that practice no or only minimal breast-feeding of infants. The model ancient historians have used in the past is one in which life expectancy at birth is twenty to thirty years; as has already been mentioned, it can be estimated, utilizing the Princeton Coale-Demeny model life tables, that with generalized high mortality conditions one in four newborns will die in their first year and one in two before completing their first decade. This is entirely possible, and indeed there is good evidence from more recent historical examples from Europe that show an IMR in the range of 150–250 per 1,000 live births and with extremes as high as 480 in six parishes in York in England in the sixteenth century.[36] This compares with a rate in the modern developed world of fewer than 10 per 1,000, an extreme difference as rates have dropped phenomenally since the beginning of the twentieth century. In poorer countries in the twenty-first century, on the other hand, the IMR still ranges from 50 to nearly 200 per 1,000.

But more than just infant mortality needs to be considered. Mortality did not recognize the first birthday, and turning one was no rite of passage in demographic terms. While it is true that after the age of one mortality rates

FIGURE 6.2: *An early example of a biographical sarcophagus showing scenes from a child's life.* Reading right to left: parents carry a baby in a horse-drawn carriage; the baby as a toddler pushing a baby walker, then slightly older playing with a large bird; in the final scene, the child rides with parents again. Late second century C.E. Paleo-Christian Museo prehistorica e Etnographico Luigi Pigorini, Rome. Image: Bridgeman Art Library.

drop, the ancient child remained very vulnerable. Indeed, it has been well said that in the face of childhood illnesses, ancient medicine would have been "a mere spectator" up to the age of puberty.[37] In fact, the majority of deaths in an ancient society were probably of children—the younger, the more vulnerable. Such widespread mortality would have affected all classes of society, more marked perhaps in urban than rural areas. Not surprising, this dramatic environment is evident in ancient testimony and realities. It was believed, for example, that the ancient Roman king Numa had instituted regulations regarding the extent of grief for a deceased family member: for a child of less than three years there was to be no mourning at all; for a child older than three years, the mourning was not to last more months than it had lived years, up to ten; and no age was to be mourned longer than that—"ten months was the period for the longest mourning."[38]

As was noted earlier, it is certain that infant and early childhood mortality was relatively severe in the ancient world, but it needs to be recognized that this is based on comparative evidence and demographic models. It has become clear in recent years that the standard model life tables utilized for the analysis of ancient populations may have led to an overestimation of the levels of infant mortality. The Princeton Coale-Demeny tables present a range of figures but can disguise the variability of mortality patterns over time and space: a more nuanced approach needs to consider more closely the disease environment in a demographic context. Furthermore, the relationship between infant and adult mortality levels remains uncertain. For very high mortality populations, the infant mortality levels in the model life tables have been predicted by means of algorithmic extrapolation. The Princeton Coale-Demeny tables are based on populations where e_0 (average life expectancy at birth) is greater than thirty-five years. For models such as those utilized for ancient populations, where e_0 is lower than thirty-five, figures are extrapolated from lower mortality regimes; in other words, the models ancient historians use are not based on empirical evidence. The levels of infant/early childhood mortality predicted by the Princeton Coale-Demeny tables—where e_0 is in the range of twenty to thirty years—are, as was noted, over 300 per 1,000 in the first year of life and over 450 per 1,000 in the first five years; there is good reason to believe these levels may be too high. Indeed, the Princeton Coale-Demeny tables quite probably *over*estimate infant and early childhood mortality levels and *under*estimate mortality levels in later years.

Other comparative material is available, however, to support this likelihood. Newer model life tables for high mortality populations, tables based on empirical evidence, are now available. Following that lead, most recently Robert Woods has developed two new sets of high mortality model life tables, dubbed South Europe and East Asia, based on a range of data sets.[39] To sum up some very detailed arguments: it might be more realistic to assume, if e_0 is approximately twenty-five years, infant mortality levels of 200 per 1,000 and early childhood mortality of 350 per 1,000. It should be noted, of course, that these are still, by modern standards, extremely high mortality rates.

One reason one should allow for lower levels of infant mortality than previously assumed is the probable level of breast-feeding in ancient populations. As is now well-known, breast-feeding is a major determinant in terms of both mortality and fertility levels. Breast milk provides immunological protection from diseases, protection uninfected in even the most unsanitary conditions; as a consequence, the infant mortality rate may be substantially lowered. A mother who breast-feeds may also experience a brief postpartum infertile or nonsusceptible period before full menstruation and ovulation are restored. If prolonged and regular maternal breast-feeding from birth was the norm among the lower classes of the ancient world, as it probably was for purely economic reasons, it may well have meant both lower infant mortality and lower fertility rates in comparison to the upper classes, where wet-nursing appears to have been routine, at least in Roman times.[40] Rather than concentrating on varying demographic levels resulting from social differentiation, however, it is perhaps more useful to consider differences due to urban as opposed to rural habitation. The fact that, for example, senators had to reside in Rome might have meant that any advantage in living standards they enjoyed because of their wealth were more than counterbalanced by the perils of dwelling in the eternal city.

In conclusion, it must be stressed that while there can never be total confidence in the precision of our demographic measures for the ancient world, there can be more confidence in terms of orders of magnitude, and scholars can and must consider demographic factors when reconstructing family and childhood in antiquity. What stands out more than anything is the sharp contrast with the levels of mortality and fertility in the modern developed world. An ancient family must have always been aware of the risks and fragility of life. Childhood was a period of vulnerability, and the household experienced great transitions over the course of its existence and evolution. Life-course rituals—first following surviving early infancy and then at the onset of puberty and the approach of adult privileges and duties—mark out these periods of transition. The stages of life, artificial as they seem, make explicit these self-conscious constructions of the life course. For most individuals in the Greek and Roman worlds, death and taxes were the overriding concerns. Survival was something to be celebrated and cherished as opportunity and the gods allowed. To quote Democritus,[41] "Child-rearing is a perilous business. When it is successful it is attended by strife and care. When it fails there is no other pain to compare with it."

CHAPTER SEVEN

The State

JO-ANN SHELTON

In modern societies, the involvement of the state in the affairs of the family is extensive. States enact laws that regulate, for example, marriage and divorce and prohibit the exploitation of children. States differ widely, however, in the scope of their intrusion into family matters. In ancient Athens, Sparta, and Rome, the three societies discussed in this chapter, the interest of the state was not the welfare of individual children but rather the stability of the citizen families who supplied the state with manpower and resources. Nonetheless, the lives of children were greatly affected by the state's attempts to maintain thriving families. Each of these three societies adopted different measures for balancing the desire to establish the state's authority over its citizens with the need to respect the traditional privileges of family members. In Athens, legislators left issues of child rearing to the families and supported, rather than appropriated, the roles of extended family and kin groups in confirming the legality of marriages and citizen status, punishing adultery, and ensuring family property remained in the possession of family members. In Sparta, by contrast, the state intruded into most aspects of family life and made even the raising of children a public and communal undertaking. In Rome, the traditional responsibilities of the male head of the family were diminished by the revolutionary changes advocated by Augustus, Rome's first emperor. He enacted legislation that promoted marriage and penalized childlessness and adultery, thus turning private matters into public concerns. He interfered further with the prerogatives of the family by making the ineligibility to inherit property one of the penalties for transgressing his marriage laws. This chapter examines how the societies of ancient Athens, Sparta, and Rome dealt, in different ways, with the need to sustain a vigorous population of citizens.

The emergence of the ancient Greek state is traced to the seventh and sixth centuries B.C.E., when people living in geographical proximity established a form of centralized government in which laws were enacted for the benefit of the community. Justice became, as Aristotle (384–322 B.C.E.) declared, "a matter for the state." A constitution was created that specified how and by whom the laws were formulated and administered and who was a citizen of the state. To ensure its survival, each state maintained an army of male citizens. It is important to be aware that, both in the Greek city-states (*poleis*) and the Roman state, only adult male citizens were allowed to participate in the political and judicial process. Women were denied a role in making these decisions that affected their lives. State and family were interdependent, and their interests generally coincided. Aristotle remarked that the family was the basic unit of the state,[1] and it was the family that ensured the economic, biological, and cultural reproduction of society. A major concern of early Greek states was to prevent situations that might cause the disintegration or even the extinction of a family and the consequent economic and political destabilization of the state. Although ancient states encouraged the birth and rearing of healthy children, the state's concern was always on the continuance of the citizen family rather than the well-being of an individual. This chapter focuses on legal codes because in this area we can trace the efforts of states to respond to the needs of families. Laws may reflect changes in the values of a society, but they may also create changes. Unfortunately, we do not know whether or how rigorously these laws were observed and enforced. The correlation between law and actual social practice and lived reality is a problematic issue. Nonetheless, a study of the laws and legal literature of Athens, Sparta, and Rome reveals how these societies strove to maintain traditional patterns of family life while creating a strong state.

ATHENS

In ancient Athens, public interest was understood to be the interest of the individual *oikoi* (households) that made up the *polis*. Indeed, the *polis* was sometimes envisioned as a megafamily or communal household.[2] Aristotle traced the intersection of the state and the *oikoi* back to the great lawgiver Solon (ca. 640–ca. 558 B.C.E.), whose law code is thought to date from 594 B.C.E. Solon's legislation was prompted, according to Aristotle, by a severe economic

and social crisis in which many poor citizens had incurred so much debt that
they needed to deliver themselves or their children into slavery to satisfy their
creditors. Solon may have hoped to solve these economic and political problems
by building a society in which the poor were less vulnerable to the predations of
the wealthy. He did not, however, attempt to dismantle existing social groups,
in particular the *phratria* (phratry, or kinship group).[3] The *kyrios* (head) of
every *oikos* (household) was a member of a phratry, and the phratries served
as an extended family by providing material and moral support. Although the
polis took over some of the functions of the phratries, especially in the sphere of
implementing justice, the phratries retained a fundamental role in the structure
of the state. Nonetheless, Solon tried to construct a system in which the *oikoi*
looked to the *polis,* rather than to phratries, for economic security and justice.
At the heart of his legislation was an intention to keep the property of the poor-
est families in their possession, thus preserving the state by ensuring its citizens'
survival. Among Solon's measures to stabilize the *oikoi* were cancelling all existing debts, forbidding lenders to accept a person's body as security on a loan,
and prohibiting the sale of children into slavery.[4] This last measure certainly
benefited children, but its main function was to prevent the loss of citizenship,
which would have resulted in the state cumulatively losing citizens.

The formation of an *oikos* began with a marriage, and the purpose of marriage was to produce children who would eventually inherit the property of the
oikos. Because the *oikos* was the reproductive unit of the *polis,* the state had
an interest in the parentage of the individuals to whom it extended privileges
and protection. In Athens, a child's entitlement to the rights of citizenship was
dependent on two factors: the status of his or her parents as citizens and their
status as partners in a marriage. However, there was no legal definition of
matrimony, no legally validating ceremony, and no requirement that a marriage be formally documented by public officials. Indeed, Aristotle commented
that there was no word for the union of man and woman. Nor were there
words that corresponded to the English *husband* and *wife.*[5] Marriage in Athens should be understood not as a legal moment but rather as a social process
with several components. A series of events confirmed the legitimacy of a marriage. The presence of witnesses was essential: serving as the eyes of the state,
as it were, they could later verify that particular marriage events had taken
place—from the betrothal, with its contract that specified the amount of the
dowry, to the public wedding party for the members of the phratry. Later, public observation would confirm whether the couple was living together or had
children. Hence, through the observation of parental behavior, a child's legal
status was confirmed as that of a family member and citizen.[6]

In 451 B.C.E., the Athenian assembly approved a law proposed by Pericles (ca. 500–429 B.C.E.) that "anyone who has not been born of two citizens should not share in the *polis*." Prior to this date, only the status of the father had been taken into account. The new law restricted the conferral of citizenship to those whose parents were both Athenian citizens and formally married to one another.[7] This legislation created a new class of children—not foreigners or slaves, equally not citizens either, yet biologically related to Athenian citizens. This could be seen as a measure, driven by ideology, that actually weakened the state and disrupted the survival of Athenian families.

The coincidence of state and family interests can be seen in the response to adultery. Because marriage was the foundation of both the *oikos* and civic status, sexual behavior that compromised a marriage or called into question the paternity of a child born to a conjugal couple was perceived by the state as a threat to public security. Traditionally, a man sought to restore his honor through deeds of revenge (the destructive nature of vengeance was a prominent theme in Greek drama), but the state had been designed to end this type of retaliatory and disorderly behavior. Therefore, *polis* leaders had an interest in curbing violence both by prohibiting sexual violations and by regulating private vengeance. The laws of Solon addressed adultery and the seduction or rape of women who were not slaves. A woman who had sexual relations with any man other than her husband was censured. A married man committed adultery only if he had sexual relations with the wife of an Athenian citizen. However, he was guilty of debauchery if he defiled, through rape or seduction, a citizen's unmarried daughter, sister, or mother. Although adultery, rape, and seduction are quite different behaviors, the Athenians considered all of them to be violations that injured not just the woman, but also her *kyrios*, whose reputation was damaged by the insult to his authority.[8] One law stated that a man would not be prosecuted for homicide if he killed a man who had violated a woman of his *oikos*.[9] Previously, *oikos* members, often with the assistance of phratry members, had assumed responsibility for avenging an injury. Interestingly, the *polis* did not take responsibility for punishing the offender; instead, it regulated the vengeance taken by a wronged citizen. Vengeance killing in this particular instance was a case of justifiable homicide. The state allowed (but did not require) a *kyrios* to kill with impunity a man who had violated members of his *oikos*. Thus, the lawmakers of the early *polis* strove to resolve the difficult issue of establishing a public sphere while not interfering unduly with the private. However, the state created harsh penalties for a wife caught with a violator. Her husband was required to divorce her, which meant she was expelled from the *oikos* of her marriage and separated from her children.[10] She brought shame upon her natal *oikos* and, unlikely to find another husband, became a burden. She was, moreover, prohibited from entering public sanctuaries and, thus, socially isolated from having any role in the state.

The main purpose of marriage was the production of legitimate heirs to inherit and manage the property of the *oikos*. An infant born to a legally married couple became a legitimate member of an *oikos,* and hence of the *polis,* only after he or she had been formally accepted by the *kyrios* of the *oikos.* There were several reasons why a *kyrios* might choose not to accept an infant born to his wife, including sickness, deformity, the family already having as many children as it wanted or could support, or a question of the paternity of the infant. To acknowledge his acceptance of an infant, the *kyrios* carried it to the household hearth on the fifth or seventh day after its birth in a ceremony attended by witnesses. At a much later date, perhaps when a male child was a teenager, he was introduced and admitted to his father's phratry. At this time, the father swore the son was the product of a legal marriage and had citizen status.[11] A young man's membership in the phratry then became his proof of citizenship.

Traditionally, a man's estate passed, at his death, to his son. If he had more than one son, the property was divided evenly among them. However, there was the possibility of bitter disputes over the estate upon the death of a man without a son. Another article of legislation attributed to Solon was the introduction of wills, which made it possible for a man to keep his estate intact and choose the person best able to maintain it.[12] This legislation helped to preserve the *oikoi* that composed the state.

Not every *kyrios* had a son; about twenty percent of conjugal families produced only daughters.[13] A daughter was not an heiress but was instead considered to be holding the estate in trust for a male heir. A daughter who married and produced a son before the death of her father had fulfilled her duty: she had provided him with a grandson as an heir. Two years after puberty, her son would inherit the estate. However, an *epikleros*—that is, a girl without brothers—whose father died intestate before she was married, or who had not produced a child, posed a problem for the state. If she did not marry or have a child, her *oikos* would become extinct at her death. Usually, a man would find a husband for his daughter before his death. An Athenian father generally married his daughter to a close relative, as in a case reported by Demosthenes (383–322 B.C.E.). Polyeuctus, who had two daughters but no sons, gave one of his daughters in marriage to his wife's brother, whom he then adopted.[14] This young woman became both the wife and sister of her maternal uncle. If a daughter were not yet of marriageable age, her father might designate a husband for her in his will. In this case, we see another benefit of Solon's introduction of wills; it enabled fathers to settle the affairs of their daughters. If, however, a father died without having made such arrangements, her marriage became the responsibility of her *anchisteia* (her kin group). However, the marriage of the *epikleros*—or, more correctly, the survival of the *oikos*—was of such concern to the state that a state official, the archon, had the task of ensuring the *anchisteia* did indeed appoint a husband for her and that the arrangement followed the formal sequence of succession rights. First in line as her husband was her father's closest agnate: his eldest brother, the man whose duty it was to marry the *epikleros* (even if it required divorcing his wife). The purpose of this complex legislation was to ensure there was no threat to the survival of the *oikos*, but fourth-century orators were much concerned with litigation over exactly this matter.[15]

In addition to overseeing the marriage of an *epikleros*, the archon was charged with guarding the financial interests of children who had lost their parents and pregnant widows. As Pericles proudly proclaimed, children whose fathers had died in battle were supported at public expense until they reached maturity. The state also furnished dowries for the daughters of men who had records of outstanding public service.[16] However, the state provided little assistance to needy children or indigent families. We know very little about the lives of children whose parents were not legally married and the children of slaves and foreigners. Finally, mention should be made of a provision of Solon's legislation mandating that a father teach his son a trade. If he did not, the son was not obliged to support him in his old age.[17] Once again, we see how the survival of the state and the interests of the *kyrios* were entwined to promote the economic survival of the family.

SPARTA

In pursuit of military supremacy, the citizens of Sparta (the Spartiatai) developed a state that actively intervened in almost all areas of family life. The prosperity of the citizens of Sparta, whose numbers always remained relatively small, was dependent on other residents of the southern Peloponnese land the Spartans had invaded in the eighth century B.C.E. Inhabitants of villages near Sparta were called *perioikoi*—"dwellers around (Sparta)." Although not granted Spartan citizenship, their work as free craftsmen and tradesmen supported the Spartan economy. Inhabitants of other areas of Laconia and Messenia fared less well. Called helots, they were reduced to the status of serfs and forced to work the land once owned by their families but now in the possession of the Spartans. This system of enslaving the native population freed Spartan citizens from the need to do manual labor. In fact, the state forbade them from doing so.[18] Their role was to defend the state militarily against internal and external threats. Little survives written by the Spartans about themselves, and we have to depend instead on accounts written by Greeks from other states. Both Xenophon (ca. 430–ca. 355 B.C.E.) and Plutarch (ca. 46–ca. 120 C.E.) report that the Spartans had a code of laws that governed almost every aspect of an individual's life. All Spartans bound themselves to obey the "laws of Lycurgus." The intention of the framer(s) of this constitution was to create a new political system, radically different from that of other Greek *poleis*.[19] The constitution imposed laws that made military preparedness the top priority of the state, and all personal interests and relationships were subordinate to this priority.

Lycurgus (perhaps seventh century B.C.E.) or the framer(s) of the Spartan constitution recognized that the persons and property of citizen families might be threatened not only by outsiders but also by internal dissension if the less wealthy envied the rich. The cornerstone of the constitution was an effort to make all Spartan citizens equal in economic assets by distributing the land seized in Laconia and Messenia in allotments of equal size. The intent was to remove any reason for envy and to encourage citizens to value equality over personal gain. All adult male citizens were known as *homoioi*, which means both "equal" and "same." After the land distribution, Lycurgus is reported to have commented that "all Sparta looks like a family estate divided among brothers."[20]

The Spartans, in comparison to the Athenians, granted their state officials a much greater role in the lives of children. Plutarch comments that Lycurgus regarded sons not as the property of their fathers but as the common property of the state. The task of validating the infant was a public matter, and the criterion for acceptance was his potential for military service. A father presented his newborn son to state elders for public inspection, and, if the elders judged the infant to be sturdy and healthy, the father was ordered to raise him. If, however, he was judged to be weak or sickly, the father was ordered to take him to Apothetae, "the Cast Offs," a ravine near the foot of Mount Taygetus where the infant would be left to die of exposure. This ritual of inspection was the initial stage of the eugenic program of the Spartan state.[21]

The grueling indoctrination of boys into the warrior society began at the age of seven, when they were taken from their homes to be raised communally and to begin the brutal thirteen-year program designed to produce male citizens who were superlative soldiers. In contrast to other Greek states, Spartan boys were at all times subject to the scrutiny of members of the state, and any man could punish any boy for perceived misconduct because all men assumed the role of father.[22]

Xenophon implies that some boys were unable to satisfy the demands of this brutal system. Unsuccessful boys had little hope of gaining the privileges of full citizenship.[23] Any failure to conform to the standards articulated by the state was punished by an institutionalized process of merciless public shaming. Women played a role in enforcing the standards by joining in the public ridicule of those whose actions were deemed cowardly or disgraceful. Mothers took a leading part and might even kill a timorous son.[24] During this rigorous training program, boys aspired to become *homoioi* in virtuous behavior as benefited the state. Nonetheless, the state also encouraged a striving for individual achievement, creating an apparent contradiction only resolved by the spirit of competition being firmly channeled toward service and obedience to the state.[25]

At the age of twenty, young men became eligible for mandatory military service (that lasted until the age of sixty) and membership into a *syssition*—a mess or male dining group. Acceptance into a particular mess was decided on by a vote of the members. Those who were not accepted never became *homoioi*. Acceptance was an indication that adults of the mess approved of the young man's successful completion of their training. Men whose behavior did not meet Spartan standards faced a grim future; they were excluded from public activities, they were forced to wear clothing that denoted their disgrace, and they and their sisters were viewed as unfit for marriage.[26] In effect, the shunning behavior of the community served to control the genetic composition of the state.

Once accepted, a man ate every dinner with his mess companions for the rest of his life. The meals were modest, the drinking of wine was restrained, and the dinner was paid for by regular contributions from members. Nonetheless, however modest the meals, a member in financial straits might need to relinquish his membership in the mess and thus his position as a *homoios*.[27] It is certainly an indication that disparities of wealth existed among the Spartans despite Lycurgus's goal of creating a state of financial equals. This system of compulsory dining groups separated men from their conjugal families. Gender-segregated dining groups were a common feature in other Greek states, but the compulsory Spartan *syssition* institutionalized the segregation and was intended to reinforce the military culture of the state. It could be concluded that Spartans regarded the mess, rather than the biological family, as containing the people most important to their lives and their sense of identity.

Men married for the first time in their late twenties and women in their late teens. Spartan girls married relatively late (compared to Athenian girls) because it was thought that older girls were more physically mature and thus better able to cope with the difficulties of childbirth. Again we see a focus on the production of strong children. Not marrying was not an option in the Spartan state, and failure to marry resulted in shaming. Since men were required to live communally in the barracks until the age of thirty, when they reached full adulthood and citizenship, a newlywed couple did not immediately begin to live together. Their sexual encounters were, by law, limited to clandestine visits at night by the husband, who then returned to his barracks. Lycurgan law also restricted the frequency of sexual intercourse on the grounds that the children created would be stronger if the desire for sex was stronger. A contradiction here is that Spartan men were also encouraged to have male lovers.[28]

The purpose of marriage was to produce the next generation of robust Spartans, and the state encouraged such production by granting exemptions from military service to men who had fathered three sons. Lycurgus advocated that the sturdiest citizens be utilized to create children. In fact, his law code encouraged situations that constituted adultery in other Greek states: an old man with a young wife, or a man without children, was encouraged to allow a younger man to impregnate his wife. The woman's husband would then adopt the child.[29] The key issue in this and other examples of Spartan wife-sharing was that the husband gave his consent to a sexual union that was of service to the state. The paternity of children born of these unions was defined legally rather than biologically.

Spartan society was also unusual in granting a relatively high degree of responsibility to its female citizens. The frequent absences of the father of the family, on a daily basis at his mess or on military campaign, led to a situation where the women of Sparta played significant roles in the management of property as well as domestic matters. Spartan daughters inherited alongside their brothers, in contrast to the practice in Athens where daughters did not inherit (unless *epikleroi*). *Epikleroi* were numerous in Sparta, perhaps as a result of the deaths of many young men in military training and war. As a result, women may have owned about two-fifths of the land. Dowries were large to attract the surviving young men.[30] Casualties suffered in military training and the eugenics program based on Lycurgan laws demographically weakened the state. The number of *homoioi* had dwindled from about eight thousand at the beginning of the fifth century to about three thousand at the end. By about 330 B.C.E., Aristotle reported that there were fewer than one thousand.[31]

The portrait of archaic and classical Sparta that emerges from the law code of Lycurgus is of a repressive state in which military requirements took precedence over family relationships. However, the Spartan state was designed to protect the property of a relatively small number of families. As a reproductive unit, moreover, the family's efforts could be concentrated on the creation of warriors.[32] Practices such as wife-sharing, which have been labeled detrimental to marriage and family stability, were, in fact, strategies to provide an heir for the *oikos*. Similarly, sharing a wife with a brother and the extreme endogamy of permitting half-siblings to marry indicate a strong desire to keep the property of the *oikos* within the possession of family members and, in the case of half-siblings, not to split the property. The retention of a system of private property transmission through family members indicates the Spartans considered family connections of prime importance, despite Lycurgan efforts to superimpose a communal social structure.[33]

ROME

In ancient Rome, a child's entitlement to the rights of citizenship was determined by the status of his or her parents as citizens. In addition, a child's legitimacy as a family member was dependent on the marital status of the parents. Only citizens could form a lawful Roman marriage and produce legitimate children. However, no formal ceremony documented by state officials was required to make the marriage legally valid. As in Athens, marriage was a social process witnessed by community members. The conjugal family was the basic unit of Roman society and served both reproductive and productive functions. However, the kin relationship that receives the most attention in Roman legal texts is a configuration called the *familia*.[34] Based on agnatic relationships, the *familia* was headed by an ascendant male known as the *paterfamilias* (father of the *familia*) whose father and grandfather were deceased. The *familia* consisted of him, the children born to him in a lawful marriage, and the children of his sons. Like the Greek word *oikos*, the Latin word *familia* sometimes also denotes the property, including slaves, managed by the ascendant male. Under Roman law, the *paterfamilias* had absolute power—called the *patria potestas*, "the paternal power"—over all his legal descendants. All the property of the *familia* resided in his possession, and all legal contracts and business transactions entered into by *familia* members needed his approval. His consent was required for marriage and divorce, and the decision to expose (or keep) an infant born to members of the *familia* rested with him. He had the legal right to inflict corporal punishment on his descendants or even put them to death. This power lasted for his entire lifetime. The jurist Gaius (ca. 110–ca. 180 C.E.) claimed there were no other cultures in which fathers wielded so much power over their children. We should not, however, conclude that the theoretical powers delineated in legal texts describe social reality. In practice, the behavior of the *paterfamilias* was undoubtedly tempered by the emotional bonds between him,

FIGURE 7.1: *Coin of Hadrian representing the restoration of freedom (*Libertas restituta*).* The emperor is seated in a curule chair before a woman with two children. The emperor restores not only freedom for men but also women and children living in the state. Coin is in the Hunter Coin Cabinet at the University of Glasgow no. 333. (illustration: Henry Buglass).

his wife, and his dependents. The jurist Marcianus (third century c.e.) recommended that *patria potestas* be exercised with affection and respect (*pietas*).[35]

The *familia*, as a legal construct of citizens arranged according to male blood descent and under the authority of the ascendant male, served as a means of establishing public order. It enabled the state to identify units of close kin and, in disputes, determine the person responsible for the actions of the members of that unit. It also served to encourage the sound management and orderly transmission of property. The *paterfamilias* was, in effect, the trustee of the property of the *familia*. His responsibility was to preserve it for his children and future generations of his *familia*. If a *paterfamilias* died intestate, the property of the *familia* was distributed according to agnatic succession. Over the centuries, Roman law was modified, albeit slowly, to adapt to the needs and wishes of Roman citizens in regard to family relationships and obligations. Civil rules of succession and intestate inheritance were expanded. People often wanted to keep property in the family but not restricted to the agnatic *familia*. Changes in the laws of succession reflected the high value people placed on the bonds between mothers and their children and on non-agnate relatives—that is, kin related by blood (cognates), such as a maternal uncle or a sister's children; or kin related by marriage, such as a wife's brother or nephews.[36]

Rome's first emperor, Augustus (ruled 27 b.c.e.–14 c.e.), was responsible for perhaps the greatest change in the relationship between the state and the family. Although his position as the state's supreme authority was unprecedented, he cleverly utilized the existing cultural associations of family to present himself as a conservator of traditional institutions. He fostered a public image of himself as the savior of Rome by virtue of being the restorer not only of military and political order in the empire but also of moral order. In the aftermath of the civil wars (44–31 b.c.e.), one of the most innovative elements of Augustus's program was his linkage of moral restoration, family responsibility, and civic duty. He reminded Romans that they had both a private and a public duty to produce children, and he sponsored several laws designed to encourage Roman citizens to marry, stay married, and raise families by penalizing celibacy, childlessness, and adultery. He thus made matters traditionally considered to be private now matters of public concern.[37] Two sets of laws, one passed in 18 b.c.e. and known as the *lex Julia*, the other passed in 9 c.e. and known as the *lex Papia-Poppaea*, regulated marriage and adultery. Much of our knowledge about these laws comes from later summaries and commentaries by jurists, who tend to conflate the two laws. It is thus difficult to distinguish between the original Augustan legislation and later revisions and interpretations. Modern scholars, therefore, continue to debate the content and purpose of the legislation.[38] However, the ramification of the laws is clear: they authorized the intervention of the state in the structure of the family. Augustus's reasons for sponsoring such remarkable legislation are unknown. Whatever his reasons, he chose to view the population problem as an issue of the reluctance of people to have children. He was troubled that some men chose not to marry and that some married couples chose to be childless. Childlessness could indicate infertility, but it could also indicate a couple had taken measures to avoid parenthood through contraception, abortion, or the exposure of a live-born infant.[39]

Among the provisions of the legislation were penalties for a failure to marry or remarry after a death or divorce. Men who remained unmarried between the ages of twenty-five and sixty, and women between the ages of twenty and fifty, were ineligible to receive inheritances or legacies. Clearly the intent of the law was to persuade people of childbearing years to marry. The *lex Julia* allowed widows a term of one year from the death of a husband, and six months from the time of divorce, to remarry—that is, a grace period within which they were not subject to penalties. The *lex Papia-Poppaea* extended the grace periods to two years and a year and six months, respectively. Married men between the ages of twenty-five and sixty with no legitimate children, and married women between the ages of twenty and fifty with no children, could receive only half an inheritance or legacy.[40]

The Augustan laws also offered incentives for marriage and the production of legitimate children. Men who had three or more legitimate children were rewarded with preference in candidacy for political office and more rapid promotion in their public careers. The emperor was able, however, to grant a childless man the privileges of a man with three children. Freed slaves with at least two legitimate children (children born after manumission to a legally married couple) were exempt from obligatory labor for their patrons. For freeborn women who had borne three children (and for freedwomen who had borne four legitimate children), the reward was release from guardianship and, thus, the acquisition of financial autonomy. Correspondingly, men with several children were released from the requirement that they serve as guardians for their female agnates.[41]

Because many of these rewards would have been attractive only to wealthy people, especially politically ambitious men, some scholars have concluded that Augustus's legislation was directed primarily at maintaining the population of the elite class, not the working poor.[42] Political advancement and eligibility for legacies were not realistic incentives for the working poor. And most freedwomen had no financial resources to gain autonomy over even if they were able to bear four legitimate children after the age of thirty, which was set as the minimum age of manumission by the *lex Aelia-Sentia* of 4 C.E.[43] If propertied men engaged in public careers were indeed the main focus of Augustus's legislation, it suggests that wealthy people saw children as economic liabilities rather than investments because of the expenses of funding their public careers and supplying large dowries. Tacitus (ca. 55–ca. 117 C.E.) commented that the Augustan legislation failed to be effective because childlessness still offered too many advantages.[44]

Other provisions of the legislation suggest the emperor was also interested in reinforcing class distinctions. Men of the senatorial class were prohibited from marrying freedwomen. Freeborn citizens were barred from marrying people considered disreputable: pimps, prostitutes, actresses, and women convicted of adultery or other crimes. However, Cassius Dio (ca. 150–235 C.E.) reports that Augustus allowed all men, except those of senatorial rank, to marry freedwomen because the freeborn population contained far more males than females. His statement may suggest that the exposure rate for female infants was higher than that for male infants.[45]

In addition to encouraging the creation of families, the Augustan legislation promoted the stability of families by taking the radical step of making adultery a crime. A woman was guilty of adultery if she had sexual intercourse with any man other than her husband. However, a man, whether single or married, was guilty of adultery only if he had sexual intercourse with a respectable married woman and thereby challenged the authority of her *paterfamilias* and husband. Sexual activity with a woman who was a slave, freedwoman, prostitute or actress, or even shopkeeper was not considered adultery. The sexual seduction of an unmarried respectable woman was also a punishable offence, again because it threatened to destabilize her *familia*. Under the Augustan legislation, a father was permitted (though not required) to kill his daughter and her partner in adultery if he caught them in the act in his own home or the home of his son-in-law. A husband was permitted to kill his wife's partner if caught in the act of adultery in his home and if the partner were disreputable—that is, if he were a pimp, actor, gladiator, criminal, or slave. In the first instance, the law preserved the traditional prerogative and duty of the *paterfamilias* to control the behavior of the members of his *familia*. In the second instance, the law preserved the right of the head of a household to maintain security by killing an intruder. Although a husband was not allowed to kill his adulterous wife with impunity, Augustan law required he divorce her. And if he did not prosecute her and her partner for adultery, the husband could be punished as a pimp. Women convicted of adultery were punished by confiscation of half their dowry and a third of their property and by exile to an island. Male adulterers were punished by confiscation of half their property and exile to an island, though not the same island as their partner. If the father or husband failed to initiate prosecution, it could be initiated by someone outside the family. Private behavior was now everybody's business, and monitoring one's neighbor became a civic duty that contributed to the health of the state. Augustus himself was bound by this law to send his only child, his adulterous daughter Julia, into exile in 2 B.C.E.[46]

As noted earlier, Tacitus reported that Augustus's measures to encourage the formation of large, stable families were unpopular and unsuccessful. Although we cannot verify the accuracy of Tacitus's statement, we learn from Pliny's letters, written about one hundred years after the enactment of the Augustan legislation, that childlessness was still an issue, at least among the elite. Pliny (ca. 61–ca.113 C.E.) himself voiced distress about remaining childless despite three marriages. He and several friends required imperial grants of the three-children privilege in order to advance politically.[47] The difficulty of maintaining a family line is illustrated by the fact that both Pliny and his third wife were only children and seem not to have had any first cousins.

Although Augustus's legislation may not have succeeded in increasing the population of freeborn Romans, particularly of the elite class, it was an unprecedented invasion of privacy and therefore created a radical and critical change in the conceptual relationship between the state and the family. The state now took on responsibility for the oversight of family behavior. Augustus's promotion of family life produced a rhetorical link between appropriate family behavior and a citizen's patriotic duty. The laws encouraged citizens to act in a responsible and respectable manner for the good of the *res publica*.[48]

Augustus also drew on the traditional cultural construct of family to define his unique position and shape the nature of his relationship to other Romans. In 2 B.C.E., he accepted the title of *Pater Patriae*, "Father of the Fatherland." By representing himself as the *paterfamilias* of the entire Roman community, he articulated the basis of his authority over Rome and its empire. As *paterfamilias*, he was the source of moral guidance and was entitled to monitor the marriages, procreation and sexual behavior of his wards. His actions could be construed as dictated by *pietas*, a deep concern for the welfare of his family members, and they were expected to respond with *pietas*—that is, devotion and obedience. In this same period, children, who had rarely been represented in the art of the Roman republic, appeared in public sculpture, most notably on the Altar of Augustan Peace.[49] The images on this monument of the happy and harmonious family suggested that Augustus's laws encouraging marriage

FIGURE 7.2: *Detail from the Ara Pacis (Altar of Augustan Peace) in Rome (dedicated 9 B.C.E.)*. The inclusion of male and female children alongside male and female adults provides the viewer with a representation of the imperial family at the very center of the state (photo Ray Laurence).

and childbearing had been successful, even as they highlighted Augustus's distinctive role as an exemplary father to both his immediate family and his empire-wide family (see figure 7.2). The fertility and chastity of his own family, moreover, were provided both as a model for emulation and an assurance of the future stability of the state through the continuity of his dynasty. Augustus's rhetoric appears to have influenced public discourse, and many of his subjects adopted his ideology of valorizing the family. During the Augustan period, it became fashionable, especially among freed slaves, to commemorate the ideal (if not the reality) of a happy and satisfying family life by including representations of spouses and children on funerary sculpture and by commissioning funerary inscriptions that drew attention to family relationships.[50] Children remained a focal point of imperial ideology for at least the next two centuries, and the emperors who followed Augustus continued to exploit the political advantages of presenting themselves in a paternal role. Like him, they utilized coinage and sculpture to promote *pietas*, fecundity, and family harmony (see figure 7.1).[51] They also offered practical assistance, in the form of *alimenta*, the system of loans and support for children (see chapter 2), and *congiaria* (public distributions of money). We see the development of the idea that it was the role of the state to nourish its citizens and of the emperor, as *pater patriae*, to foster the program. The emperor was not just the father of the country but also of the citizens and their families on which the state was maintained.

The states of ancient Athens, Sparta, and Rome developed in societies in which the male head of the family traditionally held the responsibility both for ensuring family members married and then produced and raised legitimate children and for protecting the family property for the welfare of future generations. Although the development of these states required the subordination of some family interests to the regulation of public authority, the success of each of these states depended on its ability to maintain a stable population of citizen families. Nonetheless, each state adopted different measures to achieve this goal. Athens and Sparta provide stark contrasts in the level of state intrusion into the private lives of citizens and the raising of children. In imperial Rome, Augustus created a revolutionary change in the conceptual relationship between the state and the family by connecting responsible behavior as a family member with patriotic duty as a citizen.

CHAPTER EIGHT

Faith and Religion

VILLE VUOLANTO

In all cultures, children have participated in religious life—as actors and spectators in rituals as well as objects of religious education. Not surprisingly, children in antiquity were surrounded by the world of gods from the moment of birth. The newborn child needed the acceptance and protection of divine powers. Later in life, religion was present in their homes, at the family altars, in prayers, at feasts and festivals, in rites of passage, and in their acculturation into family traditions and the values of the community.

Interestingly, there are relatively few studies of religion and faith in what has become a relatively prolific literature on childhood and the family in antiquity. There are some important exceptions that point the way to an effective appreciation of religion and faith in the lives of children in the ancient world—studies of Athenian girls and the Greek rites of passage on the edge of puberty are among the most important.[1] For Greek childhood, Mark Golden's development of the study of children in their own right, as opposed to the earlier emphasis on themes of emotional attachment, draws our attention to the importance of religious life in the socialization process.[2] By comparison, few scholars of the Roman world have directly addressed the subject.[3] The situation is similar for the Christian period; Odd Bakke's monograph on Christianity and children and Patricia Horn's paper on children's play and Christianity are important exceptions.[4] Of course, there has been considerable debate over what difference Christianity made in the lives of children, but in the absence of a full account of the role of other religions from antiquity the answer has proven rather elusive. Hence, this chapter sets out a new outlook that high-lights the importance of religion in the socialization of children in antiquity.[5] It seeks to identify the significance of religion in the lives of children in the ancient world and the way in which religion and ritual acculturated children to their social roles. In discussing these two central questions, another arises: what dif-ference did the religious orientation of a child's parents have for the experience of childhood? Due to the limitations of ancient sources and the constraints of this chapter, most examples come from classical Greece, the city of Rome, and mainstream Christian discourse, with glimpses into other traditions. Variation in religious experience needs to be recognized; after all, there was no single version of Christianity in antiquity, and when the Judeo-Christian tradition is brought into view, the idea of a uniformity of religious belief and ritual practice becomes precarious.

RELIGIOUS PROTECTION IN EARLY CHILDHOOD

In antiquity, the birth of a child necessitated both its inclusion into the social world and into the world of gods. In Athens, an infant's admittance to the fam-ily cult was marked with sacrifices and the ritual carrying of the child around the family hearth (*amphidromia*). In these rituals, the child was presented to the gods, and an olive branch at the front door proclaimed the birth to the community. In the Roman world, the front door was decorated with flowers, and sacrifices were made to the household deities and goddesses of childbirth, both in the family home and in the houses of family friends. Purification rites and name giving followed in close sequence.[6] In classical Athens, boys under one year were further presented to a phratry (see chapter 7), and elite male children soon after their birth were presented to their *genē* groups. Both these groupings were formed around the cult of a common ancestor, the founder of the line.[7] In these ways, children were brought into cult activities within the family and community at a very early age.

In early Christian culture, infant baptism—and the adjoining confirmation—became common during the third and fourth centuries C.E. It is easy to see infant baptism as a continuation of the Jewish and Greco-Roman rituals of ac-cepting the child into the religious community and ensuring divine protection against evil. An important part of baptism was exorcism, and many parents considered baptism a remedy for illnesses. There is no clear information about earlier Christian rituals linked to the birth, religious and social inclusion, and naming of the child. Most probably these practices followed those of the ma-jority of the local population. Tertullian, for example, regarded the traditional

Roman name-giving ceremonies as acceptable for Christians. On the other hand, regardless of encouragement for infant baptism among ecclesiastical writers, as late as the fifth century even the most pious parents often delayed baptism if there was no immediate fear the infant was in mortal danger.[8]

Childhood was a fragile period characterized by illnesses that could potentially result in death. During their early years, most children participated in rituals and practices to gain divine protection against the evil spirits that brought illnesses and death. At birth, an array of gods was asked for protection and good fortune. The lists of deities associated with birth and early childhood as given by Augustine (354–430 C.E.) are exaggerations aimed at ridiculing the polytheistic pantheon, but they illustrate the cares of parents, the need for divine protection at birth, and the presence of the religious sphere in the everyday life of families.[9]

Healing in antiquity was intimately linked with magic, and even toys could have apotropaic effects. In Greece, infants and children wore protective amulets and other charms against evil.[10] In the Roman tradition, these amulets were even developed as childhood symbols of free birth: a pendant with an amulet (a *bulla*) was given to an infant on the day of purification (see figure 8.1); boys wore it until receiving the *toga virilis* at the age of majority. Amulets are frequently mentioned as characteristic symbols of childhood, and Pliny the Elder (23–79 C.E.), for example, mentions some charms especially suitable for infants, like amber, dried brains of boa, and horns of scarab.[11]

Amulets and cross pendants were used to heal children and protect them from disease and demons in early Christian contexts, even if some ecclesiastical writers frowned on these magical practices: "some ablute their children in polluted water and water from arena ... some tie amulets on their children, handcrafted by men."[12] In Antioch, there was a custom to bind gospels onto the necks of children. John Chrysostom (ca. 354–407 C.E.) did not see the magical function of amulets problematic, but the association of the custom with Jewish practices created some unease.[13] The use of *tefillim*—boxes containing parchment inscribed with biblical verses carried above the forehead and on the arm and thought to have both spiritual and protective function—is well attested in ancient Judaism. *Tefillim* were used as soon as a child was considered mentally fit to understand their significance, at the age of thirteen at the latest—using them, however, did not imply a passage to adulthood.[14] Private relics and blessed objects (*eulogia*) were also used to protect Christian children from danger and keep them in good health. The *eulogia* from the shrine of Simeon the Stylite (ca. 390–459 C.E.), for example, are described as having cured many children back home. Illnesses frequently brought children into connection with

FIGURE 8.1: *Detail from the Ara Pacis (Altar of Augustan Peace) in Rome (dedicated 9 B.C.E.) showing a child wearing a* bulla (photo Ray Laurence).

the cult of saints. According to Gregory of Tours (538–594 C.E.), a bit of dust from the church of St. Martin was more powerful in curing a child than the charms of local diviners and soothsayers.[15] As part of their families, children were acculturated not only to proper religious practices but also to culturally valid beliefs.

PARENTS, CHILDREN, AND RELIGION

Religion played an integral part in family life in the ancient world. The introduction of children into the family cult was, therefore, a crucial part of their education. In this, they were both socialized into family membership and learned skills for their adult lives and for the preservation and continuity of the family cult. As early as the Greek archaic period (eighth to sixth centuries B.C.E.), children appear as dedicators of votive offerings and as worshippers of gods and heroes alongside their parents. A common scene is a parent

FIGURE 8.2: *Man, woman, and child before an altar offering a sow as sacrifice to Demeter and Kore.* Praxiteles, ca. 400–330 B.C.E. Louvre, Paris. Image: Bridgeman Art Library.

presenting and commending a child to the god's care, as in a relief dedicated to the river god Kephisos by Xenokrateia. The visual material reflects two inter-twined motives on the part of the parents: first, to present the children to the gods and submit them to divine protection; and secondly, to make public the piety and continuity of the family. It was the gods who acted as witnesses and guarantors of family unity.[16]

Sacrificing in the ancient world was often a family affair, and the pres-ence of children is highlighted in many visual sources. Children were not just bystanders; they assisted in making the sacrifices (see figure 8.2). Making a sacrifice together with children and/or grandchildren was commonplace in Athens.[17] In Rome, children assisted in everyday family sacrifices and on special occasions such as birthday celebrations and harvest sacrifices. Ovid de-scribes the annual sacrifice to Terminus (god of boundaries) celebrated by the household—the family was silent and dressed in white, the boy threw corn to the sacrificial fire, and the girl added slices of a honeycomb.[18] The cult of the household deities, the *lares* and the *genius*, brought a religious element to the everyday experience of children within the Roman house. Children could even carry out rituals for household deities on their own. Children also took part in family feasts and banquets, and they had roles at the sac-rifices and in the ritually correct serving of food at daily meals. Slave chil-dren attended the rituals of the household and could be used as assistants in sacrifices if there were no freeborn children available.[19] Presumably these practices continued as long as Roman traditional religion lasted, and the last attestation for these practices comes from the fourth century C.E.

In the cultures of the ancient Mediterranean, the presence of children as family members at funerals and in funeral processions was taken for granted. Girls were introduced to the preparation of the corpse for burial and to the rituals of lamentation, and boys learned to make offerings to the dead. Com-memorating the dead and visiting graves were family matters involving children as well as adults. These acts all formed part of a process by which the proper religious rituals and a sense of family continuity and identity were transferred from one generation to the next.[20]

Children had also special functions in Greek and Roman marriage ritu-als. In marriage ceremonies in Athens, a child with both parents living (*pais amphithales*) distributed bread from a cradle-shaped basket to the guests and accompanied the groom prior to the ceremony. In Rome, the tasks of children in marriage rituals were linked to bringing good luck, expelling evil spirits, and ascertaining fertility, even if the actual tasks—like washing the feet of the bride, shouting obscenities, noisily picking up nuts thrown by the groom, carrying the torch for the new hearth, and leading the bride to her new home—varied according to time. Moreover, the sacrifices and processions held in connection with marriage rituals involved boy or girl assistants and choirs of children.[21] There is no information on the annual celebrations of personal birthdays in Greece, but in Rome, birthday parties of family members included prayers for divine protection, ritual food, and incense and fire on the domestic altar. Children learned these rituals by attending the birthdays of older family members as well as celebrating their own birth.[22]

There were various rituals linked with coming of age. In Attica, sixteen-year-old boys made sacrifices to mark their majority and entry into the full membership of their phratry. These sacrifices were pointedly social events. Boys also dedicated their toys to gods, especially to Hermes. Similarly, before assuming the adult *toga virilis*, Roman citizen boys dedicated their *bulla* to the household gods. Sacrifices followed, and, starting from the early empire, the toga was put on at the temple of Mars Ultor in Augustus's forum. For Greek and Roman girls, marriage signified the end of childhood, and rituals such as dedicating dolls and toys to the gods (especially Artemis and Venus) were carried out. Athenian girls, moreover, made a sacrifice to Athena. The dedication of clothes, especially wedding garments, could also take place. Toys—like whips, knucklebones, tops, and hoops—most likely dedicated to Dionysus in connection with initiatory rituals also signify this kind of transfer to the adult world.[23]

In Christian contexts, religious education depended on everyday religious practices in individual families. There was some continuity of family rituals not associated with polytheistic practices. As Tertullian commented, it was not a problem for Christians to attend celebrations of *toga virilis*, betrothals, marriages, and the naming of children, as these were social events.[24] He does not mention birthdays—in their Roman form they were not social but pointedly religious rituals. For Christians, their real birthday was the day of baptism.

As soon as children could reason, parents were expected to teach them the rudiments of faith. For Jewish culture, this meant learning the meaning of the major religious festivals (and, naturally, participating in the festivities) and the essential passages of the Torah. Particular importance was placed on religious education; there were Rabbinical scripture schools from the first century B.C.E. (some with female pupils), and instruction of the young was concentrated on the Torah and oral religious traditions.[25] Christian families introduced their children early to prayers, singing hymns and psalms, and blessing themselves with the sign of the cross. Both the hagiographic stories and the pedagogical treaties presuppose that a seven-year-old child could know the Creed and could

FIGURE 8.3: *Internal space of Roman house (House of the Menander, Pompeii) showing the shrine to the household gods in the atrium (photo Ray Laurence).*

understand it as a proclamation of faith. Logically, the early penitentiaries presupposed that children made confessions. It is only in early Christianity that it is possible for the first time to see the separation of secular schooling from spiritual upbringing. This is a quite distinct feature of Christianity when compared to polytheism or Jewish practices. In the early medieval west, it became a task for godparents to teach the Creed and the Lord's Prayer to their godchildren.[26] Socializing the child in the proper religious praxis was a family matter, and it was the prerogative of the child's parents and godparents.

FESTIVALS AND RITUALS: CHILDREN IN PUBLIC

In public life, religious participation often revealed the status of a family, and both adults and children had prominent roles. Children took part in public religious rituals, carrying out tasks that were often gender specific. Sacrifices, prayers, hymns, and religious processions constituted the frame in which the other festival activities took place. In the Christian context, the sacrifices were replaced with the Eucharist, and although the association of the theater and the *ludi* (games) with the polytheistic cults aroused Christian opposition, religion retained its prominence in public life.

It was common practice in Greece for girls from seven to twelve years old to perform certain religious rituals. As a rule, some aristocratic girls served in the principal cults of their communities; for example, there were nine girls chosen (*agretai*) each year at Kos to take care of the local cult of Athena. In Athens, there were many occasions for girls to serve their community in religious festivals. *Kanēphoroi* (basket carriers) were selected from elite girls over ten years old approaching marriageable age, and at festivals they carried items for the performance of the sacrifice, including knives, barley, and ribbons. Four girls (the *arrēphoroi*), aged between seven and eleven, participated in the cult of Athena with a nocturnal journey to the Acropolis while weaving the robe (*peplos*) for the goddess. During their period of duty, they lived on the Acropolis and even had a playground there, forming a small community of their own.[27] This practice continued into the Roman period in Athens. However, there was a shift in their visibility. Beginning in the late third century B.C.E., fathers, other family members, and even the *polis* itself began to honor the *arrēphoroi* and *kanēphoroi* with statues. A similar development took place in the Eleusian mysteries. Each year, "a child of the hearth" was elected to offer prayers and sacrifices, acting as an intermediary between the initiates and the divine. The practice was in use in the fifth century B.C.E. and continued into Roman times. Originally, the child was selected by lot from the candidates, and all the known participants of the classical period were boys. When these children began to be honored in statues in the Hellenistic period, all but one were girls.[28]

More girls were included in the cult of Artemis at Brauron, even if not all the Athenian citizen girls could serve the goddess as *arktoi* ("bears," which symbolized Artemis at Brauron). There was, in addition to the rituals at Brauron, a special sacrifice and procession from the shrine to Athens every four or five years encompassing those girls who had served the goddess since the previous festival. In the fifth and fourth centuries B.C.E., this rite was an important socializing event for the seven- to eleven-year-old girls attending, with the renewal of acquaintances from Brauron and the whole community as onlookers.[29] Girls acting as *ergastīnai* (weavers) are first attested in 103/102 B.C.E., when there were about 120 girls working the wool for the *peplos* of Athena and performing the procession. This seems to have served as a counterpart for the service by the *ephebes* (young men). The office of the *ergastīnai* allowed greater participation than the other more selective duties, but the girls still came from the leading families.[30]

In Athens, well-born girls also served as tray bearers in sacrifices, as statue washers of Athena on the Acropolis, and by grinding corn to make cakes offered to Athena. All these tasks offered opportunities for citizen girls to take part in religious life and for elite families to proclaim the honor and piety of their daughters—and themselves. Moreover, many of these tasks were connected to the quotidian tasks of young women. Girls "served the gods in ways women served their households."[31]

While girls have aroused more attention in studies on Greek rituals, boys were also active, with tasks in accordance with their future roles—for example, assisting in the rite of animal sacrifice.[32] For example, at Choes (the second day of the Athenian Anthesteria festival), two-year-old boys were allowed to taste the new wine together with adults in a transitional ritual celebrating their survival of early childhood and in anticipation of adult *symposia*.[33] The rites of Oschophoria concerning the coming of age of boys included fables and cross-dressing on the part of young men in honor of Dionysus; at the Pyanopsia, boys with both parents alive went from house to house in procession, carrying olive branches wreathed with wool and decorations symbolizing fruitfulness and singing songs of plenty.[34]

The Greek *poleis* sent their representatives to other Greek shrines; thus, for example, Kos sent both chosen girls (*agretai*) and boys to Delos to serve at the shrine of Apollo. Two Locrian maidens were sent yearly to Ilion to serve Athena at her shrine—this tradition seems to have continued from the late sixth to the early second century B.C.E. Seven Corinthian girls and seven boys from elite families spent a year at the temple of Hera Akraia near Corinth.[35] The cultic life gave some Greek children unique opportunities to experience a world beyond the city of their birth and to form contacts with their peers, even those of the opposite sex. In this context, as representatives of their families, their kin, and their community, these events were important for the formation of their own identity as distinct from children of other *poleis*.

In Rome, the presence of *camilli* and *camillae* (boys and girls with both parents alive) was a visible part of religious rituals from the third century B.C.E. to the fourth century C.E. They had similar functions to the children involved in Greek rituals, frequently carrying vessels with different utensils—such as incense boxes, trays of fruit, jugs of wine, dishes, and towels—at sacrifices,

FIGURE 8.4: *Chorus of Greek girls/women.* Libation bowl from Athens, ca. 450 B.C.E. Museum of Fine Arts, Boston. Edwin E. Jack Fund. Photograph © Museum of Fine Arts, Boston.

processions, and weddings. In the visual representations of Roman religion, *camilli* are central figures, as can be seen in the relief with Marcus Aurelius offering a sacrifice as a part of his triumph in 176 C.E. with a *camillus* standing close to him holding an incense box. The *camilli* not only participated in the rituals of the annual Compitalia festival at the crossroad altars but their presence was also celebrated and perpetuated in the everyday cityscape in altar reliefs. Female *camillae* are rarer, but their existence needs to be noted.[36] Outside the city of Rome, both boys and girls took part in different kinds of youth organizations, all of which had a religious aspect. Children played the lyre in a number of religious contexts and acted as servants for priesthoods.[37]

In some of the older priesthoods, child assistants had a special place. At meetings of the Arval brethren, aristocratic *camilli* (themselves Arvals, perhaps) assisted the priests. The rituals carried out by the *Flamen* and *Flaminica Dialis* were conducted with both a male *camillus* and a female *camilla* present—the children were needed to create a familial analogy.[38] A special case of children involved in Roman religious life were the vestal virgins, who were recruited from elite girls before the age of puberty. Thus, at any given time until the abandonment of the cult in 394 C.E., at least one of the six vestals was a prepubescent child with a visible presence in Roman public religion.[39]

Athletic competitions at the religious festivals were an important way for Greek children, especially boys, to participate in religious life. In all the pan-Hellenic games, for example, there were age classes for boys—a feature that continued into the Roman period. During the Hellenistic period, girls' races were attached to religious rituals throughout the Greek world; the most famous occurred every fourth year at Olympia during the Heraia festivals.[40] In Roman religion, children's sports had less significance, but Augustus introduced the ritual of the Troy games in which high-ranking boys from seven to fourteen years old performed equestrian rituals. Later, Domitian created the Capitoline games, which included foot races for both girls and boys. Both Augustus and Domitian were adapting Greek models for the new context of Rome's empire.[41]

Choirs of boys and girls were an essential part of religious life throughout the ancient world. In Athens, choirs of boys, such as the five choirs of fifty boys at the Thargelia festival, were a regular feature. Girls' choirs were more common in other Greek cities. In Sparta, a choir of adolescent girls presented Alcman's *Partheneion* every year, and Delian girls honored Apollo with a chorus, dancing, and singing. Dancing in honor of the gods was a significant part of the religious life of girls in their transition into adult life throughout the Greek world. These forms of public performance must have given young participants "a powerful sense of belonging to the community."[42]

In Rome, elite children figured prominently as members of choirs, especially at religious occasions, including the dedication of temples or public funerals. Children and choirs seem to have been connected with purification, highlighting the continuity of the community. In 207 B.C.E., for example, there was an expiation ceremony involving a procession of three choirs of nine virgins singing and performing a solemn dance. The use of such choirs continued at least to the third century C.E., as did dances by girls performed in connection with other religious occasions. For example, in the cult of Diana at Tusculum, girls were among the priestesses leading sacred dances in the processions.[43] The presence of children was noted at the secular games (*ludi saeculares*) symbolizing the new, peaceful, and prosperous times. In Augustus's celebration of the *ludi*, the main event involving aristocratic children was the *Carmen saeculare* ("Song of the Ages"), sung twice by choirs of twenty-seven boys and twenty-seven girls. On the coins promoting the secular games of Domitian (88 C.E.), children are shown holding branches and accompanying the distribution of the purificatory material. It seems that in times of violent crises, or their aftermath, the *pax deorum* (peace of the gods) was sought with the help of boys and girls equally as representing the population, but when the threat was directed at the fertility and renewal of the community—for example, in cases of prodigies (human or animals born with birth defects)—only girls—future mothers—were involved.[44]

On the whole, the visibility, maybe even the participation, of girls in public rituals at least in Athens gradually increased during the Hellenistic period.[45] This trend was not continued under Roman influence. Except for the presence of *camilli*, there seems to have been far fewer religious roles available for Roman children, especially girls, at the public festivals of the sacral year. The context of children's festival activities was often shaped by Greek models adopted under the empire, but there was nothing comparable to the Choes or the rituals of the *arrēphoroi*; the Roman rites of passage seem more family centered. However, children were visible in Roman official rituals. On the Ara Pacis (Altar of Peace 9 B.C.E.), for example, children were represented in various religious roles: as *camilli*, as young vestals, as the offspring of the leading members of the elite in a religious procession, and as symbols of continuity and fertility in the arms of the goddess. Elite children were acculturated into society and its values by their religious duties, which simultaneously brought honor to their families.

The visibility of girls in Christian rituals is scarce. For boys, the situation was different: at least by the fourth century C.E., many of the readers (*lectores*) in the liturgy were children or young men, who usually started from the age

of eight; their tasks involved reading the scriptures, singing, blessing the offerings, and providing water for washing the officiating priest's hands. Some
boys were appointed lectors as early as five years old. In the west, the order of
child *lectores* died out after the Carolingian reforms (eight and ninth centuries
C.E.). For the whole period, boy choirs were common in churches around the
Mediterranean. Among some Christian groups, there is also some evidence for
boys performing liturgical dances.[46]

In the context of the Christian ascetic movement, there evolved a practice
of dedicating children to God. Even if the sources highlight the free will of the
children in making their decision (or even depict conflicts between parents and
children), in practice the decision for minors to enter ascetic life was almost
without exception made by their parents.[47] These children lived in the homes of
their parents and received religious education from them. The number of such
children must have been quite low during the centuries before the development
of monasticism as an institution in the fifth century C.E. For girls dedicated to
virginity, their coming of age was marked, instead of by marriage, with the
ceremony of taking the veil. In the west, the formation of the Benedictine order
in the early sixth century C.E. made child oblation a choice, although it was a
choice only for the upper class. On the other hand, some ascetics brought their
children with them to their cells or monastic communities. Later, the early medieval upper classes, east and west, customarily gave children to monasteries
to be educated and, in some cases, to have an ecclesiastical career.[48] Children
strengthened not only the earthly networks of their parents but also their bond
with God. For these children, even if only a small minority, Christianity certainly made a difference.

Families took part in public religious activities together and included their
children in these activities. In Athens, at the drama festivals in honor of Dionysus, boys were present both in audience and on stage; girls were probably also
allowed to attend the performances.[49] Aeschines (389–314 B.C.E.), in turn, was
accused of assisting his mother in the cult of Sabazios as a boy. Some children
also accompanied their parents in the Orphic rites. At Tauropolia, a women-
only festival for Artemis, unmarried girls participated with their mothers. The
religious participation of noncitizens and slaves in public cults was limited,
but their presence was not barred.[50] In the Roman world, as well, children attended religious processions and other events. Children took part in the cults
of Isis and Dionysus/Bacchus with their parents—and also in the state cult.
For the secular games of 17 C.E., for example, young people were required to
be escorted by adult relatives if they attended celebrations at night. For those
elite children active in the rituals, the experience must have been unforgettable.

Even for those participating as spectators or serving in the background—such as slave children attending with their owners or playing flutes—the festivals affected their identity and sense of belonging.[51]

Some stories in late antiquity refer to boys playing at being bishops and imitating the liturgy or the baptismal rite word by word. These stories were taken as prodigies for their future careers. In stories of Christian saints, there is an unsurprising tendency to show the heroes as pious from their earliest childhood. However, at least some children were familiar with the liturgical routines, and this was held to be normal. Families as a whole participated in the whole liturgy; even baptized babies received the Eucharist, and older children also sang hymns.[52] Children attended religious festivals and cultic performance—for example, at the feasts of the martyrs, they joined their parents on a visit to a local ascetic holy man. They were also given intercessory tasks for their communities. In the penitential procession in Rome in 590 C.E., for example, children were one of the groups representing the city dwellers.[53]

Children were full members of the Christian community in a similar way to children who participated in traditional Greco-Roman religion as full members of those earlier communities. They were fully introduced to the dominant religious and cultural assumptions and practices. To take a late example: for the eighth-century C.E. Carolingians, the religious education of the children of conquered people was a way of socializing them into new values and obedience to new rulers. Baptism was an initiation both to Christianity and to Charlemagne's realm.[54] Religious participation lay at the heart of a sense of identity and adherence to certain traditions, to a certain social stratum, and to gender roles. Hence, religion held a central place in family life, and children were socialized into the community and its values through religious events—all features that were preparation for the adult life.

CHILDREN AND RITUAL—MARGINALITY OR INTEGRATION?

Children appeared in three contexts in religious rituals. Firstly, children were at the center of the rituals concerning their own transfer from one life stage to another—at birth, name giving, baptism, and different rituals related to their protection and the passage to adulthood. Secondly, there were the rituals of family and community in which children took part as members of the group. Thirdly, in many religious practices children had special tasks. Children were also seen to possess oracular force and divine insight, and they were acknowledged to understand the wishes of the god(s), at least to the same extent as adults in the same community. Children were, accordingly, seen as perfect channels for divine contact through dreams, visions, and inspired utterances. Greek vase paintings show boys assisting in reading the livers of sacrificial animals, and insightful and portentous children appear frequently in Roman historical writing.[55] The divine insight of children was valued also in later Christian cultures as exemplified in the Rule of Benedict: "The Lord often reveals to the younger what is better." A child's shout of "Ambrosius episcopus!" ("Ambrose for bishop") was understood as a divine voice that resolved the election of the bishop of Milan in 374 C.E. Divination by children was also used in the *sortes biblicae*, in which a child opened the Bible at random. Also "sleeping with the martyrs" for divine contact through dreams was practiced by children.[56]

It has often been asked why these faculties were connected to children in the first place. Was there some specific symbolic meaning attached to children, or was there a deeper functional reason for their presence? The traditional view, which links children with sexual innocence, has aroused much criticism. The idea of sexual purity is mentioned in many contexts regarding children and religion, but it is not a sufficient condition for explaining the presence of children in religious rituals.[57] Mark Golden and Thomas Wiedemann have proposed that the most important reason was the marginality of children at the edge of (adult) society. They are "not yet wholly integrated into social world of the *polis*, they are interested outsiders," and, thus, they are perfect mediums between the gods and the mortals.[58] However, children actually were well integrated in the religious life of families and communities. In many cults, children acted in the propitiatory roles for their communities and represented a section of the population alongside freeborn men and women. The most prominent example can be seen in their involvement in the secular games, in which children stood not only for the young people in general and for elite families but also for the future of the community. If the reason for their appearance was their marginality, however, why were rituals not populated by other marginal groups such as female slaves and noncitizens?[59] Not once did ecclesiastical writers refer to the marginality of children in urging parents to promise their offspring to a life of asceticism; quite the opposite, in fact.[60] This aspect of belonging can even be revealed in the context of Phoenician child sacrifice; inscriptions highlight the children's freeborn status and their preciousness to their parents, thus communicating the children's membership in the community rather than their otherness or marginality.[61] Children represented their families and communities in the face of divinity as individuals belonging to the community—this could not be the case if they were outsiders to the social structures.

An explanation can perhaps be found in the emphasis placed on the social role of children. The central concepts are not marginalization and sexual innocence but integration and social innocence. Children are, through their lack of experience, "outside the usual areas of citizen interaction," and as such they are more than innocent.[62] This kind of qualified outsider position does not lead to their marginalization but rather to their social inclusion: it allows them to become the perfect medium for the performance of ritual within the community. Moreover, these same rituals were designed to prepare children for community life.[63] Thus, the purity of children is not due to their lack of sexual experience but, more widely, to their inexperience of the phenomena of the social world. They were exemplary in their simplicity and guilelessness as they had not yet learned to lie and deceive, and, ideally, they had only minimal contact with the pollution of broken human relations—especially death, but also divorce.[64] This might also be the reasoning behind the custom of burying children within houses or inside the city limits, which with older deceased would cause pollution. Similarly, the same logical reasoning might lie behind the use of children's body parts in recipes for magical concoctions. A child buried near the living may even have had a propitiatory function.[65]

In associating childhood with purity, Christianity was no exception.[66] The nature of exemplary children, as presented in Mark 10:13–16, aroused discussion, but generally the ecclesiastical writers pointed out that the newly born are not in any way impure. Early accounts, like that of Cyprian (ca. 200–258 C.E.), are rather imprecise, but later ecclesiastical writers generally refer to children as exemplary in their innocence: children were not corrupted by passions or false worldly values.[67] Augustine, however, disagreed, stressing that no one is sinless or pure; the *innocentia* of children simply meant they were not able to harm others. This became the prevalent interpretation of the nature of children in the west until the sixth century. However, later writers like Isidore of Seville (ca. 600–636 C.E.) and Gregory the Great (ca. 540–604 C.E.) returned to stressing the innocence and purity of children. This was the prevalent line of thought at the beginning of the high Middle Ages.[68]

CHILDREN AND RELIGION: SOME CONCLUSIONS

In antiquity, religion in family life was all embracing, and religion needs to be recognized as a key feature in the life course of children. The roles of children in religious life were more varied, and their participation more widespread, than their legal and social status otherwise would suggest. Actual religious tasks

in connection with public rituals were limited to well-born children, but participation in public festivals, domestic cults, and prayer—alongside the ubiquity of
shrines, temples, and churches—ensured there was a religious framework for
everyday life. "Children growing up could not escape a consciousness of the
role of the gods in their private and public lives."[69] Even if family was the primary context for religious experience and participation for children, religious
life offered a central way for children to appear in public.

Children were important as symbols and mediating actors in the rituals:
the social innocence and integrity of children meant they were uncorrupted
by (mis)information. In general, the roles of children in cults stem from a gendered view of the social world. As the requirement for purity was stricter for
women, the role of girls was emphasized in tasks dealing with ritual purification: the purity of a community was best manifested and represented in virgin
girls. However, as assistants in domestic and public rituals requiring "a child,"
boys were preferred—or, at least, their presence is more often remarked upon.
It is a curious fact that girls had considerably more visibility in the public rituals of classical and Hellenistic Greece than in those of the Roman republic or
Empire or later Christian contexts. In Christian practice, except for the veiling
of virgins, there were no public roles for girls; the assisting tasks in the liturgy
were reserved for male acolytes, and singing was reserved for choirs of boys
and virgins.

Religion created a sense of belonging through participation. The family
itself was very much a religious unit. Learning domestic rituals was an important part of the socialization of children. Moreover, religion was an important
way of making social contacts: religious practices constituted the most important way in which children could be visible and interact in public life: "religion
provided the main avenue for children into the life of the *polis*."[70] Religious life
tied children to their family traditions, to the values and ways of interaction in
society, and to the mythic past of their communities, whether Greek *polis* or
Christian *ecclesia*.

There is no evidence that Christianity advanced the religious equality and
status of children with infant baptism: already Greek and Roman religious tradition presented children to the gods from the moment of birth; they were seen
to have a special relationship with the divine, and they were included in the
major public and private rituals. In fact, they were equal to adults in receiving
the divine gifts and in having "a rightful share in the service of the gods."[71]

Little can be said about children's own faith and their commitment to religious ideas. Naturally, generation after generation, religious practices were
embraced and perpetuated by people who had learned them as children. There

are also scattered indications that children, on their own, practiced religious rites for the *lares* at the altars within a Roman house or by playing the liturgy. Some glimpses of everyday faith are filtered through the adult gaze and interpretation. There is, for example, a fifth-century anecdote told by Theodoret of Cyrrhus (ca. 393–466 C.E.) about a group of boys who subjected the ball with which they were playing to a purification ritual for fear it might have been polluted (as it had passed between the feet of an ass).[72] This story suggests that the boys in question had accepted society's prevailing ideas on pollution and its remedies in their everyday life and experience. This proves, if proof was needed, that children in antiquity shared with adults in the community the same rites and the same beliefs and were far from marginal to the practice of religion.

CHAPTER NINE

Health and Science

PATRICIA BAKER

In spite of recent work on childhood in the classical world, there remains a common misconception that the lives of children and infants held little value in Greco-Roman society because of high mortality rates.[1] Evidence for medical treatment in this period, however, reveals an opposing point of view. From the fifth century B.C.E. to late antiquity, medical and philosophical treatises contain information about the care and healthy development of infants and children from conception to puberty, the age at which Galen (second century C.E.) said childhood ended.[2] Although much of the information survives in fragmentary form or as passing references in works devoted to areas of health outside pediatrics, the fact that children are discussed indicates they were considered worthy of care in some circles of society.

Medical literature informs us about past conceptions of early development and the role the family played in rearing infants and children through the different stages of youth. There is a growing interest in the definition of the terms *child* and *childhood* in different periods, and ancient medicine provides insight into how Greco-Roman children were perceived through their physical constitution and age. Medical concepts and definitions not only permeated philosophical arguments but wider social understandings and customs as well—linking the science of medicine to the health of the wider population There was no prescribed family health care service because uniform family medicine is a modern conception. Most medical texts were written with reference to the health of the adult male. When exceptions were made for the health of women, children, and the elderly, the differences were clearly indicated. Hence, the evidence for pediatrics provides a means of observing the relationship between children and the family in regards to medicine and science. In certain instances, the health of an adult had a significant impact on the family as seen in the impact of major epidemics.

MEDICINE AND ITS POSITION IN ANCIENT SCIENCE AND PHILOSOPHY

The fields of medicine, science, and philosophy were not mutually exclusive; they had indistinct boundaries and influenced one another. This is most clearly seen in ancient discussions on embryology, the health and development of infants and children, the family's role in raising children, and the incorporation of medical ideas and definitions into more mundane aspects of life in antiquity, and these are the focus of this chapter.

In antiquity, the boundaries between the fields of philosophy, science, and medicine did not exist to the same extent as today. Of course, it can be argued that there were some differences between philosophy and medicine, but the two areas intersected insofar as medical writers were mentioned as philosophers and philosophers were counted amongst physicians in doxographical texts.[3] This overlap is also apparent in the topics considered by both philosophers and medics. For example, philosophers such as Aristotle (384–322 B.C.E.) wrote on embryonic development, as did writers of medicine such as Diocles of Carystus (fourth century B.C.E.) and the Hippocratic writers (fifth to third centuries B.C.E.)—they were all concerned with fundamental questions about the nature of life. The same links can be found between natural science and medicine. The development of embryos was often compared to the growth of plants, and embryological calendars seem to have been influenced by Pythagorean mathematics.[4] Hence, philosophical theories about the natural world that would be the provenance of science today not only influenced medicine but were also integral to it, making it difficult to define boundaries between the subjects.

HUMORAL PATHOLOGY

Humoral pathology, age, and gender were fundamental to ancient medicine. When writing on wounds, Celsus (first century C.E.) says that age, constitution, mode of life, and the season have some influence on how they will heal, indicating a conceived relationship between the body and its health and the natural world—a primary consideration when attempting to maintain a healthy

Humoral Pathology

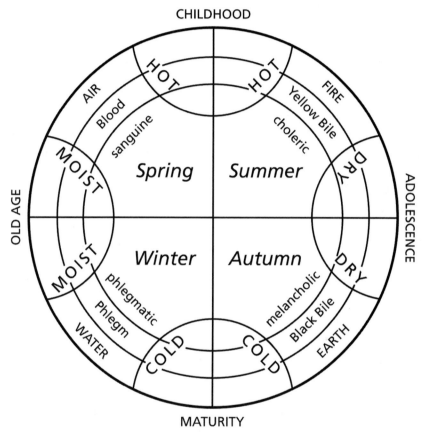

FIGURE 9.1: *Humoral pathology (illustration: Henry Buglass)*. This was copied from Peter E. Pormann and Emilie Savage-Smith, *Medieval Islamic Medicine* (Edinburgh: University of Edinburgh Press, 2007), fig. 2.2.

constitution.[5] The constitution Celsus was referring to was related to humoral pathology, the concept that the body was composed of four humors, or fluids, ultimately derived from the four elements: earth, air, fire, and water.[6] The humors consisted of blood, which was hot and moist and associated with the element air, the season spring, and childhood; yellow bile, which was hot and dry and related to fire, summer, childhood, and adolescence; black bile, which was cold and dry and related to autumn, earth, and adulthood; and phlegm, which was cold and moist and associated with water, winter, and old age.[7] Women were thought to be moister and cooler than men, who were hotter and dryer. Aging came about as the body went from a warm and moist state to one that slowly cooled.

A healthy person was considered to have a fairly equal balance of these fluids or qualities. Illness meant the humors were not in equilibrium and one had become dominant over the others, which could be caused by environmental surroundings or a lifestyle change such as diet or exercise. When an illness occurred, the practitioner would determine the nature of the disease and provide a treatment to restore the humoral proportions. The treatments were generally contrary to the illness. If it was deemed there was too much moisture or blood in the system, bleeding was likely to be recommended, and if someone was too hot and dry, moist foods, liquids, medicines, and/or bathing were suggested.

The principles that location and balance were important to health are also found outside medical literature. When writing on the best location to place specific rooms in a house, Vitruvius (first century C.E.) said a cool, shady room was best for the heat of summer while a sunny room, blocked from winds, was best for the winter.[8] The fourth-century writer Vegetius continued to promote these concepts by informing his readers of the most salubrious location to build military camps that were away from bad waters and had protection from extremes of heat and cold.[9]

CONCEPTION, FETAL DEVELOPMENT, PREGNANCY, AND CHILDBIRTH

A variety of views existed about the contribution of each parent in conception. Certain theories stated that only the father contributed seed while the mother's womb provided a space for fetal development. Others noted that both the male and female contributed seed based on the premise that children tend to look like both parents.[10] In spite of the various arguments, what is important is that both parents were deemed to play a role in embryological development.

In certain respects, the mother had more control over conception than the father on account of her options to use birth control or have an abortion. Soranus (late first/early second century C.E.) stated it was healthier for a woman to use a form of contraception than to use an abortive because abortives, either through medicines or expulsion by jumping and shaking, were harsh on her body. There is some difficulty in defining whether expulsion was seen as a form of birth control or abortion. This is compounded by the fact that throughout history there have been different ideas about when life began. Even if certain practitioners did not provide abortions, others did, as demonstrated by the recipes for abortifacients found in Soranus.[11]

Moreover, a story told in the Hippocratic work *On the Nature of the Child* (ca. 420–400 B.C.E.), which is repeated in Soranus and Galen (second century C.E.), tells of a woman who owned a valuable singer who would attend to men.[12] It was the writer's belief that if the male seed was not expelled from the uterus after intercourse, the woman had conceived. In the story, the singer noticed the seed had not left her body. The Hippocratic writer suggested she jump up and down, which caused the expulsion of an egg-like mass. This writer might have thought this was a form of contraception given that it was only a few days after coitus and the egg-like mass was not described as having life. From the evidence that survives, it is clear women did have the option of abortion, but expulsion through violent jumping and shaking seems to have been preferred to the use of medicines. However, Soranus, on the basis that it was healthier for a woman to avoid pregnancy, suggests ways to prevent conception.[13] He recommended that intercourse be avoided during times when conception was most likely, which he believed was when menstruation was abating. At this point, the uterus would be empty and would contain the correct balance of warmth and moisture for the seed to develop. This method of birth control did not always work, so it was also advised that women practice the opposite of what was recommended for the healthy development of the seed, such as eating harsh foods and doing strenuous exercises to expel the seed from the womb.[14]

Christian writers on these topics were, on the whole, clearer, though debate about the beginning of life did continue into the Middle Ages. Tertullian (second century C.E.) believed that the seed already contained life and that birth control and abortion should not be practiced. Christian ascetic texts noted that the mother's integrity was violated through conception, pregnancy, and childbirth, all of which were symbols of sexual desire. Desire was a need for procreation but at the same time was a pleasure of the flesh and a symbol of mortality.[15]

In contrast, if a woman wanted a child, she could help the seed develop in her womb by treating her body gently.[16] Once secure, the seed was understood to take shape, and ancient writers speculated on this and formulated a number of different theories of fetal development. Some writers divided fetal development into three stages: formation, movement, and delivery or miscarriage.[17] Galen argued that there were four stages. In his first stage, the seed from both parents was mixed in the uterus, forming an amorphous mass filled with blood that was not considered a fetus because its form was inarticulate. Development was thought to reach the second stage when the mass began to take shape. Galen's third stage was marked by the emergence of the fetus, which meant it had acquired limbs and more human characteristics. The fourth stage occurred when the fetus moved, or the point at which it gained sensation and life.[18] Different views about the stages of development were, in some cases, expressed by the same author—for instance, Paul of Aegina (seventh century C.E.) sometimes said there were three stages and other times four.[19]

The time it took for development varied according to the sex of the infant: males were thought to form in three months and females in four months.[20] The sex of the child was also determined by heat, as males emerged from warmer seed than females. In some cases, males were said to develop on the right side of the womb and females on the left. The Hippocratic writer of *Aphorisms* stated it was possible to tell whether a pregnant woman was carrying a boy or girl by her appearance—good complexion indicated a boy, the opposite a girl.[21]

Fetal formation was also compared to the growth of a plant or tree. The limbs were comparable to tree branches and roots. Like tree roots that gain sustenance from the ground, the limbs of the fetus obtained their nourishment from the mother. It was therefore advised that she nourish herself well in order to nurture the child. Soranus provided further guidance about how a woman could help in the development of the fetus by maintaining her health during pregnancy. He said the mother should behave in accordance with each of the three stages of pregnancy to help the fetus grow properly, though he does not give precise times for the stages. In the first stage, she was expected to preserve the seed by not agitating the womb, her food should be neutral and regular, and she should bathe in warm water to maintain the seed. The second stage was intended to alleviate symptoms such as pica, or food cravings, while the third was to help with the perfection of the embryo and train the woman to endure parturition.[22]

The embryological calendar was complex. For the most part, it was believed a healthy child could be born in the seventh, ninth, and tenth months of pregnancy. With the exception of a single manuscript from the writer Damastes (fifth century B.C.E.), a child born in the eighth month was regarded as an omen of bad luck. The eighth-month child was generally not expected to survive. Aristotle even suggests that if an eighth-month child survived, the dates of gestation should be revised to create a pregnancy of seven or nine months—confirming and maintaining a belief in ill luck associated with the number eight.[23]

When childbirth was imminent, a midwife was called upon to assist with the birth. Soranus suggested that a good midwife be older (more experienced), calm, disciplined, and sober. Physically, she should have long fingers with short nails and sound limbs.[24] She was expected to be well prepared by bringing a number of tools to assist with the task. Along with the birthing chair, a symbol associated with Greco-Roman midwives, she was expected to bring sponges for cleaning the mother and infant, pleasant-smelling fragrances for inhalation, bandages to swaddle the infant, and a pillow on which to lay the infant while the afterbirth was being expelled from the mother. She was also expected to have tools in case of a difficult labor, including fetal hooks and a decapitating knife (birthing forceps were not known at the time).[25]

Problematic deliveries and miscarriages attracted the attention of medical writers because they caused the most difficulty for the mother and midwife. Since there was a great deal of danger involved in childbirth, warning signs and causes of difficulties were mentioned frequently. Not only could difficult labors be caused by the size of the fetus, its presentation, or a physical deformity, but the constitution of the mother also might have contributed. Diocles said that women of moist and warm constitutions were likely to have problems. A common warning sign for an impending miscarriage was if the breasts of a pregnant woman regressed suddenly.[26] Soranus mentioned this Hippocratic idea of shrinking breasts as a sign of a natural miscarriage, and he also quoted Diocles as saying that heaviness in the loins and coldness in the thighs also marked possible problems. Miscarriages caused by abortifacients were associated with the secretion of a watery discharge resembling the color of liquid used to wash meat. In addition, heaviness and pain in the loins, hips, and lower abdomen were noted.[27]

To relieve a difficult birth, some suggested shaking the female to release the fetus. Men were asked to assist with this particularly if the fetus died in utero. Soranus disagrees with this action because it might damage the womb. Milder suggestions included having a woman walk up and down steps and lie down. In the most extreme cases it was recommended that the fetus be extracted by the means of hooks and a possible embryotomy, a surgical procedure performed by crushing the head of the fetus. This was carried out if the head was too large to pass through the opening of the uterus, especially in cases of hydrocephalus.[28] A less aggressive method was mentioned by Celsus, who provided a recipe for the expulsion of a dead fetus or placenta using ammoniac salts or Cretan dittany. For a difficult labor, he suggested hedge mustard in tepid wine be administered to an empty stomach.[29]

If the infant survived, the midwife was in charge of its first moments. First, she inspected it to determine if it was worth rearing by seeing if its parts were intact and its orifices all open. In addition, the mother's pregnancy was considered; if the mother had not been healthy during parturition, the infant could be weak. The length of gestation was also important. Soranus mentioned that a healthy child was born in either the seventh or ninth months; he did not mention the eighth month, implying that he too may have thought it was an ill omen. Following the inspection, the infant was placed on the ground to see if it cried with proper vigor. A baby who remained quiet or cried quietly showed signs of weakness. The omphalotomy was then performed. This could be done with a number of objects, such as a steel knife, potsherd, or hard crust of bread. The child was then bathed—first with a sprinkling of salt washed off in warm water, and then the process was repeated but with warmer water. Finally, the infant was swaddled into its natural shape and then laid down to sleep.[30]

INFANCY AND PEDIATRIC CARE

Following the birth, the development of a healthy infant was mainly the responsibility of his or her mother, but in some instances a wet nurse was employed to give the infant nourishment while the mother recovered from her pregnancy. The milk of a woman who had recently delivered was thought to be corrupted through the strains of childbirth. Spoiled milk would ultimately harm the infant, and, therefore, lactation was discussed by many medical writers.[31] Medics recommended that the ideal wet nurse was a woman between the ages of twenty and forty who had given birth two or three times. A young mother was considered to be ignorant of rearing children, with a careless mind and childish ways. Although an older woman may have had experience, her milk was thought to be watery and therefore unhealthy. Even if a wet nurse met the first two requirements, it was not guaranteed that her milk would be of good quality, so it was advised that she be of a large bodily frame, indicating a strong and healthy constitution. The wet nurse also had to adhere to a strict regimen through moderate exercise and maintaining a diet of good juices and neutral foods that would not cause digestive problems for the infant.[32]

Weaning was only recommended to occur when the infant's body started to become firm at roughly six months old. Food was not recommended for delicate constitutions; it was argued that infants had narrow pores that would not allow solid food to pass through in order to nourish the body. Their earliest victuals were crumbs of bread and sweet or honey wine. Later, spelt soup and porridge were added to their diets. Providing the infant with more solid food would aid in the weaning process because it satiated the baby, giving them less cause to want breast milk. The optimal season for weaning was spring because of its well-tempered climate. Autumn was a bad season to begin weaning because the entire body was disposed to disease; it was best that there was no change in regimen at this time.[33]

Diet was only one means of ensuring the healthy growth of a child. The infant also had to be molded physically so he or she would develop a healthy appearance. The term *mold* is used in both a literal and figurative sense because children were not only cared for through a healthy regimen of bathing, diet, and even education, but their bodies were physically shaped through swaddling and carefully timing their movements, such as walking and sitting upright. Physical appearance was linked to both aesthetics and good health, and a child required help, particularly from the mother, to develop properly. For example, when the umbilicus fell off, the mother was supposed to form lead into the shape of a spinning whirl and lay it on the umbilicus. This had a cooling effect that would cicatrize the wound, or heal it by the formation of scar tissue. The weight of the lead would also help mold the umbilicus into the cavity. Although the naval could protrude after strong weeping or a sneeze, blow, or fall, the damage caused by an umbilical hernia seems not to have been the main concern in medical literature but rather the appearance of an outwardly protruding navel. Paul of Aegina recommended wrapping it in bandages soaked with different medicines to stop its outward growth.[34]

Parents were also in charge of the malleability of the infant. If the infant sat up too soon, its spine could bend because it was not strong enough to support its head, causing it to become hunchbacked. Early walking created distorted legs. Soranus described how Roman mothers, as opposed to Greek ones, were not as careful in looking after their infants and permitted them to walk too soon. The heaviness of their bodies on their little legs supposedly made them disfigured.[35]

One would not normally place a child's education in the realm of medicine, but since medical writers were also philosophers, sometimes their thoughts about a child's development extended beyond the physical shaping of the body and the healthy regimen of diet and exercise. Although Soranus said that the child's education does not belong to the sphere of medicine, others do mention it.[36] Paul of Aegina stated that a young person's regimen also included teaching. At the age of six or seven, a child should be handed over to a calm teacher to inculcate manners. A tranquil teacher who taught leisure and joy would help improve a child's disposition.[37]

CONSTITUTION AND CHILDHOOD DISEASE

Another aspect of infant and childhood development was dependent upon keeping their bodies warm and moist. The Hippocratic writer on *Aphorisms* said growth was connected to warmth.[38] As people aged and grew, they developed a cooler constitution; or, as Soranus noted, growth led to a solidification of the body. According to Rufus of Ephesus (first century C.E.), "the [bodily] heat of children is not a [very strong] one corresponding to their moisture. This can be deduced from the slackness, feebleness and numbness of their bodies, and the weakness of their voice."[39] Although it is evident that most writers agreed a child's body was warm and moist, the significance and understanding of these features varied. There were three general positions: (1) the heat of the infant remained the same from birth to puberty, an opinion Galen was keen to promote; (2) the heat was at its highest at birth and slowly dissipated from that point, an argument put forth by Areteaus of Cappadocia (second century C.E.); and (3) the heat gradually ignited from birth, a position of Rufus of Ephesus.[40] Healthy growth depended upon keeping the child's body warm and moist.

Certain times throughout childhood were thought to hold special dangers for health. These were on the fortieth day, the seventh month, the seventh year, and at puberty.[41] It is common to read that children developed in seven-year stages, or *hebdomads*, although, as with gestation, these seven-year stages are not confined to a precise or rigid system.[42] The Hippocratic writer on *Aphorisms* mentioned that particular maladies were common at specific stages of development, ideas also found in later writers. In *Aphorisms*, newborn infants suffered from mouth ulcers, vomiting, coughs, insomnia, nightmares, inflammation of the umbilicus, and discharge from the ears. As infants grew older, tonsillitis; deflections of the vertebrae of the neck; asthma; stones; priapism; swellings in the cervical glands and other tumors; and infections with round worms, such as ascaris, were common. Those approaching puberty not only suffered from the diseases of older children but also often had long-continued fever and epistaxis.[43]

As mentioned earlier, health was also affected by the seasons and geographical location. The Hippocratic work *Airs, Waters, Places* emphasizes that doctors should not only consider the patient's symptoms but also his or her surroundings because winds, water, the season, and the weather also promoted certain conditions and agitated others. Moreover, these properties affected people on account of their age. Celsus, for example, noted that children and adolescents enjoyed their best health in spring and were safest in summer.[44] Pregnancy was also influenced by the weather, as a damp mild winter followed by a dry spring with a north wind tended to produce miscarriages in women who were expected to deliver in the spring.[45] Children born under these conditions tended to be weak and were expected to die soon after birth. If they lived, they were thought to remain frail.

Although children of certain ages were thought more likely to suffer from specific illnesses, there were also conditions that only affected children. Dentition receives considerable discussion in medical texts, most likely because it was a traumatic period that caused stress and illness. Not only did teething cause painful gums, but teething infants were likely to suffer from fever, convulsions, and diarrhea. These symptoms were expected especially during the eruption of the canines and in plump children or those with hard stomachs. Soranus wrote a detailed section on the subject of dentition. According to him, it was normal for teeth to begin growing in the seventh month, which possibly adheres to the Hippocratic aphorism that this was a dangerous time for an infant's health. Inflamed and pitted gums were signs of the onset of dentition. To help make the experience less agonizing, parents were advised to ensure infants did not masticate before teething because it would bruise and harden the gums, making them calloused and difficult to split when the teeth grew. In order to soften the gums, an infant was supposed to suck on chicken fat while in the bath from the fifth month. Once teeth began to appear, the child should not have butter or fat because food remnants could get caught between the teeth and gums. At this time, the wet nurse should drink little more than water and, when feeding the infant, should force the milk up from her breast because the infant would damage itself when sucking. Other treatments suggested were to rub the brain of a land hare on the infant's gums, bathe the child frequently, and feed him or her sparsely.[46]

Moisture in the ears was also a problem thought common to infants and occurred, according to Rufus of Ephesus, because the child had too much moisture in his or her food. The simple cure was to avoid feeding the infant in the evening, allowing the ears to dry.[47] Paul of Aegina mentioned that in some children the proliferation of flesh forming in their ears was caused by the moistness of their bodies.[48]

Siriasis was mentioned by more than one writer as be common to infants and children. There are different concepts of it in ancient literature, but it seems to have been some form of heat stroke. Two stories survive that explain the illness's name. Demetrius of Apamea (third/second century B.C.E.) wrote in his book *Semiotics* that the illness was nothing but a burning fever and because of this might have been named after the dog star, Sirius, which appeared during the hot and dry summer. However, another sign of siriasis was that the bregma—the juncture of two parts of the skull on the top of the head—sunk inward; because of this change the illness might have been named after the *serios*, a hollow object in which farmers threw and kept seeds. The skin also became pale and the body dry.[49] Paul of Aegina said it was a swelling alongside the membrane covering the brain. An accompanying symptom was that the

FIGURE 9.2: *Relief depicting a visit to the doctor with Greek inscription.* Roman first century C.E. Museo della Civilita Romana, Rome. Image: Giraudon/Bridgeman Art Library.

parietal bone and the eyes sank in and the color of the body became yellow and dried out, which is similar to the description given by Soranus. Since it was a disease of heat, one treatment was to use cucumber to help cool the child.[50]

Other diseases common to infants were inflammation of the tonsils; thrush, a superficial ulcer in the cavity of the mouth; coughing and wheezing; exanthemata (blisters) and itching; flux of the bowels; cradle cap, a term used for ulcers found on the heads of children; and diarrhea.[51] The general rule for treatment was to rebalance the body with an opposite treatment to harden, loosen, cool, or heat the body. Additional measures included placing both the child and the wet nurse on specific diets to help to restore balance.

When it came to diseases suffered by both adults and children, it is clear that many writers thought each person should be cured in accordance with their constitution and age. The Hippocratic writer of *Aphorisms* stated the old were able to undertake fasting as a treatment most easily, followed by adults, much less youths, and least of all children.[52] The more active someone was, the less able they were to bear fasting. Bleeding was only practiced on strong children.[53] Stones in the urethra were a considerable worry in the past because the treatment was surgical and therefore of greater danger to the patient. Children suffered from stones, it was believed, because they were caused by warmth.[54]

Epilepsy, or the sacred disease, also had different effects on children in comparison to adults. Those who suffered from epilepsy as children were thought to grow out of it. Infant deaths might be explained by copious amount of phlegm, the cause of epilepsy, which could not be absorbed in their small blood vessels. Phlegm was regarded as a cold substance with the power to cool down the heated blood, resulting in seizures and death. Adults, on the other hand, generally did not die from the disease because their vessels were regarded as larger; they had more blood in their system and so would not succumb to the coldness associated with phlegm.[55]

Fevers were mentioned frequently in ancient medical texts, and here, too, there are differences in the ways children are treated in comparison to adults. For example, children were considered likely to have convulsions if they suffered a high fever along with constipation. This was most commonly associated with children under the age of seven.[56] In cases of pestilent fevers, Celsus suggests, as with any disease, that a child should not be treated like an adult and that more caution is needed. He advised not to let blood regularly, nor clyster, nor torment the child with wakefulness, hunger, or excess thirst.[57] Rufus said the temperament of children during fever contained something harmful to them. Because of this, a child could suffer a strong pain, stupidity, and quasi-insanity.[58]

Surgery was rarely recommended for children. The most common opera-
tions mentioned are the removal of stones and scrotal hernias.[59] Presumably,
surgery was considered too extreme an intervention for a child to endure, or
perhaps, in the absence of anesthesia, surgery could not be performed on a
mobile and agitated child. The regimen used to maintain an infant's health was
also different from that of adults. Children were recommended to bathe for
long periods in warm water, and their wine should be warm and diluted. Wine
was better for children if it was mild and not harsh on the stomach.[60] These
ideas were thought to promote growth and a good complexion.

MENTAL AILMENTS

Mental illnesses (understood today within the paradigms of Freudian psychia-
try) were defined quite differently in the past and were mainly problems for
adults, with the exception of fever-related madness. Mental imbalances were
described in vague terms such as "madness," "melancholy," and "hysteria,"
and writers provided different symptoms, though for the most part mental
illnesses were thought to be caused by imbalances in the humors. Often the
conditions were temporary and curable. Madness was commonly found to be a
symptom of fever, perhaps explained as hallucinations brought on by the high
temperature, and often ceased when the fever had abated. Melancholia was a
sadness associated with an excess of black bile, and those with a melancholic
disposition were said to sometimes suffer from insomnia, fits of anger, agita-
tion, and loss of appetite.[61]

Hysteria was a disease of women, and it was linked to the ancient conception of the womb. For example, Plato described the womb as a living creature
in the *Timaeus*.[62] Its movement was seen as a cause of shortness of breath and
other diseases. Yet there were many different conceptions of this malady, and it
cannot be certain that the causal link between hysteria and mental anxiety was
the same as that found in eighteenth- and nineteenth-century medical writers.[63]

In Byzantine texts, another cause of madness discussed by Christian writers
was demonic possession. Possession, like hysteria, also had various interpretations, not all of which were seen as mental ailments. In general, unusual behavior could be caused by possession, and children could be possessed. It could be
cured by visits to saints' shrines.[64]

Those who suffered from some form of diminished mental capacity, possibly through a head trauma or birth defect, appear, as adults, to have been perceived of and treated as children. One example is the skeleton of an adult male
found in the Athenian Agora, dating to the Iron Age, that had signs of cranial

damage received later in life. The damage was severe enough to have left the man mentally incapacitated, needing the help and care a child would receive. It is evident from the regrowth of bone that someone did look after this person, but who it was cannot be determined. Overall, though, from medical texts and archaeological evidence there is a suggestion that people with different mental impairments received help, perhaps from their families.[65]

EPIDEMICS AND PLAGUES

Plagues attract much attention in Greco-Roman medical history because graphic descriptions of the symptoms of the diseases and their effects on society survive.[66] Since the symptoms were described, modern diagnosis has been attempted. Yet retrospective diagnosis is problematic because diseases were described differently without the clinical medical terms used today. Furthermore, the descriptions were usually made by historians rather than medics and there are inconsistencies between writers. Thucydides also admitted to omitting symptoms that differed in various people in his report of the Athenian plague,[67] suggesting that the necessary information to make a proper diagnosis of the epidemic has not survived into the twenty-first century. Although there are many epidemics recorded, they were usually mentioned in passing without explanations of their social and medical effects. The three with the most information are the Athenian plague (430–427 B.C.E.), the Antonine plague (165–169 C.E.), and the plague of Justinian (541–544 C.E.), which led to a pandemic that lasted for roughly two hundred years and ended in about 749 C.E. These plagues affected people from all walks of life and were noted for their devastation both on an economic and social level. Little direct reference to the effects of epidemics on children and families is actually made other than that sometimes entire families died: in the Athenian plague, the healthy were afraid to go near the ill, often leaving entire households to fend for themselves; during the Antonine plague, both the young and the old were affected; and in the plague of Justinian, whole families were placed on the same pyre.[68] In regard to medical philosophies, it is possible that during plagues and epidemics, similar to other diseases, the care of certain age groups was based on the constitution of the body, age, and location.

Galen was alive during the Antonine plague and recorded how it killed soldiers and citizens alike. On his return to Pergamon to escape the plague in Rome, Galen recorded how he saw the population dwindling along the way.[69] The high mortality of the plague affected the population economically as there would have been fewer people working and producing food, which could lead to other economic and social problems.[70] Although there are no direct statistics or literature indicating the effects epidemics had on families, such devastation would have left orphans, single parents raising children, and smaller extended families, which could have caused possible impoverishment, poor health, and disturbances to family welfare.

Medics might also have succumbed given the devastation of some epidemics, leaving some places without professional medical treatment; hence, parents, children, and other members of their extended families might have been left to care for one another. It can be speculated that the care they offered to one another might have been based on folk remedies rather than the theories mentioned in the medical texts discussed in this chapter. However, without further evidence it is difficult to provide specific details of the effects disease outbreaks had on the health of families.

FROM SCIENCE TO HEALTH CARE IN THE COMMUNITY

Care was offered by various means to children and families. In the Roman period, the *paterfamilias* was in charge of the health of the family, and nowhere is this better shown than in the works of Cato the Elder, who in his *de Agri Cultura* (*On Agriculture*) listed a number of medicinal recipes based on early Roman remedies, most of which involved the use of cabbage, an ingredient he saw as a panacea. However, doctors and folk healers were also available to the family. No records exist about the frequency with which families approached doctors, but from the high numbers of references to them in ancient literature, papyrology, and epigraphy, it is clear families had a number of options to maintain their health. Although some doctors specialized in certain ailments, there are no specialists in pediatrics recorded, but the midwife, nurse, and parents might have filled this role.

Records also show that doctors were both male and female. Female doctors (*medica*) were mentioned in Galen and on inscriptions. It is uncertain whether these women treated women alone and focused on female problems or if they were trained in all forms of medicine and offered care to male and female alike.[71] Most of the records describe male doctors (*medicus, iatros*), and it is fairly apparent they treated everyone.

In antiquity there were no regulations in medical training, so anyone could set themselves up as a healer. However, a common way of gaining medical training was through apprenticeships or by visiting cities such as Athens, Alexandria, and Pergamon to study at the libraries. In larger cities, it was possible for doctors to specialize in specific types of healing, such as eye care or surgery.[72] There were also those who specialized in folk remedies, but given the diverse and unregulated nature of medicine, it is actually difficult to see the boundaries between the folk healer and the *medicus*. Doctors did not work in the bounds of modern perceptions of rational (using philosophical argument and observation) and irrational (based on magic and religion) healing because the two were combined, as can be seen in medical schools set up in healing sanctuaries to Asclepius, the god of medicine. Doctors also left altars to healing deities, demonstrating how they sought divine help in their cures. The most famous sanctuaries were dedicated to Asclepius and are found at Epidauros, Pergamon, Cos, Athens, and in Rome on an island in the middle of the Tiber. There were other healing sanctuaries associated with Salus, Hygia, and Apollo. Healing mainly occurred through incubation. The patient slept in the sanctuary, would receive a dream of the god curing him or her, and awoke in a healthy state.[73]

Treatment was offered in many other locations. It seems that patients were commonly treated in their homes and looked after by their family. On the other hand, if someone was well enough to travel, he or she could visit doctors at their residences.[74] Surprisingly, the evidence for hospitals is not only slim, but, more significantly, definitions of what a hospital was have changed over time and have been affected by cultural conceptions of how patients should be treated. In the Roman period, a *valetudinarium*, translated as hospital, is known to have existed from passing literary references and inscriptions, but no precise archaeological examples have been found. Celsus is the only writer who mentions these establishments outside a military context, but he does not describe their layout, where they were located, or what sorts of activities took place in them.[75] From inscriptions it is known that *valetudinaria* existed in some military fortifications, but the inscriptions were not found *in situ* and are not associated with particular buildings. The identification of specific courtyard-style buildings as hospitals has been reassessed to demonstrate the tenuous nature of these identifications.[76] Hence, little can be said about these places with the exception that they existed and probably offered treatments.[77] Treatment was also available in public baths as can be seen from milk teeth with indentations from forceps used during their extraction that were found in the drains of the baths at Caerleon.[78]

The influence of Christianity on medicine in the third and fourth centuries is demonstrated in the construction of *xenodocheion* (the house of strangers) and *noskomeion* (the house of the sick) because Christians were supposed to care for the ill, poor, and less fortunate in society. These structures are thought to have acted as hospitals, but they were more likely places that offered comfort and rest to the poor, the sick, and travelers.[79] There is no categorical evidence that demonstrates some proprietors were trained in medicine and offered practical care. The physical appearance and arrangement of these structures are not known as nothing survives in the archaeological record.[80]

The Christian ascetic emphasis on the importance of the soul had an impact on changes in medical care, yet it is clear that earlier medical ideas persisted (e.g., in the works of Paul of Aegina). Many people were probably in agreement with Basil (ca. 330–379 C.E.) that God put medicines on this earth to help with the health of the flesh. Healing practices that took place in pagan sanctuaries also continued, but Christians visited sanctuaries dedicated to saints. Some of these sanctuaries were established at older pagan sites, such as the sixth- and seventh-century shrine dedicated to Cyrus and John (a few miles outside of Alexandria at modern Abuqir), which was particularly important for curing eye diseases through incubation. Cyrus was a doctor trained in Galenic methods and John was a soldier.[81] Even the congregation of Augustine (354–430 C.E.) practiced cures that appear to be forms of pagan/magical ritual by bringing children to baptism for healing, using the four gospels as amulets, and placing the Eucharistic host on a child's eyes to cure disease.[82] The patron saints of healing were Cosmos and Damian, both of whom were trained in Galenic medicine, and they could be prayed to for help just as someone might have prayed to Asclepius, showing a continuation of medical practices and beliefs.

CONCLUSION

This chapter establishes that understandings of family health care in antiquity can best be located in medical descriptions of infants and children. The most significant point in the health of the family appears to be the role parents played in their child's development from conception to puberty. It is also evident that there were various interpretations of the humoral construction of a child and the effect of the humors on health, and it becomes clear that children were cared for and seen to be different from adults. Given these points, surviving medical descriptions provide scientific or medical insights into familial relationships that offer unique perspectives on other aspects of childhood and the family in antiquity.

CHAPTER TEN

World Contexts

MARY HARLOW AND RAY LAURENCE

Childhood and the family in antiquity existed in a world context focused on a shared tradition rooted in the cultures of classical Athens (fifth century B.C.E.) and the Hellenistic world (fourth to second centuries B.C.E.). These cultural traditions evolved as a consequence of the vast geographical expanse of the Roman Empire and the myriad communities encompassed within it. On the one hand, the presence of the Roman Empire gives the impression of a unified political and cultural space that stretched from modern Scotland in the north to Egypt in the south and from modern Portugal in the west to Iraq in the east; and at the same time, this seemingly homogenous Roman world was full of different societies each with their own social systems, living arrangements, and aspirations. Importantly, it is within the family and the wider external community that a global concept of a civilized Greek or Roman identity was negotiated.[1] These issues are difficult to define given the nature of the evidence available, and this chapter references three groups: Jewish Diaspora families; Egyptian families; and Germanic, or barbarian, families of the first century C.E. In these examples, it is possible to get some idea of the variety of family structures and childhoods that existed within the world of antiquity. However, antiquity did not simply cease to exist with the deposition of the last Roman emperor in the west (476 C.E.); instead, it continued to have an influence on the cultures, families, and children in Europe through at least 800 C.E. (if not to the present). The final period of antiquity is evaluated here to examine the change in world context and how that change may have affected families and childhood, a subject that has been somewhat neglected in the current debates on the transformation of the Roman world and the early Middle Ages.[2] It is evident that during the early Middle Ages, some of the classical ideas of family and childhood were maintained, particularly through Christian rhetoric, while others were downplayed.

COMMUNITIES OF THE JEWISH DIASPORA

Jewish children and families living under the Roman Empire provide our first view into the world contexts of antiquity. The Jews had a unique identity when compared with other ethnic groups in the ancient world. This identity centered on the rites and rituals of their monotheistic religious belief and on maintaining ancestral traditions. In Diaspora communities, the family became the locus for the continuation of this identity in the face of outside social and cultural influences. Like Christianity, Judaism was also a religion of the book—sacred texts and laws provided rules for living that were different from those utilized by others in the same communities. Jewish parents inculcated their children in the rituals and tenets of Judaism, and the rules of the Sabbath and food regulations created a very clear "consciousness of difference."[3] Jewish children were aware of who was Jewish and who was not from they type of food they could eat and who they could eat with. This would have been reinforced by the celebration of the Sabbath. No other group in the Greco-Roman world celebrated a regular day of rest in this period, and the domestic setting of the Sabbath ritual must have reinforced the family as a special type of community. These factors make the Jewish ethnic identity easier for modern historians to identify and make it possible to examine how Jewish families and their children lived within a Roman as well as a Jewish context.

Jews were incorporated into the world context of the Roman Empire, and the state recognized Jews as an identifiable group regardless of their geographical origins. This definition was particularly significant after 70 C.E. when a tax was imposed on Jews. Estimates put the Jewish population in Rome in antiquity in the region of twenty to sixty thousand (in the first to second centuries C.E.). Jewish secular and religious identity were identical: however fervently a person worshipped the Syrian god Jupiter Dolichenus, that person would not become a Syrian. In contrast, converts to Judaism became Jews. In consequence, inscriptions set up to commemorate African and Syrian Jews in Rome might have assumed their ancestors came from Israel, but their only known ancestors may have been from Rome itself. Within the family context, evidence found in epitaphs suggests that the majority of the Jewish population in Rome used Latin or Greek names, with only about thirteen percent using Semitic names.[4] The use of the Greek language not only in the vast majority of epitaphs but also in the synagogues of Rome created a distinction between this community and that of others living in Rome.[5]

Yet this does not mean that Jewish families and their children lived apart from the world context of the Roman Empire. Even in Palestine, it can be difficult to define cities as specifically Jewish through comparing the material and textual remains to other cities of the eastern Mediterranean.[6] The 1989 publication of the archive of a woman called Babatha caused a fundamental reinterpretation of our understanding of the impact of Roman social practices on the empire's Jewish population. The archive was discovered in a cave in the Roman province of Arabia (although most documents had been composed in the province of Judaea), and items referring to such issues as marriage contracts, guardianship, and other family matters ranged in date from the first to third centuries C.E. Fascinatingly, the documents—written in Greek—have more in common with Roman law than with contemporary Rabbinic law.[7] When set in the context of other Jewish marriage contracts and legal documents, Hannah Cotton found there was a far greater assimilation of the Jewish population into local cultures in the eastern Mediterranean than might be expected of a group the state identified as different. Papyri from Egypt provide no evidence for Jews using Jewish courts or Jewish laws.[8] Moreover, the dating on these documents uses the Roman system rather than the Jewish calendar. It is too easy to see Roman and Jewish culture in confrontation, as scholars did in the nineteenth century; as has been suggested in the reinterpretation of this new evidence, Roman law and cultural practices could have been utilized by Jews to create new synergies or hybrid forms.[9]

How much impact Roman family and child-rearing practices had on Jewish communities is hard to judge, and it is necessary to look to the evidence from epitaphs in their local context. Diaspora Judaism was a fundamentally decentralized religion, and Jewish communities interacted with quite different local versions of Roman-ness. The epitaphs of Jews in Rome, written in Greek rather than Latin, show a commemorative pattern very similar to that found in non-Jewish epitaphs from Rome, and emphasis is placed on the commemoration of young children. This pattern is less apparent in epitaphs of Jews in Egypt or Jerusalem. This demonstrates the impact of the local community on Jewish children and their families, which suggests that Jewish childhoods in the Roman Empire did not follow a distinct structure. Jewish families were subject to the same influences as other ethnic groups resident in the Roman world.[10]

FAMILIES IN ROMAN EGYPT

A wide variety of family experience existed in Greco-Roman Egypt—and any-where in the ancient Mediterranean—but what makes Egyptian family rela-tionships noticeable in their own time, and in modern scholarship, is the high incidence of brother-sister marriage. The exact nature of sibling marriage in Roman Egypt is yet again a subject keenly debated in the modern literature, and it seems unlikely any one answer will solve the issue of why ancient Egyp-tian society embraced a practice that goes against an incest taboo assumed as fundamental in most societies.[11] Evidence for this practice and others is not derived, as it so often is in antiquity, from literature written by the elite, but rather from personal letters, wills, marriage contracts, divorces, and household accounts preserved on papyri. These reveal the existence of a multiplicity of household groups—from small conjugal units (nuclear type) to complex and extended families.[12] A subject that was also commented upon in passing by a number of Greek, Roman, and Jewish authors was the different marital prac-tices of the Egyptians as contrary to the general custom of antiquity.[13] As a consequence, evidence in Egypt provides us with the possibility of understand-ing the intersection of the wider context of the Roman Empire with that of the family and childhood at a local level.

Census returns from the first to third centuries C.E. seem to confirm that en-dogamous marriage was the favored system; sibling marriage was not unusual, and, indeed, it was more common in cities than in rural areas. In these en-dogamous marriages, it is likely the bride and groom would have known each other before the marriage—even more so in sibling marriage, obviously. A new husband may not have noticed much change in his location, but his bride, unless a sibling, would move to a new household, even if it was very close to her natal one, and deal with a different set of social dynamics. Egyptian girls usually married in their late teens. Topographical registers demonstrate that families sought to acquire neighboring properties as they expanded, and while the shape of the families that occupied the space might change over time, ex-tended families tried to maintain property holdings among themselves. A new bride may have had her birth family as very near neighbors. The diversity of family structures and living arrangements even in the snapshots of census re-turns is salutary. For example, one return presents a household of at least five illegitimate co-resident siblings. In this family, two of the siblings are married to each other and one to an outsider. Another return shows a household of twenty-seven individuals that contains the husband's ex-wife (his sister), the new wife, and all their mutual children.[14] These examples of families drawn from the papyri challenge expectations and are of such complexity that they are viewed as quite different from what might be described as the Roman family as set out in chapter 1. This can be best understood with reference to an example in detail.

The intertwined nature of families is shown by the life course of Tryphon, a weaver, whose family dealings are known from a number of documents dating from the first century C.E. Tryphon was the eldest of the four sons of Dionysios and Thamounis. In his midtwenties, he was deserted by his wife, Demetrous, who took some of his property with her. Within three years (36 C.E.), Tryphon was living with another woman, Saraeus. Their relationship had some drama: a daughter was born within the year, and in the following year Saraeus was attacked by Tryphon's first wife and her mother. In 49–50 C.E., the couple was accused of stealing a child whom Saraeus was wet-nursing and claiming it as their own. Since a wet nurse must be lactating (must have given birth herself in the recent past), this shows that Tryphon and Saraeus had more children of their own in the interim and begs the question of what happened to them. Tryphon's relationship with his extended family is demonstrated in his financial dealings: he secures a loan from Thoonis, son of Thoonis, who could be his cousin or nephew (both Tryphon's uncle and brother were named Thoonis). He bought a share in a house that was owned by a maternal cousin, property that had originally been owned by Tryphon's mother, Thamounis, and her sister. This property was neighbor to Thamounis's own dwelling and to a house owned by a female cousin. Other documents show Thamounis herself active in family life, arranging an apprenticeship for one son and registering another as missing.[15] Tryphon's convoluted family life demonstrates the close and intertwined relationships that could exist in a single family group and reminds us of the variability of family life, even if detailed evidence does not survive for most families from the period.

Papyri in the form of letters also give insight into family life, reflecting concerns over childbirth and the well-being and education of children as well as more mundane issues such as lost clothing. Women could also be property owners in their own right, such as Thamounis and her sister in the aforementioned story. There is also evidence of women running estates either in their own right or in their husband's absence. Apollonous wrote to her husband, "Rental in kind and all the seed will be entirely available. And do not worry about the children: they are well and attend (lessons with) a woman teacher. And with regard to your fields, I relieved your brother from two *artebai* of the rent."[16] The unique evidence found on the papyri from Egypt reminds us of the diversity of family structures that existed in antiquity and the varied social and gender dynamics they encompass. Endogamous marriage practices present a different set of expectations about the role of family, but even so, the conjugal group—perhaps consisting of more than one couple—seems to be the center of the wider relationship network.

ROMANS ON THE BARBARIAN FAMILY

Just as Greek and Roman writers viewed Jewish and Egyptian families and childhoods as different from their own, they also saw the barbarian context as creating distinct family structures and unique childhood experiences. In 98 c.e., the Roman historian Tacitus wrote a treatise on the Germans (at that time defined as those who lived across the Rhine). The subtext of Tacitus's work was to comment on the behavior of upper-class Rome in his own time by implicit comparison with so-called barbarians, a people whom the Romans considered a great deal less civilized than themselves. The text highlights how childhood and family in the Roman Empire were discussed not only in terms of a simple representation of practice but also with the intent to make a cross-cultural comparison—representing both German practices and a critique of the family, and specifically child rearing, in Rome itself. In the world context of the Roman Empire, barbarian social practices could be presented as better than those found in Rome. The form of analysis found in Tacitus allows for the possibility of a re-evaluation and even the incorporation of barbarian social practices into the world of Greco-Roman antiquity.

On the matter of family, Tacitus's observations reflect a certain admiration for the cultural context under discussion. He noted that the German marriage codes were strict and "no part of their manners more praiseworthy. Almost alone among barbarians they are content with one wife, except a very few of them, and these not from sensuality, but because their noble birth procures for them many offers of alliance." Unlike the Romans, the husband rather than the wife brought a dower to the marriage, and it did not consist of "fripperies or luxuries" but articles such as oxen, horses, and weaponry. Once her family had approved the goods, the bride was considered married, and she gave her husband a gift of arms. The yoked oxen and weapons of the dowry symbolized for the bride that she would share the life of her husband in work and war. Tacitus went on to claim that adultery was virtually unknown as the Germans were a society without the stimulation of public shows and feasting—the sort of activities Tacitus thought encouraged moral degeneracy in Roman social life. If a woman was caught in adultery, her husband had the right to cut off her hair and, in the presence of her kin, strip her naked and flog her through the village. A woman who suffered such a punishment was unlikely to marry again. Tacitus also commented on domestic arrangements: "In every household the children, naked and filthy, grow up with those stout limbs which we so much admire." He also commented that the Germans did not limit the number of children they had and raised them all and that every mother nursed her own children and never handed them over to servants. This was a society in which there were no advantages to childlessness. All these comments stem from Tacitus's perception of the ills of his own society where, in his view, couples preferred to remain childless to avoid inheritance problems and wives were too busy committing adultery to nurse their own children. The warlike nature of Germanic society was also reflected in the domestic arrangement: when the men were not at war or hunting, they did not attend to their estates or run their households; rather, they left these in the hands of women, old men, and other weaker members of the family. Little is known about the upbringing of the children of these families, but it can be assumed that gender roles were inculcated early in life. Young men were as interested in owning fine horses and hunting as any young man in Roman Italy, although in Germany young men were preoccupied with warfare and following a chief. Similar to the Spartans, German mothers and wives treated the wounds of their menfolk and were critics of their performance in battle.[17]

Tacitus was looking into a society outside the frame of reference of the Greco-Roman world set out in previous chapters, but his observations and reflections were designed for an audience based within that Greco-Roman world. Tacitus defined German society through the absence of features that were normative within the Greco-Roman context. In consequence, the strength of kinship relations is asserted due to the absence of written law and wills. Children were automatically the heirs of their parents, but if there were no offspring, the next in succession to the property were brothers and uncles on both sides. Inheritance practices clearly favored males. A contrast is made between the Germans, who valued wide kin relations—the more numerous relations a man had, the more honored he was in old age—and the Romans, who did not. The *Germania* is not an ethnographic survey in any modern sense, but Tacitus recognized differences in family relations that he thought worth noting. The very act of recognizing value within a society different from one's own might provide us with an understanding of a key feature of the Roman world context: social practices that were different or distinct could be evaluated for their qualities, rather than being simply rejected as alien and different. Even the barbarians could have a place in that world context.

FIGURE 10.1: *Detail from the Ara Pacis (Altar of Augustan Peace) in Rome (dedicated 9 B.C.E.) showing a barbarian child differentiated from his Roman equivalents by his dress.* He wears a tunic rather than a toga and a torque rather than a *bulla*, while a Phrygian cap denotes his lack of citizen status. It is likely this image represents a son of a barbarian king who grew up in Rome (photo Ray Laurence).

THE FAMILY AND CHILDHOOD AFTER THE FALL OF ROME

The changes that affected the family and childhood as the Roman system slowly collapsed in the fifth and sixth centuries C.E. require evaluation since their world context is quite different from that of the earlier period. The Roman roads that had formed the backbone of the communication system gradually fell into disrepair, settlements became more remote, production and exchange became more localized, and urban space contracted as the populations of cities decreased.[18] The people who now occupied the former Roman Empire had strong family traditions of their own. The society that emerges in the sources of the sixth through eighth centuries is no more homogenous than that of the Roman Empire (which could include the Jewish, Egyptian, and barbarian families discussed earlier in this chapter), and this point must be held constantly to the fore in the following discussion. The various kingdoms of the Franks, Visigoths, Ostrogoths, and Lombards interacted and assimilated local Roman traditions in varying ways. Family structures thus continued to be culturally, socially, economically, and politically determined and framed by locally specific assumptions of gender roles and age-related behavior. By the fifth century, most of the new power brokers of the west were gradually adopting Christianity, and in this period Christianity emerged as the dominant religion of antiquity. It was through the conduit of Christianity that earlier Roman customs and traditions, as well as Roman moral codes and views of family relationships, were transposed to the new post-Roman world of barbarian kingdoms.

Christianity had transformed the framework within which the Greco-Roman family existed. Its moral code impinged on areas of private life in a far greater way than earlier philosophers. In terms of power structures, the emerging Christian family had much in common with its Roman counterpart: paternal power remained a means of social control and *pietas* expected from children (and parents). Wives were expected to obey their husbands and slaves their masters. In other areas, however, church fathers tried to impose rules on sexual behavior that had not previously been articulated in such a strenuous fashion nor linked with individual salvation. The evolving doctrine of original sin and hostility to the role of sex and sexuality in the world produced a movement with the potential to undermine family life completely. Asceticism praised virginity above all other human states and brought the role of sex into sharp focus. One of the more moderate spokesmen for this way of thinking was Augustine (354–430 C.E.), who, while he held that the sexual act was innately sinful, recognized that it could be allowed if used solely for procreation. He could thus argue for the advantages of remaining celibate—something he did not manage himself until a while after his conversion to Christianity—and for the good of marriage. Such teaching was also reinforced by the traditional gendered view of society, which was now further justified by the curse laid upon Eve after the Fall of mankind. Long before the end of the Roman Empire, church fathers pontificated on many areas of family life, particularly against remarriage and divorce. This rhetoric was influential and continued throughout the Middle Ages, but the more pragmatic churchmen recognized that most of society could not or would not live up to their ideals. People continued to marry, have illegitimate unions, divorce, remarry, and produce children from all types of relationships. In the medieval period, the tension is often between the rules of the church, which appear in the sermons of churchmen and as canon law, and the lived reality of people's lives.[19]

The role of the kin group already recognized by Tacitus was a key part of social control in these new kingdoms. Like the Romans, the Germanic peoples had no word that equates to the modern sense of the nuclear family, and, like the Roman household, Germanic households contained a fluid population of blood relatives, foster children, servants, and retainers. The household was focused on the conjugal couple, which remained the locus of affection and loyalty, but the wider kin group was a strong force in the dynamics of family life. The kin group could also be fluid. It included biological kin; in-laws (*affines*); adopted, fostered, and illegitimate children; and, by the seventh century, frequently also included spiritual kin in the form of godparents and godchildren. This is a far wider group than that entertained by the Roman *paterfamilias*, and the group was expected to have a very active interest in family marriages and inheritance practices.[20]

Marriage—or some equivalent form of socially recognized union—remained the cornerstone of family structures, and the practice of a younger bride marrying an older groom persisted. Marriage was negotiated between the bride's father and the groom, and early medieval custom demanded a "morning gift" or dower from the groom to the bride. It is unclear how much say a young girl had in the selection of her husband, but canon law, following Roman law, did try to make consent part of the process. Betrothal was considered binding. While a carefully arranged marriage linking two kin groups might be the ideal, occasionally a bride might be stolen or collude in her abduction. The law codes offer varying penalties for such a practice to compensate for the loss of a valuable asset.[21]

On marriage, a bride moved to live with her husband and his kin. Germanic marriage customs allowed for several different types of union. In Germanic society, women had fewer legal rights than under the Roman Empire and were for the most part under the legal authority (*mundium*) of their father, husband, or male kin. Among royal circles it was also not uncommon for men who could afford it to have more than one wife. Churchmen may have spoken out against this practice, but the Merovingian kings set a different example. The work of Gregory of Tours (539–594) provides several instances of apparent polygamy; for example, King Clothar I (511–558) was asked by his wife Ingund to find a rich husband for her sister, Aregund. Clothar, a womanizer (he had seven wives in total, though not all simultaneously), claimed he had looked around for someone suitable and decided he himself was the best candidate. Clothar had seven children by three women. He was not unusual among the Merovingian kings, and his sons followed his example. Such close kin marriages were increasingly prohibited by the church, and unions between kin of varying degrees were gradually outlawed.[22]

The main aim of marriage was, of course, procreation. Merovingian kings generally seem to have recognized all their children by their various relationships, so legitimacy might not have been the issue for them that it was for the Romans, although the situation was different for ordinary Franks. However, these seemingly liberal attitudes toward sexual behavior recorded by Gregory of Tours are not found in Christian rhetoric or the law codes, where much stricter sexual codes existed. As in the Greek and Roman worlds, these rules were applied much more to women than to men: the sexual integrity of a wife and mother reflected the integrity of the household and its male head, the legitimacy of its heirs, and the honor of the wider kin group. Adulterous women could suffer disfigurement and loss of status. Following late Roman practices, husbands could divorce wives, but it was much harder for a wife to leave a marriage of her own accord. Outside the royal family, women's legal rights and access to property ownership were restricted. They did not often inherit except in the absence of sons. Marriage at an early age followed by motherhood, and perhaps remarriage, remained the expected life course for most women. The only viable alternative to the traditional female life course was the religious life.[23]

Little is known of the lives of young children in the early medieval household, but there is plenty of evidence to suggest that parents rejoiced at their birth, grieved at early deaths, and were concerned about their upbringing. As in the classical period, underlying assumptions about gender roles were influential in shaping children's lives. Girls learned domestic skills that would aid the economy of their natal home and then that of their husband's: weaving, household management, and so forth. Boys, like their Greek and Roman counterparts, enjoyed far greater freedom than their sisters. Young men learned the skills suitable for their status. Among the peasant classes the difference between childhood and adulthood might be the type of labor that was undertaken, but even here marriage came late for young men. Among the upper classes, young men might move to the house of their lord or a kinsman, training as warriors in the lord's retinue and learning manners commensurate with their station. They, too, married later, and a period of sexual freedom was both anticipated and socially acceptable.[24]

The Germanic custom of *wergeld*, which put a monetary value on an individual's life, recognized some stages of the life course as more valuable to the community than others. In the Frankish codes (early sixth century), the standard *wergeld* for a freeman or woman was 200 *solidi*, but for a man of warrior age or a woman of childbearing age it increased to 600. There is archaeological evidence from Metz, almost contemporary with the Frankish codes, that seems to support this valorization. A study of burials has shown that women who died in their childbearing years were often buried with extensive grave goods: jewelry, keys, and weaving implements. Young men between the ages of twenty to about forty were also marked in burial with weaponry. Children and older men and women were often buried with minimal goods or nothing at all.[25] The law codes from Visigothic Spain (fifth to seventh centuries) reflect similar ideas about the status and value of individuals, suggesting the men able to fight as warriors and women of childbearing age were more highly valued by their families and the community.[26] It was not only the status of the individual but also their stage in the life course that gave them value.

Throughout the early Middle Ages, Christian thinking offered a commentary on family life and the roles of family members. The writings of the church fathers were founded in the classical tradition, and they inherited and manipulated traditional stereotypes of the family from Roman, Jewish, and New Testament traditions. Christian opinion expressed in sermons, canon law, hagiography, and penitentials all commented on all aspects of family life. The church tried to insist on monogamy, to reiterate the power of parental consent in choosing one's marriage partners, and to speak against divorce. Churchmen also spoke out against contraception, abortion, and the exposure and abandonment of children. Abandonment, however, remained a common response for those who could not afford to raise another child, and councils passed rulings stating that children should be left in public places, such as church doorways, so that the priest could ensure they were properly raised.[27]

Competing ideas about the child and childhood emerged: on the one hand, the child was seen as pure and innocent, an exemplar of humility; on the other, the infant was already stained by original sin as was evidenced in infant

FIGURE 10.2: *Ivory diptych of Stilicho, his wife, Serena, and son, Eucherius, ca. 400* C.E. *Stilicho was of Vandal origin but rose to be regent of the western Roman Empire.* Basilica di San Giovanni Battista, Monza, Italy. Image: Alinari/Bridgeman Art Library.

tantrums. The realities of a child's life could be brutal, short, and with few comforts. This situation did not change in the early Middle Ages, but the idea of the Christian child was a new vision of childhood. Hagiography offered an alternative to the traditional family, one in which a child could choose a different path from that assigned by his or her parents. Christian teaching supported the child in any family tension this might cause as the choice was often between marriage and the celibate and religious life. A child who chose not to marry had implications for the wider kin group in terms of the inheritance of property, and, however much spiritual capital might accrue to the family through having a holy person in their midst, the practicalities of life were likely to be the main concern of parents.[28]

THE RECEPTION OF IDEAS OF CHILDHOOD AND THE FAMILY FROM ANTIQUITY INTO THE EARLY MIDDLE AGES

The conception of the child and childhood in the Middle Ages owes much to the thinking of antiquity, and for this reason it is possible to see the world contexts of antiquity as extending into this later period. The Roman Empire disseminated a concept of culture fundamentally different from that found outside its borders. Rome reproduced Hellenistic concepts of childhood and stages of life that clearly influenced medieval and early modern thinking in both the Christian and Muslim worlds. One of the best examples of this can be seen in the work of Isidore of Seville (ca. 560–636 C.E.), in particular the *Etymologies*. As archbishop of Seville in the early seventh century, he was clearly part of the medieval world, yet the thinking behind his work reproduced concepts from the pagan world of the Greco-Romans. In *Etymologies* book IX.4, he details the familiar concept that the state is formed from its citizens based in households composed of biological children and their parents. In the next section, he defines family relations. For Isidore, there were six stages of life: infancy (birth to seven), childhood (seven to fourteen), adolescence (fourteen to twenty-eight), youth (twenty-eight to fifty), maturity (fifty to seventy), and old age (from seventy). His explanations of the nomenclature for each stage are based on an unusual interpretation of etymology: for example, *iuventus* (youth) is derived from *iuvare* (to help) as this is the age at which a person is most capable of assisting others, whereas *adolescens* was derived from the concept that a man was *adultus* (old enough) to procreate. Etymology, rather than earlier practice, causes Isidore to place *adolescens* prior to *iuventus*, in contrast to a number of earlier age systems.[29] While there is a clear connection to classical age systems, Isidore's work is a product of his own world. Classical age systems were all predicated on males; for the first time in Western literature, Isidore also includes the female life course, but in this the influence of Christianity is manifest. He regards the word virgin (*virgo*) as derived from *viridior*, meaning a "greener age" or a sprout (*virga*), or, alternatively, from *virago*, the word for a heroic maiden based around *vir* and *agere*. Classical learning was therefore combined with biblical tradition. The *virgin* can be as strong as a man, whereas the word woman (*mulier*) was used to define the weaker sex, since Eve had only existed in this form according to Genesis 2:2. Isidore repositioned the entire nexus of ideas derived from antiquity within a framework of biblical origins that encompasses both Romans and barbarian worlds. The work as a whole draws together the classical tradition, the Christian tradition, and the origins of former barbarians while making these traditions available to the governing class of Visigothic Spain in relatively simple Latin.[30]

The relationship between the Muslim world of the early Middle Ages and that of antiquity has for sometime been recognized in the fields of the history of science and medicine. There has been far less study of the reception of social institutions from antiquity into early Muslim cultures. Yet there is a need to recognize that the body of knowledge developed in the classical world with respect to childhood and the family seeped into the Muslim world of the early Middle Ages. The translation of Greek texts into Arabic was not an uncommon phenomenon, and numerous examples survive from the ninth century onward. For example, Ishāq b. Hunayn translated a work attributed to Plato on the moral education of young men in the late ninth or early tenth century. These translations of original Greek works became so thoroughly assimilated into Arabic scholarship that even the most authoritative Islamic theologians' views on the upbringing of children—for example, Ibn Miskawayh's work *Tahdhīb al-akhlāq* (The Refinement of the Soul)—are based to a great extent on ancient Greek ethical, philosophical, and pedagogical thought. The medical concepts of the child discussed in the previous chapter, based on the works of Hippocrates and Galen, can be found in Arabic medical compilations made from the tenth century onward; however, there was perhaps a greater emphasis on pediatric medicine in these Arabic texts than in Greek medical writing.[31] Ibn al-Jazzār expanded on the Greek tradition to produce the fifteen-chapter *Book of Child Rearing* at the end of the tenth century. What is striking for a student of antiquity is how the medieval Muslim world contains so many familiar concepts that might have originated in Greco-Roman civilization, including treatises on consolation composed from the thirteenth century, such as Sulaymān b. Banīn b. Khalaf al-Daqīqī's *Consolation for the Steadfast Person on the Loss of a Child*. The relationship between these treatises and Greco-Roman traditions of *consolatio* has not yet been fully investigated. Treatises on the education on children in Arabic draw heavily on the works of Aristotle and the Neo-Pythagorean writer Bryson's work, *Oikonomikos*, yet no major studies have looked at how the original texts have been repackaged for their new social, cultural, and religious context.[32]

There is one final aspect that needs to be considered before we discuss the significance of childhood in antiquity within the frame of a world context. Historians of age in antiquity have become attuned to the use of certain age stages in the past and may too easily see the continuation of some customs into later periods—for example, military service at the age of seventeen. In respect to the introduction of different ages of suffrage, it is easy to suspect politicians and civil servants in the late nineteenth and early twentieth century of borrowing (implicitly or explicitly) from their reading of classics at school and university.[33] Often these suspicions cannot be proven, but they lead us to wonder if, instead, the repetition of age systems from antiquity over time resulted in the natural-ization of childhood and its stages. For example, in December 2007, the British government issued a new ruling that all children over the age of seven would learn a foreign language at school. Why seven? There is undoubtedly some educational research behind this, but it but it brings to mind how the ancients' thinking about the transition in childhood at age seven may have been received and rearticulated over time to create seven as the natural point within child-hood to establish a boundary between those who must have language lessons and those who need not. It may also reflect the views of many civil servants and politicians formed from their own experiences in public (and private) schools of learning languages from the age of seven.[34] Could the system of age and child development from antiquity be subconsciously reproduced in the twenty-first century?

Of the volumes in the *A Cultural History of Childhood and Family* series, this first on antiquity has the longest chronological range (800 B.C.E.–800 C.E.); within this long time frame, the concept of childhood and the family was devel-oped and maintained across a vast geographical area eventually unified under Rome. At the level of the state, the family was based on marriage for the pur-pose of procreation and the maintenance of the family unit. However, at a local or individual family level, numerous possibilities affected the structure of the family and the lived experience of the child, as we saw in the case of Tryphon in Egypt. This is not to say that there was no global conception of the family but rather to observe its variation and to understand how the concept of family could affect the lived reality of family life—as it did both globally and locally in the case of the Diaspora Jews living under the Roman Empire. The strength of these conceptions of family and childhood can be most effectively seen in the study of the family and childhood after Rome. Barbarian social institutions were incorporated or merged with the institutions of the former Roman state, most notably in law codes and through the church as a conduit of continuity of Roman practices, albeit transformed for the new dispensation. In all cases discussed in this chapter, the ancient family can be seen as a social institution that was flexible and capable of incorporating others into its framework, thus maintaining the family, as a social institution, over time.

NOTES

Introduction

The editors would like to thank all the contributors to this volume for their time, hard work, and patience. We would also like to warmly thank Henry Buglass and Graham Norrie from the University of Birmingham for the maps, illustrations, and digitization of some of the images.

1. Joshel 1992: 3–24 provides discussion of muted groups and the use of literary stereotypes in antiquity.
2. Crawford and Lewis (2008) review the bibliography and associated approaches; see also Sofaer (2006: 117–143) on the separation of approaches in osteoarchaeology from the interpretative practices within social archaeology.
3. Australian National University. 2004. *Children conquered Roman hearts*. Available at http://info.anu.edu.au/mac/Newsletters_and_Journals/ANU_Reporter/Autumn_2004/Roman_children.asp. Accessed November 2008.
4. de Mause 1974; Ariès 1962; Rawson 1997, 2003.
5. Eyben 1972, 1993.
6. See chapter 6 in this volume.
7. Rawson 1991a; Rawson and Weaver 1997.
8. Rawson 1986a: 237–239.
9. George 2005: 1–3.
10. Rawson 1986a: 238; see also discussion in Evans Grubbs 2002: xi–xiv.
11. Garnsey 1991; Bradley 1986: 221; Dixon 1992: 98–108.
12. Rawson 1986a: 245.
13. For Australia: Dixon 1988, 1992, 2001b; Rawson 1986a, 1991a, 2003, and with Weaver 1997; for North America: Bradley 1991; Saller and Shaw 1984; Saller 1987, 1994; Shaw 1987.
14. Rawson 1995.
15. Dixon 2001a especially 1–25 for discussion; compare to Rawson 2005.
16. Shaw 2001.

17. Dixon 2001a.
18. Rawson 2003: 3; Wiedemann 1989: 2–3.
19. For the paucity of evidence for Hellenistic Greece, see Golden 1997; compare for the Roman Empire—Saller and Shaw 1984; George 2005.
20. James and James 2004; James and Prout 1990; Sofaer 2006: 129–138.
21. For example, see Saller 1994 on the nature of patriarchy.
22. See Dixon 1988: 104–141 on young child; compare with 168–210 on adult sons.
23. See papers in Dasen 2004.
24. Jenks 1996; Steedman 1995.
25. Saller 1994; Hallett 1984; Andreau and Bruhns 1990; Wiedemann 1989.
26. See Gardner 1998 for a discussion of adoption; on the role of adults, see Golden 1990; Rawson 2003; and papers in Mustakallio, Hanska, Sainio, and Vuolanto 2005.
27. See Néraudau 1984.
28. Compare papers in George 2005; also Nathan 2000: 1–2.
29. See Cooper 2007; Nathan 2000; Evans Grubbs 1995 for recent discussion of the latter, with comments by Rawson 2005: 8–9.
30. See Nathan 2000; Cooper 2007 for discussion.
31. Interpretations vary on the impact of Christianity; compare Nathan 2000 and Cooper 2007.
32. See chapter 6 for discussion.
33. See Harlow and Laurence 2002 for a discussion of the Roman life course.
34. Ziolkowski 1993 for further discussion and details.
35. Cassius Dio *History of Rome* 44.30.6–8.
36. Laurence 2000; Uzzi 2005: 142–155.
37. Crawford and Lewis 2008; Sofaer 2008.
38. For example, Allison 2004a, 2004b, and 2006.
39. Lillehammer 1989 is regarded as the first work on the archaeology of childhood; see more recently Wileman 2005; papers in Baxter 2005; papers in Sofaer Deverenski 2000; papers in Crawford and Shepherd 2007; and Sofaer 2008 for the interaction of osteoarchaeological approaches to the body with theories drawn from interpretative archaeologies of society.
40. Henneberg and Henneberg 1998.
41. Gowland 2007.
42. Perhaps in the manner of Dixon 2001a on women.
43. Dixon 1997.

Chapter 1

1. Aristotle *Politics* 1.1–3; Cicero *On Duties* 1.54.
2. Aristotle *Politics* 1.2–3; Lacey 1980: 15–32; Golden 1990: 23–38.
3. Blundell 1995: 116–117; Lacey, 1980: 28; Cohen, 1989: 163–180; Maffi 2005: 254–266; Patterson 1998: 70–106.
4. For a discussion of inheritance patterns see chapters 3 and 7 in this volume; Blundell 1995: 116–119.

5. *Digest of Justinian* 50, 16.195 (Ulpian); Gaius *Institutes* 1.49, 55.

6. For a discussion of changes in marriage patterns see Treggiari 1991a: 16–36; Dixon, 1992: 41–43.

7. Saller 1984: 336–355; 1994, 74–101; Bradley, 1991: 4–5.

8. Saller and Shaw 1984: 124–156.

9. Bagnall and Frier 1994; Alston 2005: 129–158.

10. Wickham 2005: 551.

11. For the Anglo-Saxon family see Crawford 1999: 8–10.

12. Aristotle *Politics* 1.12; Ephesians 5:22–6:9; Colossians 3:18–4:1; 1 Peter 2:18–3:7.

13. Blundell 1995: 114–124; Lacey 1980: 100–124, 167–172; Just 1989; Cohen 1991.

14. See Aristophanes *Lysistrata, Thesmophoriazusae, Women in the Assembly*. For a discussion of the image of women presented in Greek drama see Blundell 1995: 143, 172–180 and her references.

15. Xenophon *Oeconomicus* 7.5ff; see Pomeroy's commentary 1994: 268–282, which also discusses the role of women in ancient Greece in general; Plutarch *Advice to Bride and Groom*.

16. Segregation and seclusion have been a matter of much discussion: see, for example, Cohen 1989: 135–145; Just 1989: 106–125; Nevett 1994; Blundell 1995: 135–138.

17. Xenophon *Oeconomicus* 3.15. See Pomeroy's commentary (1994), especially chapters 4 and 5 on the relationship between spouses.

18. Xenophon *Oeconomicus* 10.

19. For example, Democrates 41.17–19; Lysias 32.11–18 in which a mother is prepared to speak out against her sons' guardian about misappropriation of their inheritance; Demosthenes 59 for Neira the courtesan and her ambitions. See also Henry 2008 for discussion.

20. See, for example, *Corpus Inscriptionum Latinarum*. 1.1007; 6.11602, 29580, 34268; 8.11294; 9.1913 all cited in Gardner and Wiedemann 1991: 52–54. For Roman wives in general see Dixon 1988, 1992, 2001a; Gardner 1986.

21. Pliny the Younger *Letters* 4.19.

22. Pliny *Letters* 6.4, 7.5; for a discussion of Pliny and Calpurnia see Shelton 1990.

23. Cicero *Ad Familiares* 14.4. For a good example of using Cicero as a case study see Bradley 1991: 177–204.

24. Dixon 1984: 78–101.

25. For a précis of the indifference debate see Harlow, Laurence, and Vuloanto 2007.

26. See, for example, Engels 1980; Harris 1982; Boswell 1988; Evans Grubbs 1993: 133–137; Corbier 2001; Bakke 2005: 110–130.

27. Soranus *Gynaecolgy* 2.19; Tacitus *Dialogues* 29; Bradley 1986: 201–229; 1994; French 1986; Joshel 1986; Fildes 1988: 4–25; Garnsey 1991; chapter 9 this volume.

28. Pliny *Letters* 6.3; Augustine *Confessions* 1.6.7, 11.

29. Golden 1990: 82–89; Blundell 1995: 141–142 for references from drama; Plutarch *Consolation to His Wife;* Oakley in Neils and Oakley 2003.

30. Images of Greek childhood appear in a number of media. For a very accessible collection see the catalogue from Neils and Oakley 2003, which also has many relevant articles. For images and a discussion of the iconography of Roman childhood see Huskinson 1996, 1997, 2005: 233–238; Rawson 1997: 205–232; Uzzi 2005.

31. Dixon 1988 for the Roman mother; Neils and Oakley 2003 for other images.
32. Crook 1967: 113–122; Saller 1994: 123–124, 218–220.
33. Saller 1994: 12–41, 122–124.
34. For guardianship (*tutela*) see Saller 1994: 181–203, 229–231. For the implications for women see Gardner 1986: 3–29.
35. Cicero *On Duties* 2.11.46, *Republic* 6.16; Valerius Maximus 5.4; Saller 1994: 102–132.
36. For discussion and images see Neils 2003: 145–147 and catalogue 284–287; Golden 1990: 42–43, 125–126.
37. "Brother and sister stele" in the Metropolitan Museum of Art, New York (cat no. 11.185). Image and discussion in Neils and Oakley 2003: 179–180; Golden 1990: 128–129, and on siblings generally, 126–136.
38. Aristotle *Nichomedean Ethics* 1161b18–1162a; Plutarch *On Brotherly Love.* Golden 1990: 117–178.
39. Saller 1994: 47–66; tables show the nature of kin relations, including siblings.
40. Cicero *Ad Atticum* 5.20.9; Bannon 1997: 101–115, esp. 103–105; Harders 2008.
41. Rawson 2003: 243–250, including reference to Cicero, Tullia, and Marcus; Harders 2008.
42. Hallet 1984.
43. On the potential relationship between slavery, children, and violence in Athens, see Golden 1990: 154–168.
44. Suetonius *Nero* 35; for Constantine and Fausta see Zosimus 2.29.
45. *Confessions* 9.9; Schroeder 2004.
46. *CJ* 5.17.8, 449 CE; *NJ* 22.15. See Nathan 2000: 103–105.
47. Quintilian *Institutes* 1.3.13 argued that beating made a child like a slave; Golden 1990: 64; Saller 1994: 133–153. See chapter 5 in this volume.
48. Seneca *On Anger* 2.21; Plutarch *On the Education of Children*; Laes 2005.
49. Bakke 2005; Nathan 2000: 133–159.
50. Elvira, canon 12 306 CE; *Theodosian Code* 5.9.2. See Evans Grubbs 1993 for discussion; Nathan 2000: 137–138.
51. *Novels of Justinian* 153; Boswell 1988.
52. Laes 2003; McKeown 2007.
53. Corbier 1999b; Rawson 1986a, 2003: 251–255; Bellmore and Rawson 1990.
54. For images see Kleiner 1977.
55. *Apostolic Constitutions* 4.1–2; Finn 2006: 70–84.

Chapter 2

1. For example, Laurence 2007.
2. Xenophon *Memorabilia* 3.6.14; Hansen 1997b: 11; Wallace-Hadrill 1994; Hansen 1997b: 12–15; compare Morgan and Coulton 1997.
3. For male spaces (or the absence of women and children) see Aristotle *Politics* 1270a 31; Hansen 1997b: 26–27; Wileman 2005. Wallace-Hadrill 1994.
4. Tacitus *Agricola* 21.

5. Strauss 1993: 11; Sissa 1996; Patterson 1998: 180–225; Saller 1994; Golden 1990: 40–41.

6. Golden 1990: 38–35; Strubbe 1998.

7. Aristotle *Politics* 3.1278a 4; Golden 1990: 39. The age of majority was eighteen years in Athens, twenty-five years in the Roman Empire; Strauss 1993: 67; Harlow and Laurence 2002: 54–78.

8. On Socrates see Plato *Apology of Socrates*; Euben 1997. On Catiline see Sallust *Catilinarian Conspiracy*. For Tiberius Gracchus see Plutarch *Life of Tiberius Gracchus* 8. For Agricola see Tacitus *Life of Agricola* 4.

9. Harlow and Laurence 2002: 69–72.

10. For demographic context see chapter 6 in this volume; Parkin 1992; Saller 1994; and papers in Scheidel 2001a.

11. Cicero *On Duties* 1.76, *Rhetorica ad Herennium* 4.68; Lintott 1994: 62–77 for narrative based on later sources; compare Laurence 1994.

12. Plutarch *Life of Gaius Gracchus* 4.

13. Aristotle *Politics* 5.11.1313a-b; Schmitt-Pantel 1990; see Golden 1990: 62–65 on Athenian schools.

14. Kennell 2006 for evidence for the *Ephebia*; Della Corte 1924 read with Coarelli 2001; Laurence 2007: 168–173; Rostovtzeff 1900; Jaczynowska 1970; De Ruggiero 1948–1958: 4.317–320.

15. Schmitt-Pantel 1990: 210.

16. Coarelli 2001; *Inscriptiones Graecae ad res Romanas pertinentes* 4.454; Jones 1940: 220.

17. *Digest of Justinian* 50.9.4.2, 27.1.6.2.

18. Link 2004: 1; on Spartan education see Ducat 2006; Kennell 1995; Rawson 1969; Cartledge and Spawforth 1989: 176–184.

19. Apuleius *Metamorphoses* with Millar 1981; Suetonius *Life of Nero* 26; Champlin 2003.

20. Tacitus *Annals* 14.17; *Corpus Inscriptionum Latinarum* 4.1293; Moeller 1970.

21. Nippel 1995: 85–100; Coulston 2000.

22. On the rashness of youth see Thucydides 6.12–13; Strauss 1993: 149; Kagan 2003: 256–261. Aristotle *Rhetoric* 2.12–14; Harlow and Laurence 2002: 69–71. On Alcibiades see Thucydides 6.16; compare Champlin 2003 on actions of Nero in Rome.

23. Thucydides 6.26–27; Kagan 2003: 262–274.

24. Thucydides 6.60–61; Longrigg 2000.

25. Compare Scheidel 2002; Bruun 2007.

26. Plutarch *Life of Alcibiades* provides a list of morals to avoid. Alcibiades is quoted by Plutarch in *Life of Alcibiades* 22.

27. Cicero *Pro Caelio*; Laurence 1994 on role of rumor. Other examples from antiquity: the Bacchanalia scandal (Beard, North, and Price 1998: 91–98) and the Catilinarian conspiracy (Wiseman 1994: 342, 346–358; Gruen 1974: 416–433; Seager 1964; Yavetz 1963).

28. For Numerius Popidius Celsinus see *Corpus Inscriptionum Latinarum* 10.846, for translation Cooley and Cooley 2004: C5. Child councilors at Pompeii: Kleijwegt

1991: 318–319 lists forty-nine examples; Laes 2006a; Cooley and Cooley 2004: G21, G24 for two examples from Pompeii. At Canusium: *Corpus Inscriptionum Latinarum* 9.338; Mouritsen 1998 with full bibliography.

29. *Digest of Justinian* 50.2.6.1; Kleijwegt 1991: 325.

30. See debate: Mouritsen 1988; Biundo 1996; Mouritsen 1999 and Biundo 2003.

31. Castrén 1975: 114–118 for full list of supporters. For women, Savunen 1997: 13–47 is fundamental; also see Bernstein 1988.

32. Savunen 1997: 26, Table 4 for the data and evidence.

33. Mouritsen 1988: 52–60.

34. Ovid *Metamorphoses* 9.669–706 compare the line from the Greek comic poet Posidippus fragment 11, "Everybody raises a son even if he is poor, but exposes a daughter even if he is rich"; Blundell 1995: 131–132; Patterson 1985 on evidence in Greece; and Harris 1994 on Rome. The idea of unequal sex ratio exists at the level of hypothesis only, Patterson 1985: 120–121.

35. For Judea see Cotton 1994 for the text and commentary; for Sparta see Xenophon *Constitution of the Spartans* 1.3; Aristotle *HA* 9.608b 15.

36. For Rome see Huskinson 1999; Hemelrijk 1999; for Greece see Xenophon *Oeconomicus* 7.30; Plato *Laws* 781c; Walker 1983; Nevett 1999; Cahill 2002; Nevett 2002; and papers in Ault and Nevett 2005; Milnor 2005: 94–139.

37. Cato *On Agriculture* 143.

38. Lycurgus *Against Leocrates* 40; Theophrastus *Characters* 28; Thucydides 2.45.2; Blundell 1995: 135–136; Laurence 2007: 161–162; Wallace-Hadrill 1994, 1997; Allison 2004a; Wiedemann 1996. For women interacting with neighbors, etc., Blundell 1995: 131–132, 137 for these instances in drama and literature.

39. See Oliver 2000 on jewelry; *Digest of Justinian* 34.2.23 on gender and clothing; see McGinn 1998: 154–161; 2004: 151–152; Milnor 2005: 141–185.

40. Fagan 1999: 26–29 takes the rational view that some baths were men only, others women only, and others mixed. Eger 2007 on the sensory experience of bathing.

41. Harlow and Laurence 2008; Bradley 2005; see also chapter 9 in this volume.

42. Dixon 2001a: 47–49.

43. Sourvinou-Inwood 1988: 27–30, 35–37, 39–40, 42, 44–45, 57, 60–61; King 1983; Demand 1998: 75–77. On betrothal see Harlow and Laurence, in press.

44. King 2004, 1998; Cooper 1996: 74–78; Sourvinou-Inwood 1988: 30, 51–53; Younger 1997; Lefkowitz 1981: 50–52; Staples 1998: 131–136; Beard 1980, 1995; also Sissa 1990.

45. Wiedemann 1989: 38–39, 113–114, 159–162; Nicolet 1980: 89–148.

46. Compare Plutarch *Life of Tiberius Gracchus* 8; Pliny the Younger *Panegyricus* 26.

47. Rathbone 1981: 16–19 and note 32; Fentress 2000, 2004.

48. On exposure see Aristotle *Politics* 1265b and 1335b; on urban decline see Hopkins and Burton 1978; Brunt 1971; on the cessation of colonies see Harris 2007: 525, 515–517.

49. Musonius Rufus 15 (for translation see Lutz 1947).

50. *SEG* 1.366 (for translation see Hands 1968: 176).

51. Veyne 1990; Hands 1968: 26–61, 89–92; Duncan-Jones 1982: 264.

52. Woolf 1990 for discussion with data from Duncan-Jones 1982 chapter 7 and appendices 5 and 6.

53. See Aurelius Victor *Epitome de Caesaribus* 12.4; Woolf 1990: 204; Patlagean 1977; *Theodosian Code* 11.27.1–2; Woolf 1990: 205; Gebbia 2006 on the sale of children.

54. Woolf 1990: 214–215.

55. Liebeschuetz 1991 outlines the difference in terms of "a way of life" within the cities; Lavan 2003. Compare the town of Cosa and its neighboring villas, in particular Settefinestre.

56. See Casiodorus *Variae* 8.31 on use of the forum, baths, and the city as something worth defending from enemies; Riché 1996. Liebeschuetz 1991: 19–20; Matthews 2000.

57. Cassiodorus *Variae* 9.14; Lepelley 1996: 71.

58. Patlagean 1977: 144–148; James 2004; Halsall 1995: 72–86.

59. Liebeschuetz 2001: 318–320; Jones 1964: 1007, 1405 note 52.

60. Theodoret *Ecclesiatical History* 4.18; Jones 1964: 997.

61. This matter is discussed by Jones 1964: 1005–1007.

62. MacPherson 1989: 126.

Chapter 3

1. Aulus Gellius *Attic Nights* 17.21.44.

2. Fantham, et al. 1994: 228f; Golden 1990: 23.

3. Shelton 1988: 30; Corbier 2001: 58–65; Rawson 2003: 117–119, with further references.

4. Golden 1990: 106–107.

5. On children's education see Fantham, et al. 1994: 59; Rawson 2003: 195. On the issue of Greek women being able to read and write see Cole 1981.

6. Hemelrijk 1999; Rawson 2003: 197–209.

7. On the age of marriage for girls see Shaw 1987; Harlow and Laurence 2002: 90–91, 95–99; Evans Grubbs 2002: 88–91. On betrothals see Evans Grubbs 2002: 88; Harlow and Laurence 2002: 58–60; and Harlow and Laurence, in press, with an exhaustive discussion on betrothals in Roman imperial times.

8. Harlow and Laurence 2002: 95–97.

9. Lefkowitz and Fant 1992: 55–56, no. 76; Saller 1994: 205–206.

10. On dowries in classical Athens see Pomeroy 1975: 63; on Roman dowries see Treggiari 1991a: 95–100; Gardner 1986: 97–102; Treggiari 1991: chapter 10; Evans-Grubbs 2002: 91–98.

11. Schaps 1979: chapter 6 with appendix 1; Golden 1990: 132–134; see Polybius 31.26–27 on the family of the Scipios; Fantham, et al. 1994: 263; Saller 1994: 206.

12. On Roman dowries and divorce see Gardner 1986: 105–114; Treggiari 1991: 467f; Evans Grubbs 2002: 191–192, 198–210.

13. Gardner 1986: 46–47, 74–75; Treggiari 1991: chapter 11; Evans Grubbs 2002: 98–100 with examples from Roman law on these issues; Harlow and Laurence in press. For late antiquity see Kuefler 2007: 357–359 with further references.

14. For inheritance rights in Greece/Athens see Lysias 10.15: Aristotle *Politics;* Pomeroy 1975: 69; Schaps 1979: 31–32; Golden 1990: 119–120.
15. On Roman inheritance see Gardner 1986: 164–169; Fantham, et al. 1994: 263; Evans Grubbs 2002: 219. For the example of Antonia Minor see Kokkinos 1992: 11.
16. For changes in inheritance rights in late antiquity see *Codex Theodosianus* 3.8.2; Evans-Grubbs 2002: 230f; and Kuefler 2007: 345–347 for further references.
17. Gardner and Wiedemann 1991: 68.
18. See Suetonius *Life of Augustus*: 74 for women of the imperial family and wool work. Treggiari 1991: 243; Gardner and Wiedemann 1991: 68, 70.
19. Cato *On Agriculture* 135.1.
20. On the concept of *otium* see Cooper 2007: 93f. See d'Arms 1981 for a more extensive discussion of the involvement of Roman elite families in trade and business.
21. For more examples on slave prices in antiquity see Scheidel 2005: 1–17, which includes further bibliography on the slave economy, including other publications by Scheidel.
22. Varro *On Agriculture* 1.17; Duncan Jones 1974: chapter 2; Brunt 1987: 707; Bradley 1991: 114.
23. See Joshel 1992 for an extensive study of occupational inscriptions from Rome.
24. For children's work see especially Bradley 1991: 106–109, Table 5.1. On Roman work in general see Cicero *On Duties* 1.42; Joshel 1992; Dixon 2001b. The gold spinner Viccentia, deceased at age nine, is documented by a funerary inscription, *Corpus Inscriptionum Latinarum* 6.9213. For further examples of working children who died young see Bradley 1991: 115.
25. Ariès 1962.
26. Jewell 2007: 48.
27. Wickham 2005: 554–557.
28. Brown 1988: 115, 174; Cooper 2007: 80f, 104–107. See also Cooper and Hillner 2007 *passim*.

Chapter 4

I would like to thank Mary Harlow and Ray Laurence for inviting me to contribute to this volume and for their support throughout the production of this chapter. A version of this was presented at the European Social Sciences and History Conference in Lisbon in March 2008, and thanks go to the audience for their feedback. I am also grateful to Alison Moore, Yvonne Marshall, and Tim Champion for their help and advice on the family and age in general. Penny Copeland provided information on child labor at Mons Porphyrites and Ray Laurence the age data for Thugga.

1. Holloway and Valentine 2000.
2. Morris 1999.
3. Jameson 1990; Nevett 1999.
4. Walker 1983.
5. Xenophon *Oeconomicus* 9.2–5; Nevett 1994, 1995, 1999.

6. Lysias 1.9–10.
7. Nevett 1999: 4–10.
8. Hales 2003.
9. Wallace-Hadrill 1994; Zanker 1998.
10. Harlow and Laurence 2002; Laurence 2006.
11. Ellis 1988, 1991, 2000.
12. Cunliffe 1988; Horden and Purcell 2000.
13. The literature on Romanization is vast; influential collections include Blagg and Millett 1990; Keay and Terrenato 2001; Mattingly 1997; Metzler, Millett, and Slofstra 1995.
14. Ward-Perkins 1984.
15. Woolf 2005: 231.
16. Zienkiewicz 1986: 223.
17. Sofaer Derevenski 2000.
18. Peacock 1982; Smith 2005: 122.
19. Revell 2009.
20. Lillehammer 2000.
21. Diodorus 3.12.
22. Hong, et al. 1994, 1996.
23. Gratton, et al. 2002.
24. King 2001.
25. Swan 1992.
26. Hajnal 1965.
27. Saller 1987; Saller and Shaw 1984; Shaw 1987.
28. Saller and Shaw 1984: 138; also Edmondson 2004.
29. For example, Strabo *Geography* 3.4.18.
30. The argument for local recruitment has its origins in the work of Mommsen, in particular Mommsen 1884. It has been modified by the work of Saller and Shaw 1984 amongst others. See also Haynes 2001: 66.
31. Phang 2002.
32. van Driel-Murray 1995.
33. The original figures were estimated in Cheeseman 1914 and revised in le Bohec 1994: 96.
34. Although such figures are by their nature rough estimates, Willems estimates that in the first century C.E. the population was from thirty to forty thousand constituting from four to six thousand households. If the community was maintaining units of approximately five thousand five hundred men, then, on average, each household would have provided one soldier to the Roman army (Willems 1984). See also Haynes 2001; van Driel-Murray 2002.
35. Nicolay 2002.
36. Millett 2001: 167; Tranoy 1981: 176–178.
37. The evidence is discussed in Guijarro 1997, who argues for different family types in the area based upon their housing; see Table 3.1 for summary.
38. Smith 1997.
39. Alston 2005. See also chapter 10 in this volume.

40. Bradley 1991: 13–36.
41. Smith 2005: 115–147.
42. A fuller account is given in Revell 2005.
43. Harlow and Laurence 2002.
44. *Corpus Inscriptionum Latinarum* 9.4810.

Chapter 5

1. Huys 1996.
2. Morgan 1998: 25–32 on encyclical education; Veyne 2005 on Roman culture being essentially Greco-Roman; Kah-Scholz 2004 on gymnasia.
3. Kaster 1983; Vössing 1997: 563–574; 2003.
4. Naerebout and Singor 2001; Veyne 2005.
5. Brown 1971.
6. Aristotle *History of Animals* 588a 31–b3. See Gourevitch 1995 on ancient concepts on babies and their irrationality; Néraudeau 1984: 91–98; Wiedemann 1989: 5–11, 17–25; Golden 1990: 5–7; Bakke 2005: 15–22 on the link between children and irrationality. On molding see John Chrysostom *On Vainglory and the Education of Children* 20.
7. Cicero *On the Ends of Good and Evil* 5.42–43, 5.48, 5.55; Plato *Laws* 788d–793d (zero to three years), 793d–794c (three to six years); Aristotle *Politics* 1336a2–b37 on child development to age seven. On Quintilian and Augustine, see van Nieuwenhuizen, Brand, and Claassen 1994.
8. Plato *Laws* 789a-d (womb); 790c–791c (gymnastics by midwives and nurses). *Educit enim obstetrix, educat nutrix, instituit paedagogus, docet magister* (Nonius Marcellus *Handbook of Instruction* 718, ed. Lindsay).
9. Soranus *Gynaecology* 2.10–11. For a telling comparison, see Plato *Theaetus* 151a-d; 157c-d, where Socrates warns not to act irrationally like the mother who became angry with the midwife who found a baby unable to survive and secretly removed the infant. Soranus *Gynaecology* 1.3–4 on the ideal midwife. See also chapter 9 in this volume.
10. On the value of children see Laes 2009; Cilliers 2005 (on Vindicianus, a sixth-century medical writer); Hummel 1999 on Arab medicine. See Orme 2001: 15–16 on medieval practice and rituals of midwives; Rollet 2001: 203–217 on the medicalization of the profession and the rise of medical centers.
11. Bradley 1986: 202.
12. On storytelling, see, for instance, Plato *Republic* 377–378 and *Laws* 887d; Tacitus *Dialogues on Oratory* 29.1; Strabo *Geography* 1, 2, 3, and 8; Massaro 1977. On Spartans not being swaddled see Plutarch *Lycurgus* 16.4, and on Spartan nurses being popular in other cities see Plutarch *Alcibiades* 1.3, so one may suppose that other Greek children were not swaddled. See Deissmann-Merten 1986: 291.
13. See Manca Masciadri and Montevecchi 1984 for nursing contracts on papyri; Joshel 1986 and Dixon 1992: 98–132 offer ample dossiers with attention to cross-cultural references. Also see aside remarks in Manca Masciadri and

Montevecchi 1984: n. 198 (father being angry because his son-in-law does not hire a nurse); Phaedrus *Fables* 3.15 (a lamb considers a she-goat as its real mother since she gave her milk). Bradley 1986, 1991; Eichenauer 1988: 274–283 for Rome and the provinces; Vilatte 1991 for nurses in ancient Greece (an understudied subject); Crespo Ortiz de Zarate 2005, 2006.

14. Demosthenes 57.42; Aristotle *Athenian Constitution* 7.456 (epigram); ps. Plutarch *The Education of Children* 1d–2a; Tacitus *Dialogue on Oratory* 28–29 (traditionalist discourse, on which see Joshel 1986: 9–10).

15. Manca Masciadri and Montevecchi 1984: n. 6 (baby being raised outside the house) and n. 19 (discussion about its identity); Seneca *Controversies* 4.6 (changing of babies). Raising a child outside the parents' house did occur according to *Codex Theodosianus* 9.31.1. On orphanages, see Miller 2003 (the famous Orphanotropheion of Constantinople was probably founded during the reign of Emperor Constantius and still functioned as a large institute nine hundred years later in the fourteenth century). On nurses being valued see Demosthenes 47.55; Suetonius *Nero* 50 (nurses caring for Nero's corpse); Pliny *Letters* 6.3.1 (Pliny donating land and a farm).

16. Cicero *On Friendship* 20, 74; Seneca *On Anger* 2.21.9. Gellius *Attic Nights* 12.1 (Favorinus); Soranus *Gynaecology* 2.19.

17. Golden 1990: 141–168 (alliances in Athens); Laes 2004, 2008 (Roman pedagogues); Julian *Orations* 241c–d; *Beard-Hater* 351a–352c; Suetonius *Claudius* 2.4 (pedagogue enforcing his will).

18. In connection with the Persian educating system: Herodotus 1.136; Valerius Maximus 2.6.16. On fathers in Greek comedy see Aristophanes *Lysistrata* 878; *Clouds* 1380. In Hellenism, Theophrastus *Characters* 20.5.

19. On Athens see Deissmann-Merten 1986: 294; Rome: Bradley 1994: 150–152. On epigraphic evidence see Laes 2006b: 87–95; 2007. *Carmina Latina Epigraphica* 1535A 5; *L'Année Epigraphique* 1981 673, 3–5.

20. On sarcophagi see Huskinson 1996; toys see Willemsen 2003. *Infancy Gospel of Thomas* 2–3; Plutarch *Consolation to his Wife* 608c.

21. Pindar *Olympian* 2.94–96. Marrou 1964: 73–75 on the first schools in Athens and aristocratic opposition. Aeschines *Orations* 1.6 states that the statesmen Dracon and Solon actually regulated upbringing, but this does not equal with free institution or schooling for every citizen.

22. Plato *Laws* 7.794c and Aristotle *Politics* 7.1336b 36 (age seven); Plato *Clitopho* 407b–c and Plato *Laws* 7.809e–810b; Aristotle *Politics* 8.1337b 23–32 (reading and writing, gymnastics, music, and drawing). See Morgan 1998: 9–21 on the background of education in classical Greece.

23. There is evidence of a school (with one teacher?) of 60 pupils on Astypalea (Pausanias 6.9.6) and 120 on Chios (Herodotus 6.27.2). Golden 1990: 62–64. Plato *Protagoras* 326c (music and gymnastics for the wealthy; only the rich continue with school).

24. Exemption for schoolteachers only occurs in an edict by king Ptolemy Philadelphus in Hellenistic Egypt (third century B.C.E.): *Dikaiomata* (ed. Graeca Halensis 1913) 1.260–265. See Cribiore 2001: 62. No exemption in Roman times: *Digest*

of Justinian 50.4.11.4, with a possible exception for a mining district in Lusitania: *Inscriptiones Latinae Selectae* 6891.

25. Aesop *Fables* 45. The story was found several times on papyri, copied by pupils or school teachers, with many mistakes. See P. Rainer Unterricht 117–132.

26. Bonner 1977: 165–188.

27. Proverb in *Comica Adespota* 20. See Booth 1981 and Laes 2007: x (negative discourse on school teachers). See Laes 2007 for a collection of inscriptional evidence.

28. See *Supplementum Epigraphicum Graecum* 27.950 for a Christian *didaskalos* from Cappadocia. Marrou 1964, vol. 2: 136–143.

29. Such as Chrysostom, c. 347–407 C.E., in his youthful treatise *Comparison between a King and a Monk* or Jerome, c. 345–420 C.E., Letter 107 designing the education of two girls consecrated to an ascetic life of virginity.

30. Bakke 2005: 201–215 is an excellent account of Christian attitudes toward pagan schools. See Hippolytus *Apostolic Tradition* 16 on Christian teachers. On catechetical teaching, see Lactantius 6.3.15 and Augustine *Sermones* 138.2.10. Lector Vitalis: *Corpus Inscriptionum Latinarum* 8 453. On Sundays replacing local calendars, see Marrou 1964, vol. 1, 223–225. See Jerome *Letters* 107, and see Bakke 2005: 160–162 and 183–188 for a discussion. See Miller 2003: 45–47 on boarding schools.

31. On the absence of girls in Athenian schools: Golden 1990: 73–74. On mixed elementary Hellenistic schools: Marrou 1964, vol. 1: 218–219 (explicitly in school laws from Milet and Teos, see Dittenberger *Sylloge Inscriptionum Graecarum* 577 and 578 as well as numerous papyri; Cribiore 2001: 74–101, esp. 80–82). Roman schoolteachers teaching both girls and boys: Marrou 1964, vol. 2: 65 (see Martial *Epigrams* 9.68.2). See Booth 1979 on Roman elementary education as primarily aimed at lower classes.

32. The cynic philosopher Teles (third century B.C.E.) refers to a curriculum in which teachers of arithmetic and geometry—as well as a trainer of horse riding and teachers of gymnastics, music, and art—came to the fore after schooling with elementary teachers. This sounds like an attempt at systematization by a philosopher similar to the theories of Plato and Aristotle. As mentioned previously, the Athenian schooling system of the fifth and fourth century B.C.E. (and perhaps by extension that of other Greek city-states) was informal, and one can only state that the wealthy continued their education with the purpose of acquiring rhetorical skill (a *conditio sine qua non* for succeeding in a competitive *polis* society) or philosophical knowledge (a point the leaders of philosophical schools such as Plato or Aristotle evidently are eager to stress). See Teles in Stobaeus *Florilegium* 3.234–235, ed. Meineke; Morgan 1998: 9–21.

33. See the tables in Morgan 1998: 308–313. For school papyri, see Cribiore 1996, 2001; Morgan 1998. For grammarians from the Roman times, see the edition of the *Grammatici Latini* by Keil and the fundamental studies by Kaster 1988 and Agusta-Boularot 1994.

34. Vössing 2002 for a thorough and convincing account.

35. Pomeroy 1984 (Greek antiquity) and Hemelrijk 1999 (Roman antiquity) on learned women; Vössing 2004 for a convincing account on girls' absence with grammarians.

36. Sluiter 1988.
37. Vössing 1997; Morgan 1998: 152–189 on grammar and the power of language.
38. Morgan 1998: 190–239; Cribiore 2001, 2007.
39. Watts 2006; Cribiore 2007 for vivid accounts on students' life; Laes and Strubbe 2008: 75–99. Papyri: *P. Oxy.* 18.2190; Cicero *Letters to Friends* 16.21; *Theodosian Code* 14.9.1 (Valentinian).
40. Vössing 1997.
41. Marrou 1964, vol. 1: 39–54; Tazelaar 1967; Kukofka 1993. Plutarch *Lycurgus* 16 (not illiterate). Cicero *Tusculan Disputations* 2.34; Libanius *Orations* 1.23 (Sparta in Roman times). Xenophon *Constitution of the Lacaedaemonians* 2.12.
42. Brunner 1957: 171–172 (stock phrase on discipline); Feucht 1986; Janssen and Janssen 1990. See Diodorus Siculus 1.70.2 on age twenty.
43. Hdt. 1.136; Xenophon *Cyropaedia* 1.2.2–12; Plutarch *Artaxerxes* 3.3. On Persian education see Dandamayev 1998.
44. Lemaire 1981; Mayer 1986; Tal Ilan 1996 (girls); Dijstra 2005. See 2 *Makk.* 4.12 (tensions); *jMeg.* 3.1 (480 schools); *bBaba Batra* 21a (*Jozua ben Gamala*); *Ab* 5.21 (age five or six to seven); *bBat* 21a (maximum twenty-five) *bQidd* 29a; Luke 2:46 and 4:16 (instruction and trade taught by father).
45. See Strabo 5.233, who states that Atellanae in Oscan were performed in Rome in the first century B.C.E. Oscan survived in Pompeii until 79 C.E. See de Simone 1980.
46. Green 1995. See Caesar *Gallic Wars* 6.13–14; Pliny *Natural History* 30.13; Strabo 4.1.5.
47. Pachomius *Praecepta* 139–140; de Vogüé 1971: 1355–1368; Orme 2006: 15–32.
48. Landau 1986.
49. Laes 2005.
50. Laes 2006b: 133–197 (170–174 on apprentice contracts); Frasca 1999 (educational value of the master); Invernizzi 2002 for a nuanced approach toward child labor; Laes 2008 (on child slaves at work).
51. Cicero *On the Republic* (*frag. incert.*) 5, p. 137 (ed. Ziegler). Bakke 2005: 19.

Chapter 6

1. Solon fragment 27 [West] (as quoted by Philo *de Opif. Mundi* 35.103–104); Clement of Alexandria *Stromata* 6.16.144; Censorinus *de Die Natali* (*On Birthdays*) 14.4, 7; cf. Psalms 90:10. The standard treatment of the theme for antiquity remains Boll 1913.
2. Cod. Reg. Paris. 1630, 114v. (Boissonade 1830: 454); cf. Boll 1913: 109, 112–118, 120. The difficulty in translating age-class terms into English and the danger of equating concepts of different age classes across societies cannot be overemphasized. *Boupais*, for example, might be translated more literally as bigger child than as teenager.
3. Hippocrates *Hebdomades* 5 (as quoted in Philo *de Opif. Mundi* 36.105).
4. Censorinus *de Die Natali* (*On Birthdays*) 14.3, Pollux *Onomasticon* 2.4, Scholiast on Hesiod *Works and Days* 447; Boissonade 1830: 455–456.
5. Ptolemy *Tetrabiblos* 4.10.204–207.

6. For further references, see especially Eyben 1972 together with his important paper, Eyben 1973.
7. Aristotle *Politics* 7.1336b.
8. Censorinus *de Die Natali (On Birthdays)* 14.2; cf. Servius *On the Aeneid* 5.295; Boll 1913: 106.
9. Diogenes Laertius 8.10; cf. Diodorus Siculus 10.9.5; Ovid *Metamorphoses* 15.199–236, Boll 1913: 102–103.
10. Isidorus *Origines* 11.2.1–8.
11. Isidorus *Origines* 5.38.5, 11.2.32.
12. Isidorus *Differentiae de Numeris* 2.19.74–76 (*Patr. Lat.* 83.81); *Num.* 7.31 (*Patr. Lat.* 83.185).
13. See, for comparison, e.g., Alonso-Núñez 1982.
14. Aeschines *In Timarchum* 49 (345 B.C.E.). Plato *Lysis* 207c describes two young friends unsure which of them is the older.
15. Ausonius *Epigrammata* 20, *Parentalia* 9 [Green].
16. *Digest of Justinian* 32.69.1 (Marcellus *Liber Singularis Responsorum*).
17. Servius, Commentary *on the Aeneid* 6.114; Hesiod, fragment 321 [MW] (cf. Parkin 2003: 413); Plutarch *Lycurgus* 21.2; Aristotle *Rhetoric* 2.12–14.1388b-90b; Horace *Ars Poetica* 169–176.
18. van Gennep 1909.
19. See, for comparison, Aristophanes *Lysistrata* 638–648. A very good introduction to Athenian rites of passage, male and female, is provided by Garland 1990: chap. 4.
20. The classic account is Saller and Shaw 1984.
21. *Meditations* 11.34.
22. Regarding ancient demography the bibliography is becoming substantial. For what follows reference may usefully be made to Parkin 1992; Scheidel 2001a.
23. Bagnall and Frier 1994; Scheidel 2001b.
24. See especially Saller 1994.
25. Parkin 1992: 61–62.
26. Brunt 1971: 558–566 (appendix 9) remains the best overview in English of the Augustan marriage legislation.
27. For example, Golden 1988.
28. See, for comparison, Bradley 1991: chapter 5 on child labor in the Roman world.
29. Cicero *On Old Age* 10.33; note too the reference to four ages of life.
30. *Corpus Inscriptionum Latinarum* 3.3572.
31. See figure 6.1. Images of this (and much more *passim.*) may be conveniently found in Neils and Oakley 2003: 162, 300–301 (cat. no. 115).
32. Pliny *Natural History* 7.13.57; Cicero *Brutus* 211; Tacitus *Dialogue on Oratory* 28; Dixon 2007.
33. Aristotle *History of Animals* 7.588a8; Macrobius *Saturnalia* 1.16.36; Plutarch *Roman Questions* 102, 288c. The Augustan legislation on childbearing and the number of living children, referred to earlier, also recognizes high infant mortality rates.
34. On childhood diseases in antiquity see (e.g.) Hummel 1999 and Bradley 2005.
35. Sallares 2002.

36. On infant mortality levels from comparative evidence, see, e.g., Wrigley and Schofield 1981; Woods 1993.

37. Étienne 1976.

38. Plutarch *Life of Numa* 12.2 (cf. *Frag. Vat.* 321 for the verb *sublugere*, "to mourn a little").

39. Preston, McDaniel, and Grushka 1993, tables based on data for freed American slaves in the late nineteenth century who migrated to Liberia; Woods 2007.

40. I first explored these possibilities in Parkin 1992.

41. Democritus 68 B 275 [Diels-Kranz], quoted in Garland 1990: 106.

Chapter 7

1. Aristotle *Politics* 1253a and b.

2. Patterson 1998: 177. On the development of the Athenian state, Ober 1989; Manville 1990; Raaflaub, Ober, and Wallace 2007.

3. Lambert 1993.

4. Aristotle *Constitution of the Athenians* 2 and 5; Plutarch *Solon* 15.3 and 4, 23.2.

5. Patterson 1998: 108; Harrison 1968: 1; Aristotle *Politics* 1253 b.

6. Patterson 1998: 108–114; Cox 1998: 180.

7. Aristotle *Constitution of the Athenians* 26.3; Lacey 1980: 105. See Demosthenes 59.52 and 84 on penalties for fraudulent claims of citizenship.

8. Patterson 1998: 114–125; Cohen 1991.

9. Pluarch *Solon* 23.1; Patterson 1998: 118, 128, 171.

10. Demosthenes 59.85–87.

11. Golden 1979: 25–38; Pomeroy 1997: 79–82; Demosthenes 57.54.

12. Plutarch *Solon* 21.2. A daughter's dowry was, in effect, her inheritance—that is, her share of the property of her natal *oikos*, which she received before the death of her *kyrios*.

13. Goody 1976: 92 conjectures that about twenty-one percent of couples produced only daughters, and about seventeen percent were childless.

14. Lacey 1980: 142; Demosthenes 46.20, 41.3.

15. The *anchisteia* extended only as far as the children of first cousins, and priority was given to the father's kin (the agnates) over the mother's. Cox 1998: 97–99. Demosthenes 43.54.

16. Demosthenes 43.75; Aristotle *Constitution of the Athenians* 56.6 and 7; Thucydides 2.46.1; Aeschines 3.154, 3.258; Plutarch *Aristeides* 27.4.

17. Plutarch *Solon* 22.1. See Patterson 1990 and Ogden 1996 on bastards.

18. The ratio of helots to Spartans may have been seven to one; Pomeroy 1997: 48 suggests a ratio of twenty to one. See Figueira 1986 on population figures. Xenophon *Constitution of the Lacedemonians* 7.2; Plutarch *Lycurgus* 24.2.

19. MacDowell 1986: 2, 8–22. See Herodotus 7.104.4–5 on the role of law in Sparta; Xenophon *Lacedemonians* 1.2; Plutarch *Lycurgus* 5.2.

20. Plutarch *Lycurgus* 8.3 and 4. Hodkinson 1986 on Spartiate land tenure. Plutarch *Moralia* 239E.

21. Plutarch *Lycurgus* 15.8. Pomeroy 1997: 49 conjectures that girls were exempt from state inspection at birth, but see Xenophon *Lacedemonians* 1.3 and 4; Plutarch *Lycurgus* 14.2 for Spartan ideals of female eugenics.
22. Xenophon *Lacedemonians* 2.1–11 and 6.1; Plutarch *Lycurgus* 16.4–7, 17.1.
23. Xenophon *Lacedemonians* 3.3; Kennell 1995: 132–133.
24. Plutarch *Lycurgus* 14.3, *Moralia* 240F, 241A and B; Patterson 1998: 78.
25. Lendon 1997: 119–123.
26. Xenophon *Lacedemonians* 5 and 9.4–6; Plutarch *Lycurgus* 10 and 12; Aristotle *Politics* 1271 a 26–37; 1272 a 13–15. Pomeroy 1997: 57; Kennell 1995: 130.
27. Aristotle *Politics* 1271 a.
28. Xenophon *Lacedemonians* 1.5, 6; Plutarch *Lycurgus* 15.1–5, 17.1, 18.4.
29. Aristotle *Politics* 1270 b; Plutarch *Lycurgus* 15.7 and 8; Xenophon *Lacedemonians* 1.7 and 8.
30. Plutarch *Lycurgus* 14.1; Aristotle *Politics* 1269 b–1270 a. Cartledge 1981; Pomeroy 2002; Hodkinson 1986: 394–404; also Hodkinson 1989, 2004.
31. Kennell 1995: 134. Aristotle *Politics* 1270 a; see Figueira 1986 and Hodkinson 1989 on the population decline.
32. Plutarch *Solon* 22.2 comments that Solon needed to find occupations for Athenian citizens, whereas Lycurgus freed the Spartans of labor by repressing the helots but required the Spartans to then concentrate on war.
33. Philo *On Special Laws* 3.4.22 on the marriage of half-siblings; Pomeroy 1997: 54.
34. Patterson 1998: 108–114; Treggiari 1991a: 32, 33. For definitions of *familia* see *Digest of Justinian* 50.16.195 (Ulpian); Saller 1984.
35. *Digest of Justinian* 25.3.4 (Paulus); Radin 1924; Harris 1994; Corbier 2001. Gaius *Institutes* 1.55; Dionysius of Halicarnassus *Roman Antiquities* 2.26.10. *Digest of Justinian* 48.9.5. See also Eyben 1991 and Saller 1991.
36. Gardner 1998: 220–233.
37. Severy 2003: 60.
38. For texts, see Riccobono 1945; Treggiari 1991a: 60–80.
39. Hopkins 1965; Garnsey 1991; Riddle 1992.
40. Ulpian *Tituli* 14.1, 16, 17.1; Gaius *Institutes* 2.111 and 286.
41. Pliny *Letters* 2.13.8, 7.16.2, 10.2.1; *Digest of Justinian* 4.4.2 (Ulpian), 27.1.2 (Modestinus), 38.1.37 (Paulus); Gaius *Institutes* 1.145 and 194; Ulpian *Tituli* 29.3; Gellius *Attic Nights* 2.15.4; Tacitus *Annals* 15.19.
42. Wallace-Hadrill 1981: 58–62; Dixon 1988: 86.
43. Dixon 1988: 89.
44. Tacitus *Annals* 3.25.
45. *Digest of Justinian* 23.2.23 (Celsus), 23.2.43 (Ulpian), 23.2.44 (Paulus); Ulpian *Tituli* 13.1 and 2; Cassius Dio *History of Rome* 54.16. Rawson 2003: 117.
46. Paulus *Opinions* 2.26.1, 4, 6, 7, 8, 11, 14, and 16. *Digest of Justinian* 48.5.15 and 26 (Ulpian). Tacitus *Annals* 3.24; Suetonius *Augustus* 65. See Severy 2003: 180–184.
47. Pliny *Letters* 2.13.8, 7.16.2, 8.10 and 11, 10.2.1, 10.94.2.
48. Dixon 1988: 86; Severy 2003: 55, 56.
49. On *pietas*, Saller 1994: 105–114. See also Kleiner 1978; Severy 2003: 104–112; Rawson 2001: 21.

50. Rawson 2001: 23; Kleiner 1977: 177–179.

51. On the coinage, Mattingly and Sydenham 1923: vol. 1: 90, #350; vol. 2: 278, #461; 250, #93; 251, #105; 478, #1041; vol. 3: 271, #709; Rawson 1991: 24. On the Arch at Beneventum: Currie 1996; Kleiner 1992: 224–229.

Chapter 8

I thank Katariina Mustakallio and the editors of this volume for their insightful comments on the present chapter and Niilo Helander Foundation for financial support.

1. See, for example, Padilla 1999; Dillon 2002; Brulé 1987, all with further references.

2. Golden 1990, 2003.

3. Most importantly, Rawson 2003: 312–339; Mantle 2002: 85–106; Wiedemann 1989: 176–208; Néraudau 1984: 223–250.

4. Horn 2005 and Bakke 2005. See also the papers in Wood 1994 and Burrus 2005.

5. On socialization, see Handel 2006. The function of religion as a socializing agent is, however, seldom taken up in the modern childhood sociology.

6. Neils 2003: 143–144; Pomeroy 1997: 68–70; Hänninen 2005: 55–58; Rawson 2003: 108–111.

7. Pomeroy 1997: 76–81. Later in the Hellenistic period (or outside Athens) girls were also included, and the children could be older, maybe three. See also Lambert 1993.

8. Tertullian *On Idolatry* 16.1–2; Bakke 2005: 230–246; Wiedemann 1989: 104, 190–192; Jensen 2005: 130–135; Yarborough 1993. In the Jewish tradition, girls were named immediately after birth, boys on the eighth day, when they were circumcised (if they were—not all Hellenistic Jews practiced circumcision).

9. Augustine *City of God* 7.2 and 4.11; see also Hänninen 2005: 55–57; Néraudau 1984: 224–226.

10. Neils 2003: 143–144; Ham 1999: 206; Horn 2005: 99.

11. Pliny *Natural History* 30.47 and 37.12. Infants also had amulets in the shape of a phallus (*facinum*). For amulets and *bulla* in the Roman tradition, see Rawson 2003: 110–111, 144–155, and Hänninen 2005: 57.

12. Pseudo-Athanasius, *Homily on Virginity* chap. 95, as translated in Frankfurter 2005: 258.

13. Horn 2005; Frankfurter 2005: 258, 261, 280 (for quotation and Chrysostom).

14. It is unclear if girls used the *tefillim*. The rite of bar mitzvah at the age of thirteen was not developed until the late Middle Ages (Mayer 1986: 365).

15. Bowes 2005:196–199; Trout 2005: 178; for Gregory, see Frankfurter 2005: 277. See also Theodoret of Cyrrhus, who was cured as a child when he wore a belt of Peter the Hermit (*Religious History* 9.15).

16. See van Straten 1994: 248–265; Dillon 2002: 30–35.

17. Van Straten 1994; Golden 1990: 30–32, 138; Pomeroy 1997: 69–70.

18. Ovid *Fasti* 2.650–654. See also Tibullus 1.10.23–4. Further in Mantle 2002: 100–101.

19. Rawson 2003: 270; Mantle 2002: 101–102, 106; Wiedemann 1989: 181; Néraudau 1984: 226–228.
20. Oakley 2003: 163–167, 188–189; Rawson 2003: 334–339; Mustakallio 2005: esp. 188–189.
21. Golden 1989: 30; Mantle 2002: 99–100; Néraudau 1984: 236–238 (esp. on obscenities).
22. Rawson 2003: 134–135.
23. Phratries, see Golden 1990: 25–30 and Lambert 1993: 140. Sacrifices and dedications: Golden 1990: 54, 78; Dillon 2002: 20; Wiedemann 1989: 153; Rawson 2003: 144–145, 323; Horn 2005: 100–103 (especially for Dionysus and toys). See also Neils 2003: 148–149 for Aiora, expiation ritual connected to puberty, with girls swinging.
24. Tertullian *On Idolatry* 16.1–2.
25. Mayer 1986: 381–389 and Yarborough 1993: 41–45.
26. See chapter 2 in this volume, see also Wiedemann 1989: 193–200; Petersen 1994: 33–36. Clark 1994: 12–21; Gould 1994: 43–48; Nelson 1994: 100–103; Meens 1994: 53, 61–63.
27. Dillon 2002: 37–41, 57–60; Brulé 1987: 79–98.
28. Dillon 2002: 57–60; Mikalson 1998: 199–200, 260, 293.
29. Golden 1990: 78–79; Mikalson 1998: 40; Sourvinou-Inwood 1988.
30. *Inscriptiones Graecae* II² 1034; Brulé 1987: 99–105; Mikalson 1998: 256–258.
31. Golden 1990: 46 and 48 (quote); Dillon 2002: 57, 60–63, 133.
32. Neils 2003: 158.
33. Neils 2003: 145–147; Ham 1999: 213.
34. Golden 1990: 43–44; Dillon 2002: 89.
35. Dillon 2002: 53–63, 68–69; Neils 2003: 142; Golden 1990: 41.
36. Wiedemann 1989: 183–184; 99–100. Rawson 2003: 272–274, 315; Mantle 2002: 85, 91–96.
37. Mantle 2002: 99; Rawson 2003: 324, 339.
38. Mantle 2002: 93–97; Wiedemann 1989: 184; Néraudau 1984: 229–231.
39. Mustakallio 2008.
40. Kyle 2006: 116–120, 138–139, 143, 148, 158, 161 for boys, 217–218 for girls; Dillon 2002: 131; Golden 1990: 65–70.
41. Kyle 2006: 332–333; Wiedemann 1989: 182–183; Rawson 2003: 316, 320–321, 327; Néraudau 1984: 234–236. Girls were no longer attending the Capitoline games in the third century CE.
42. Golden 1990: 65–66, 67 (quote), 76; Dillon 2002: 66–68, 132, 140. For children and mysteries of Dionysus, see Lambrechts 1957: 329–332.
43. Cassius Dio 59.7.1; Livy 27.37; Rawson 2003: 315–317, 324; Mantle 2002: 90, 99; Mustakallio 2005: 183. See also Tacitus *Histories* 4.53: When the temple of Jupiter was reconsecrated in 70 C.E., boys and girls with both parents alive took part in the purification by sprinkling water.
44. Rawson 2003: 315–320; Mantle 2002: 86–90.
45. Mikalson 1998: 293, 322.
46. Wiedemann 1989: 186–188; Bakke 2005: 251–256; Theodore of Cyrrhus *Historia Ecclesiastica* 4.19 (on liturgical dance among the Arians in Alexandria); see also

Horn 2005: 106. Even if there were choirs of dedicated virgins (of any age), there are no mention of girls' choirs.

47. Vuolanto 2008: 118–122, cf. for example, Clark 1994: 26.

48. Clark 1981: esp. 245–249; de Jong 1996: 16–55; Clark 1994: 1–2, 16. The minimum age for children to enter monastic communities varied, but in some exceptional cases even three-year-olds were included. For the monastic education, Kalogeras 2005 and Guerreau-Jalabert 2000: esp. 275–277.

49. Golden 1990: 44–46.

50. Dillon 2002: 127–130, 159–160, 190–191; at Thesmophoria, a women-only festival, no girls were included, except for the little children too young to be left at home (Dillon 2002: 118–122, cf. Golden 1990: 76–77). It seems that there were no children initiated into Eleusian mysteries (Dillon 2002: 92–93; cf. Golden 1990: 44).

51. Néraudau 1984: 246–249; Lambrechts 1957: esp. 329–332; Suetonius *Augustus* 31.4; Rawson 2003: 275, 312, 319.

52. Paulinus *Life of Ambrosius* 2.4; Socrates *Ecclesiastical History* 1.15 (on Athanasius); see also *Apostolic Constitutions* 2.57; Horn 2005: 110–111, 114; Jensen 2005: 130–135. Bakke 2005: 246–251.

53. Gregory of Tours *History of the Franks* 10.1; Bakke 2005: 255–257; Clark 1994: 18–19, 27; see also Theodoret of Cyrrhus on himself and his parents: *Religious History* 9.14–15, 13.16–18.

54. Nelson 1994: 97–99; also chapter 2 in this volume.

55. Golden 1990: 10–11, 14; Neils 2003: 158; Néraudau 1984: 238–240. For insightful children in Roman historical writing, see Wiedemann 1989: 177–178. See also, for example, Virgil *Aeneid* 7.116–127 and Tibullus 1.3.11–12. For prodigious children, see Dasen 2005, 66–70.

56. *The Rule of Benedict* chapter 3; Paulinus *Life of Ambrosius* 6; Nelson 1994: 88. See also *Acts of Peter* 11, 15. Sleeping with martyrs: Bowes 2005: 198. For the divine insight of children in the New Testament, see Gundry-Volf 2001: 47, 59.

57. See the critique in Wiedemann 1989: 180–181; Johnston 2001: 106–107; Golden 1990: 49, all with further references.

58. Golden 1990: 44 (quote) and 85; Wiedemann 1989: 176–180, 186: "the child may serve as an acolyte just because he is not an adult, he is not really there."

59. See also Mantle 2002: 103.

60. Vuolanto 2008: esp. 189–206.

61. See Brown 1991 and Rives 1994. See, however, Moscati 1996 (with further, mainly Italian, scholarship), who claims the children had died before their offering as votive gifts to the gods. This interpretation would, of course, fit better with our modern understanding of parental attachment and belonging. (See also Golden 2003: 24 for the not necessarily negative correlation between the sacrifice of a child and attachment for it.)

62. Golden 2003: 10, 14; see also Néraudau 1984: 135.

63. Also Golden 1990: 46–48.

64. Johnston 2001: 108, 114; Rawson 2003: 315; Gould 1994: 40–41; Wiedemann 1989: 177 on the powerlessness of children. For Athens, see, for example, Golden 1990: 30, on the symbolism of boys with both parents living in the Athenian public cults.

65. Golden 1990: 85; Rawson 2003: 343; Wiedemann 1989: 178–179; Néraudau 1984: 241–242.
66. See, for comparison, Clark 1994: 20, who claims that the difference between the pre-Christian and Christian views of children lies in the fact that "the distinctive quality of children in the Greco-Roman culture was not innocence but unreason."
67. Jensen 2005: 130–131 (on Cyprian); Guroian 2001 (esp. on Chrysostom); Gould 1994: 41–44.
68. Stortz 2001 and Clark 1994: 23–25 on Augustine. For the later authors, see Nelson 1994: 86–87; Meens 1994: 65; de Jong 1996: 40 for girl oblates as "an institution-alized form of cultic purity." See also Wiedemann 1989: 180 claiming that Isidore derives the purity of children from their beardlessness—however, the text makes it clear that the main reason is the essential purity of children: "Puer a puritate vocatus, quia purus est, et necdum lanuginem floremque genarum habens ... Pro obsequio et fidei puritate" (Isidore *Etymologies* 11.2.10–11).
69. Rawson 2003: 270.
70. Golden 1990: 41.
71. Compare Bakke 2005: 256–257 on children and Christian practices. Quote from Neils 2003: 159, paraphrasing Melanippe.
72. Theodoret of Cyrrhus *Ecclesiastical History* 4.13.

Chapter 9

1. For example, Dasen 2004; Golden 1990; Harlow and Laurence 2002; Houby-Neilson 2000; Rawson 1986a, 1991a.
2. Galen 637K.
3. van der Eijk, Horstmanshoff, and Schrijvers 2005: 10–11.
4. Hippocrates *On the Nature of the Child* 23–24; Pormann 1999: 15–20.
5. Celsus *On Medicine* 5.26.6; Hippocrates *Airs, Waters, Places*.
6. Throughout this chapter, *humoral pathology* is used to refer to fluids in the body, even if not all writers used this terminology in antiquity.
7. For example, Hippocrates *On the Nature of Man* 2–8, *Fleshes* 1–3.
8. Vitruvius *Ten Books on Architecture* 5.4.1–2.
9. Vegetius *Epitome of Military Science* 1.22.
10. Galen *On Semen* 1.
11. Soranus *Gynaecology* 1.60–61; King 1990, 1998: 134–135.
12. Hippocrates *On the Nature of the Child* 13.1–3; Soranus *Gynaecology* 1.60; Galen *On Semen* 1.4.28; *On the Formation of the Fetus* 1.6 (V 653 K).
13. Soranus *Gynaecology* 1.61.
14. Soranus *Gynaecology* 1.36, 2.61, compare 1.61.
15. I am grateful to Dr. Jeremy Worthen for bringing this medieval Aristotelian debate to my attention. Tertullian *Apology* 37; Clark 1996: 212–223; 2005: 218. See Kapparis 2002 on abortion in general.
16. Soranus *Gynaecology* 1.36.
17. Aristotle *Politics* 1335 b 24, *History of Animals, Generation of Animals*; Caelius Aurelianus *Gynaecologyaecia*; Damastes [Parker 1999: 515–517]; Diocles [van der

Eijk, et al. 2005]; Hippocrates *On Food* 42, *On Generation, On the Nature of the Child*; Galen *On Semen* 1 and 2; Soranus *Gynaecology* 1.43.

18. Galen *On Semen* 1.9.12; Bertier 1996: 2162.
19. Pormann 1999: 15–20.
20. King 1990: 16.
21. Hippocrates *Aphorisms* 5.42.
22. Hippocrates *Nature of a Child* 22–23, *On Generation* 9–10; Galen *On Semen*. 1.9.11; Soranus *Gynaecology* 1.46–54.
23. This was complicated by several dating systems based on lunar months being used in Greece at one time, and, even with the development of the Julian calendar (46/45 B.C.E.), it is likely that people carried on using lunar months—see Porter 1999; Hanson 1987: 599; Aristotle *History of Animals* 7.4 584 b 12–14.
24. Soranus *Gynaecology* 1.1–4.
25. Soranus *Gynaecology* 2.2, on the midwives' chair see 2.3; Demand 1995: 275–283.
26. Soranus *Gynaecology* 4.1, 4.4; Hippocrates *Aphorisms* 5.37–38.
27. Soranus *Gynaecology* 1.59. See also Gourevitch 1996, 2004; Hanson 1994.
28. Hippocrates *Diseases of Women* 1.70; Soranus *Gynaecology* 4.1–16.
29. Celsus *On Medicine* 5.25.13–14.
30. Deyts 2004; Gourevitch 1989.
31. For example, Paul of Aegina *Pragmetia* in Pormann 2004: 95–97; Paul of Aegina in Pormann 1999: 22; Rufus of Ephesus in Pormann 1999: 22; Soranus *Gynaecology* 2.17–29.
32. Soranus *Gynaecology* 2.19, 24–27.
33. Soranus *Gynaecology* 2.46–48.
34. Soranus *Gynaecology*. 2.42–45; Pormann 1999: 49–50.
35. Bertier 1996: 2173, 2175–2176; Soranus *Gynaecology* 2.42–44.
36. Bertier 1996: 2173–2175; Soranus *Gynaecology* 2.48.
37. Pormann 2004: 104.
38. Bertier 1996: 2166. Hippocrates *Aphorisms* 1.14.
39. Pormann 1999: 57. The same idea is found in Galen 7.258 K; Oribasius Lib 131, 18; Bertier 1996: 2164–2165.
40. Bertier 1996: 2168.
41. Hippocrates *Aphorisms* 3.28. See also Bertier 1990; Bonet 1998; Bradley 2005.
42. Bertier 1996: 2164.
43. Hippocrates *Aphorisms* 3.24–27; see Pormann 2004: 104 on later writers.
44. Celsus *On Medicine* 2.1.17; Hippocrates *Aphorisms* 3.18.
45. Hippocrates *Aphorisms* 3.12.
46. Hippocrates *On Dentition, Aphorisms* 3.25; Galen 12, 874 K; Soranus *Gynaecology* 2.49; compare Oribasius 148.18–150; Paul of Aegina in Pormann 1999: 25–26; Dioscorides 2.19; Rufus of Ephesus in Pormann 1999: 62–63.
47. Pormann 1999: 60.
48. Pormann 1999: 31–32.
49. Soranus *Gynaecology* 2.55.
50. Pormann 1999: 34–36; Dioscorides 2.135.2.
51. Soranus *Gynaecology* 2.50–56; Paul of Aegina in Pormann 1999: 44–45; Paul of Aegina in Pormann 1999: 39–40.

52. Hippocrates *Aphorisms* 1.13.
53. Celsus *On Medicine* 2.10.3.
54. Hippocrates *On the Nature of Man* 12.
55. Hippocrates *Aphorisms* 5.212; *On the Sacred Disease* 11–12.
56. Hippocrates *Prognosis* 24.
57. Celsus *On Medicine* 3.7, 1 B-C.
58. Pormann 1999: 58–59.
59. Bertier 1996: 2209–2211.
60. Hippocrates *On Regimen* 6.
61. Hippocrates *Epidemics* 3.15; Hippocrates *Airs, Waters, Places* 10; Hippocrates *Epidemics* 3.2.
62. Plato *Timaeus* 91a-d.
63. King 1998: 205–246.
64. Horden 1993.
65. Baker and Francis (n.d.).
66. See Duncan-Jones 1996; Leven 1991, 1995.
67. Thucydides 2.51.
68. Thucydides 2.51; Paul the Deacon 6.5 mentioned in Jackson 1988: 175.
69. Galen K. 10.360–363, 19.17–18.
70. See Duncan-Jones 1996 for a discussion of the wider impact of the Antonine plague with reference to Roman Egypt.
71. See Flemming 2000 for a full discussion on this topic.
72. Drabkin 1944; Nutton 1995:19–22, 44–47.
73. Edelstein and Edelstein 1945.
74. Horstmanshoff 1995; Xenophon *Hellenica* 3.1.3. A man suffering from an eye disease was seen leaving a doctor's home.
75. Celsus *On Medicine* Proemium 65.
76. Baker 2004: chapter 6.
77. Harig 1971: 185–187; Jackson 1988: 65.
78. Zienkiewicz 1986: 223.
79. Horden 2006: 48–50; Miller 1997; van Minnen 1995.
80. *Bimaristans* ("houses of the ill") appear in the Islamic world in the ninth and tenth centuries, the first structures to be used in a similar fashion to a hospital—see Pormann and Savage-Smith 2007: 96–101.
81. Montserrat 2005: 230–238.
82. Nutton 1995: 74–75.

Chapter 10

1. For a discussion of this concept see Mattingly 2004 with bibliography.
2. For recent bibliography on the early Middle Ages see Halsall 2007; Innes 2007; Smith 2005; Wickham 2005, 2009.
3. Barclay 1997: 69.
4. Noy 2000: 255 *passim.*; on ethnic origin: 255–256; on Roman state and geographical origins: 258; use of Semitic names: 262.
5. Rajak 2001: 388; Goodman 2007: 286–317 defines the distinctions.

6. Schwartz 2001: 132–136, 148–149.

7. Lewis, Yadin, and Greenfield 1989; Wasserstein 1989; Cotton 1993, 1994.

8. Cotton 1993: 100.

9. See Rajak 2001: 535–557; Meyers 1992: 90–91.

10. Noy 2007: 84–87 for a statistical analysis that demonstrates the stages of Jewish childhood coincided with those found in Roman childhood.

11. Alston 2005; Huebner 2007; Remijsen and Clarysse 2008.

12. Bagnall and Frier 1994.

13. For a brief review of the ancient material see Remijsen and Clarysse 2008: 54–56 and their references. For a contrary reading of the evidence see Huebner 2007.

14. See *P.Berl.Leihg.* III.52B, AD 147; *P.Ryl.* II.111, AD 161, both from Bagnall and Frier 1994.

15. For an expanded version of Tryphon's details, relevant references, and other examples see Alston 2005: 141, 145–147.

16. *P. Mich.* 8.464 cited in Bagnall and Cribiore 2006: 79–80.

17. Tacitus *Germania* 7, 13–15, 18–20.

18. For current bibliography see note 2 and their references.

19. On paternal power in late antiquity: Arjava 1998: 147–165; on the early Christian family in general see Nathan 2000; Clark 1993; on asceticism see Brown 1988; Hunter 2007. Augustine *On the Good of Marriage.*

20. King 1972: 222–250; Murray 1983; Smith 2005: 83–87, 11–14, and her references.

21. Evans Grubbs 1995; Bitel 2002; Wemple 1981.

22. Gregory of Tours *Ten Books of History*: Guntram 4.25; Charibert 4.26; Chilperic 4.27. On marriage prohibitions see Herlihy 1995: 96–109; de Jong 1998: 107–140. On problems with understanding the Merovingian family see Wood 2003.

23. There is a growing bibliography on women and gender in the early Middle Ages; see Nelson 2002, Stafford and Mulder-Bakker 2001; Halsall 2004; Coon 1997: 120–141.

24. On children: Alexandre-Bidon and Lett 1995; Shahar 1990; Herlihy 1995: 215–243.

25. Halsall 1996. Smith 2005: 120.

26. King 1972; Herlihy 1995: 222–224; an English translation of the Visigothic law codes can be found at http://libro.uca.edu/vcode/visigoths.htm.

27. On church and children: Bakke 2005; Wood 1994; Alexandre-Bidon and Lett 1995. On exposure and abandonment: Alexandre-Bidon and Lett 1995: 15–18; Boswell 1988: 139–227.

28. On infant tantrums and original sin see Augustine *Confessions* 1.8. For competing ideas of childhood see Alexandre-Bidon and Lett 1995: 8–9; Bakke 2005.

29. See *Etymologies* 9.1–2.

30. For an excellent recent translation and introduction to Isidore's *Etymologies* see Barney, et al. 2006. For age systems see *Etymologies* 11.2, and see chapter 6 in this volume for other age systems of the ancient world.

31. Gil'adi 1992: 4, 19–34.

32. Gil'adi 1992: 5, 11–12, 45–60, 69–93; Rosenthal 1941.

33. Fully discussed by Stray 1998.

34. See, for example, Stray 1992: 25, which is suggestive that normative commencement of Latin was at age seven in the Edwardian period.

BIBLIOGRAPHY

Agusta-Boularot, S. 1994. "Les références épigraphiques aux grammatici et gramma-tikoiv de l'empire romain (Ier s. av. J.-C.—IV e s. ap. J.-C.)." *Mélanges de l'Ecole Française de Rome. Antiquité* 106 (2): 653–746.

Alexandre-Bidon, D., and D. Lett. 1995. *Children in the Middle Ages fifth–fifteenth centuries*. Notre Dame, IN: University of Notre Dame Press.

Allison, P. M. 2004a. *Pompeian households: An analysis of the material culture*. Berke-ley: Cotsen Institute of Archaeology, University of California, Los Angeles.

Allison, P. M. 2004b. *Pompeian households* online companion, http://www.stoa.org/pompeianhouseholds.

Allison, P. M. 2006. *The insula of the Menander at Pompeii*. Vol. 3, *The finds, a con-textual study*. Oxford: Oxford University Press.

Alonso-Núñez, J. M. 1982. *The ages of Rome*. Amsterdam: Gieben.

Alston, R. 2005. "Searching for the Romano-Egyptian family." In *The Roman family in the Empire: Rome, Italy, and beyond*, ed. M. George, 129–157. Oxford: Oxford University Press.

Andreau, J., and Bruhns, H. 1990. *Parenté et stratégies familiales dans l'antiquité Romaine*. Rome: École Française de Rome.

Ariès, P. 1962. *Centuries of childhood*. Harmondsworth, UK: Penguin. (Orig. pub. 1960 as *L'Enfant et la vie familial sous l'Ancien Régime*. Paris: Librarie Plon.)

Arjava, A. 1996. *Women and the law in late antiquity*. Oxford: Clarendon Press.

Arjava, A. 1998. "Paternal power in late antiquity." *Journal of Roman Studies* 88:147–165.

Arjava, A. 2001. "The survival of Roman family law after the barbarian settlements." In *Law, society, and authority in late antiquity*, ed. Ralph W. Mathisen. Oxford and New York: Oxford University Press.

Ault, B. A., and L. Nevett, eds. 2005. *Ancient Greek houses and households*. Philadel-phia: University of Pennsylvania Press.

Bagnall, R., and R. Cribiore. 2008. *Women's letters from ancient Egypt 300 BC–AD 800*. Ann Arbor: University of Michigan Press.

Bagnall, R., and B. Frier. 1994. *The demography of Roman Egypt*. Cambridge: Cambridge University Press.

Baker, P. 2004. *Medical care for the Roman army on the Rhine, Danube, and British frontiers from the first through third centuries AD*. British Archaeological Reports International Series 1286. Oxford: Archeopress.

Baker, P., and S. Francis. n.d. "Incomplete adults: The mentally impaired in classical antiquity." Paper given at the 2007 Classical Association of South Africa Annual Conference, Cape Town.

Bakke, O. M. 2005. *When children became people: The birth of childhood in early Christianity*. Minneapolis, MN: Fortress Press.

Balch, D., and C. Osiek, eds. *Early Christian families in context: A cross-disciplinary dialogue*. Chicago: Erdmans.

Bannon, C. 1997. *The brothers of Romulus*. Princeton, NJ: Princeton University Press.

Barclay, J.M.G. 1997. "The family as the bearer of religion in Judaism and early Christianity." In *Constructing early Christian families*, ed. H. Moxnes, 66–80. London: Routledge.

Barney, S. A., W. J. Lewis, J. A. Beach, and O. Berghof. 2006. *The Etymologies of Isidore of Seville*. Cambridge: Cambridge University Press.

Baxter, J. E. 2005. *The archaeology of childhood: Children, gender, and material culture*. Walnut Creek, CA: Altamira Press.

Beard, M. 1980. "The sexual status of vestal virgins." *Journal of Roman Studies* 70:12–27.

Beard, M. 1995. "Re-reading (vestal) virginity." In *Women in antiquity: New assessments*, ed. R. Hawley and B. Levick, 166–177. London: Routledge.

Beard, M., J. North, and S. Price. 1998. *Religions of Rome*. Vol. 1, *A history*. Cambridge: Cambridge University Press.

Bellmore, J., and B. Rawson. 1990. "Alumni: The Italian evidence." *Zeitschrift für Papyrologie und Epigraphik* 83:1–19.

Bernstein, F. 1988. "Pompeian women and the *programmata*." In *Studia Pompeiana et Classica in Honor of Wilhelmina F. Jashemski*, ed. R. I. Curtis, 1–17. New Rochelle, NY: A. D. Caratzas.

Bertier, J. 1990. "Enfants malades et maladies des enfants dans le Corpus Hippocratique." In *La maladie et les maladies dans la Collection Hippocratique, Actes du VI e colloque international Hippocratique. Québec, du 28 septembre au 3 octobre 1987*, ed. P. Potter, G. Maloney, and J. Dessautels. Québec: Eds du Sphinx.

Bertier, J. 1996. "La médecine des enfants à l'époque impériale." *Aufsteig und Niedergang der Römischen Welt: II: Principate* 37 (3): 2147–2227.

Bitel, L. M. 2002. *Women in early medieval Europe 400–1000*. Cambridge: Cambridge University Press.

Biundo, R. 1996. "I Rogatores nei Programmata Elettorali Pompeiani." *Cahiers Glotz* 7:179–188.

Biundo, R. 2003. "La Propaganda Elettoral a Pompei: La Funzione e il Valore dei *Programmata* nell'Organizzazione nella Campagna." *Athenaeum* 91:53–116.

Blagg, T.F.C., and M. Millett. 1990. *The early Roman Empire in the West*. Oxford: Oxbow.

Blundell, S. 1995. *Women in ancient Greece*. London: British Museum Press.

Boissonade, J. F. 1830. ANEKΔOTA: *Anecdota Graeca e codicibus regiis*. Vol. 2. Paris: in Regio Typographeo.

Boll, F. 1913. "Die Lebensalter. Ein Beitrag zur antiken Ethologie und zur Geschichte der Zahlen." *Neue Jahrbücher für das klassische Altertum* 31:89–145. Reprinted in F. Boll, *Kleine Schriften zur Sternkunde des Altertums*, ed. V. Stegemann, 156–224. Leipzig: Koehler & Amelang, 1950.

Bonet, V. 1998. "Les maladies des enfants et leur traitement d'après le témoignage de Pline l'Ancien." In *Maladie et maladies dans les textes latins antiques et médiévaux. Actes du Ve colloque international "Textes médicaux latins" Bruxelles, 4–6 Septembre 1995 (Latomus 242)*, ed. C. Deroux. Brussels, Belgium: Société d'Études Latines de Bruxelles.

Bonner, S. 1977. *Education in ancient Rome*. London: Methuen & Co.

Booth, A. 1979. "Elementary and secondary education in the Roman Empire." *Florilegium* 1:1–14.

Booth, A. 1981. "Some suspect schoolmasters." *Florilegium* 3:1–20.

Boswell, J. 1988. *Kindness of strangers*. Harmondsworth, UK: Penguin.

Bowes, K. 2005. "Personal devotions and private chapels." In *Late ancient Christianity*. Vol. 2, *A people's history of Christianity*, ed. V. Burrus, 188–210. Minneapolis, MN: Augsburg Fortress Press.

Bradley, K. 1986. "Wet-nursing at Rome: A study in social relations." In *The family in ancient Rome: New perspectives*, ed. Beryl Rawson, 201–229. New York: Cornell University Press.

Bradley, K. 1991. *Discovering the Roman family*. Oxford: Oxford University Press.

Bradley, K. 1994. "The nurse and the child at Rome: Duty, affect, and socialization." *Thamyris* 1 (2): 137–56.

Bradley, K. 2005. "The Roman child in sickness and in health." In *The Roman family in the Roman Empire: Rome, Italy, and beyond*, ed. M. George. Oxford: Oxford University Press.

Braund, D. 1996. *Ruling Roman Britain: Kings, queens, governors, and emperors from Julius Caesar to Agricola*. London: Routledge.

Brown, P. 1971. *The world of late antiquity*. London: Thames & Hudson.

Brown, P. 1988. *The body in society: Men, women, and sexual renunciation in early Christianity*. London: Faber.

Brown, S. 1991. *Late Carthaginian child sacrifice and sacrificial monuments in their Mediterranean context*. Sheffield, UK: *Journal for the Study of the Old Testament* Press.

Brown, S. 1997. "'Ways of seeing' women in antiquity: An introduction to feminism in classical archaeology and ancient art history." In *Naked truths: Women, sexuality, and gender in classical art and archaeology*, ed. A. O. Koloski-Ostrow and C. L. Lyons, 12–42. London: Routledge.

Brulé, P. 1987. *La Fille d'Athènes. La religion des filles à l'époque classique*. Paris: Les Belles Lettres.

Brunner, H. 1957. *Altägyptische Erziehung*. Wiesbaden, Germany: Otto Harrassowitz.

Brunt, P. A. 1971. *Italian manpower 225 BC–AD 14*. Oxford: Clarendon Press.

Brunt, P. A. 1987. "Labour." In *The Roman world*, ed. John Wacher, 701–716. London and New York: Routledge.

Bruun, C. 2007. "The Antonine plague and the 'third century crisis.'" In *Crises and the Roman Empire*, ed. O. Hekster, G. de Kleijn, and D. Slootes, 201–218. Leiden, Netherlands: Brill.

Bunge, M. J., ed. 2001. *The child in Christian thought*. Grand Rapids, MA, and Cambridge: Eerdmans.

Burrus, V., ed. 2005. *Late ancient Christianity*. Vol. 2, *A people's history of Christianity*. Minneapolis, MN: Augsburg Fortress Press.

Cahill, N. 2002. *Household and city organization at Olynthus*. New Haven, CT: Yale University Press.

Cameron, A., and A. Kuhrt, eds. *Images of women in antiquity*. London: Routledge.

Carleton Paget, J. 2004. "Jews and Christians in ancient Alexandria from the Ptolemies to Caracalla." In *Alexandria, real and imagined*, ed. A. Hirst and M. Silk. Aldershot, UK: Ashgate.

Cartledge, P. 1981. "Spartan women: Liberation or license." *Classical Quarterly* 31:84–105.

Cartledge, P. 1992. *The Greeks: A portrait of self and others*. Oxford: Oxford University Press.

Cartledge, P. 2002. *Sparta and Lakonia: A regional history 1300–362 BC*. London and New York: Routledge.

Cartledge, P., and A. Spawforth. 1989. *Hellenistic and Roman Sparta: A tale of two cities*. London: Routledge.

Caspar, P. 1991. *Penser l'embryon d'Hippocrate à nos jours*. Paris: Editions Universitaires.

Castrén, P. 1975. *Ordo Populusque Pompeianus: Polity and society in Roman Pompeii*. Rome: Bardi.

Champlin, E. 2003. *Nero*. London: Belknap.

Cheeseman, G. L. 1914. *The auxilia of the Roman imperial army*. Oxford: Oxford University Press.

Christie, N., and S. T. Loseby, eds. *Towns in transition: Urban evolution in late antiquity and the early Middle Ages*. Aldershot, UK: Scholar Press.

Cilliers, L. 2005. "Vindicianus' *Gynaecia* and theories on generation and embryology from the Babylonians up to the Graeco-Roman times." In *Magic and rationality in ancient Near Eastern and Graeco-Roman medicine*, ed. Manfred Horstmanshoff and Marten Stol, 343–367. Leiden, Netherlands; Boston; and Cologne, Germany: Brill.

Clark, E. A. 1981. "Ascetic renunciation and feminine advancement: A paradox of late ancient Christianity." *Anglican Theological Review* 63:240–257.

Clark, G. 1993. *Women in late antiquity: Pagan and Christian lifestyles*. Oxford: Clarendon Press.

Clark, G. 1994. "The fathers and the children." In *The church and childhood*, ed. D. Wood, 1–28. Oxford and Cambridge, MA: Blackwell.

Clark, G. 1996. "The bright frontier of friendship: Augustine and the Christian body in late antiquity." In *Shifting frontiers in late antiquity*, ed. R. Mathisen and H. Sivan. Aldershot, UK: Varioum.

Clark, G. 2005. "The health of the spiritual athlete." In *Health in antiquity*, ed. H. King. London: Routledge.

Clarke, J. R. 2003. *Art in the lives of ordinary Romans: Visual representation and non-elite viewers in Italy, 100 BC–AD 315*. Berkeley, London: University of California Press.

Coarelli, F. 2001. "Il Foro Triangulare: decorazione e funzione." In *Pompei: Scienza e Società*, ed. G. Guzzo, 97–107. Milan: Electa.

Cohen, D. 1989. "Seclusion, separation, and the status of women in classical Athens." *Greece & Rome* (n.s.) 36:3–15.

Cohen, D. 1991. *Law, sexuality, and society: The enforcement of morals in classical Athens*. Cambridge and New York: Cambridge University Press.

Cohen, S., ed. 1993. *The Jewish family in antiquity*. Atlanta, GA: Scholars Press.

Cole, S. G. 1981. "Could Greek women read and write?" In *Reflections on women in antiquity*, ed. H. P. Foley, 219–245. New York: Gordon and Breach.

Cooley, A., and M.G.L. Cooley. 2004. *Pompeii: A sourcebook*. London: Routledge.

Coon, L. 1997. *Sacred fictions: Holy women and hagiography in late antiquity*. Philadelphia: University of Pennsylvania Press.

Cooper, K. 1996. *The virgin and the bride: Idealised womanhood in late antiquity*. Cambridge, MA: Harvard University Press.

Cooper, K. 2007. *The fall of the Roman household*. Cambridge: Cambridge University Press.

Cooper, K., and J. Hillner, eds. 2007. *Religion, dynasty, and patronage in early Christian Rome 300–900*. Cambridge: Cambridge University Press.

Corbier, M. 1991. "Divorce and adoption as Roman familial strategies." In *Marriage, divorce, and children in ancient Rome*, ed. Beryl Rawson. Oxford: Clarendon Press.

Corbier, M., ed. 1999a. *Adoption et Fosterage*. Paris: De Boccard.

Corbier, M. 1999b. "Adoptés et nourris." In *Adoption et Fosterage*, ed. M. Corbier, 5–40. Paris: De Boccard.

Corbier, M. 2001. "Child exposure and abandonment." In *Childhood, class, and kin in the Roman world*, ed. S. Dixon, 52–73. London: Routledge.

Cotton, H. 1993. "The guardianship of Jesus son of Babatha: Roman and local law in the province of Arabia." *Journal of Roman Studies* 83:94–108.

Cotton, H. 1994. "A cancelled marriage contract from Judaea (*Xhev/Se Gr. 2*)." *Journal of Roman Studies* 84:64–86.

Coulston, J.C.N. 2000. "'Armed and belted men': The soldiery in imperial Rome." In *Ancient Rome: The archaeology of the Eternal City*, ed. J. Coulston and H. Dodge, 76–118. Oxford University School of Archaeology Monograph 54.

Cox, C. A. 1998. *Household interests*. Princeton, NJ: Princeton University Press.

Crawford, A., and G. Shepherd, eds. 2007. *Children, childhood, and society*. BAR International Series 1696. Oxford: Archeopress.

Crawford, S. 1999. *Childhood in Anglo-Saxon England*. Stroud, UK: Sutton Publishing.

Crawford, S., and C. Lewis. 2008. "Childhood studies and the society for the study of children in the past." *Childhood in the Past* 1:5–16.

Crespo Ortiz de Zarate, S. 2005. *"Nutrices" en el Imperio romano. 1. Estudio de las fuentes y prosopografía*. Valladolid, Spain: Crespo Ortiz de Zarate.

Crespo Ortiz de Zarate, S. 2006 *"Nutrices" en el Imperio romano. 2. Estudio social*. Valladolid, Spain: Crespo Ortiz de Zarate.

Cribiore, R. 1996. *Writing, teachers, and students in Graeco-Roman Egypt.* Atlanta, GA: Scholars Press.

Cribiore, R. 2001. *Gymnastics of the mind: Greek education in Hellenistic and Roman Egypt.* Princeton and Oxford: Princeton University Press.

Cribiore, R. 2007. *The school of Libanius in late antique Antioch.* Princeton and Oxford: Princeton University Press.

Crook, J. 1967. "Patria Potestas." *Classical Quarterly* 17:113–122.

Cunliffe, B. W. 1988. *Greeks, Romans, and barbarians: Spheres of interaction.* London: Guild Publishing.

Currie, S. 1996. "The empire of adults: The representation of children on Trajan's Arch at Beneventum." In *Art and text in Roman culture*, ed. J. Elsner. Cambridge: Cambridge University Press.

Dandamayev, M. A. 1998. "Education I in the Achaemenid period." In *Encyclopaedia Iranica.* 8:2. Costa Mesa, CA: Mazda.

D'Arms, J. 1981. *Commerce and social standing in ancient Rome.* Cambridge, MA, and London: Harvard University Press.

Dasen, V. 2004. *Naissance et petite enfance dans l'Antiquité. Actes du colloque de Fribourg, 28 Novembre–1er Decembre 2001.* Fribourg: Academic Press.

Dasen, V. 2005. "Blessing or portent? Multiple births in ancient Rome." In *Hoping for continuity. Childhood, education, and death in antiquity and the Middle Ages*, ed. K. Mustakallio, et al., 61–73. Acta Instituti Romani Finlandiae 25ae XXXIII. Rome: Institutum Romanum Finlandiae.

Deissmann-Merten, M. 1986. "Zur Sozialgeschichte des Kindes im antiken Griechenland." In *Zur Sozialgeschichte der Kindheit*, ed. Jochen Martin and August Nitschke, 267–317. Freiburg and Munich, Germany: Verlag Karl Alber.

De Jong, M. 1996. *In Samuel's image: Child oblation in the early medieval West.* Leiden, Netherlands: Brill.

De Jong, M. 1998. "An unresolved riddle: Early medieval incest legislation." In *Franks and Alamanni in the Merovingian period*, ed. I. Wood, 107–140. Woodbridge, UK: Boydell Press.

Della Corte, M. 1924. *Iuventus.* Arpinum, Italy: Giovanni Fraioli.

Demand, N. 1995. "Monuments, midwives, and gynecology." In *Ancient medicine in its socio-cultural context*, ed. P. J. van der Eijk, H.F.J. Horstmanshoff, and P. H. Schrijvers. Amsterdam and Atlanta: Rodopi Press.

Demand, N. 1998. "Women and slaves as Hippocratic patients." In *Women and slaves in Greco-Roman culture*, ed. S. R. Joshel and N. Kampen, 69–84. London: Routledge.

De Mause, L. 1974. *The history of childhood.* New York: Psychohistory Press.

Derks, T. 2006. "Le Grande Sanctuaire de Lenus Mars à Trèves et ses Dédicaces Privées: Une Réinterprétation." In *Sanctuaires, pratiques cultuelles et territoires civiques dans l'Occident Romain*, ed. M. Dondin-Payre and M. T. Raepsaet-Charlier, 239–270. Brussels, Belgium: Le Livre Timperman:.

De Ruggiero, E. 1948–1958. *Dizionaria Epigrafico di Antichita Romane.* Rome: Instituto Italiano per la storia antica.

De Simone, C. 1980. "Italien." In *Die Sprachen im römischen Reich der Kaiserzeit,* ed. Günter Newmann and Jürgen Untermann, 65–81. Cologne, Germany: Rheinland Verlag.

De Vögué, A. 1971. *La règle de Saint-Benoît. Commentaire historique et critique.* 2 vol. Paris: Cerf.

Deyts, S. 2004. "La femme et l'enfant au maillot en Gaule: Iconographie et épigraphie." In *Naissance et petite enfance dans l'Antiquité: Actes du colloque de Fribourg, 28 novembre–1er décembre 2001*, ed. V. Dasen. Fribourg: Academic Press.

Dijstra, M. 2005. "Opvoeding in de Levant." *Phoenix* 51 (2): 55–74.

Dillon, M. 2002. *Girls and women in classical Greek religion.* London and New York: Routledge.

Dixon, S. 1984. "Family finances: Tullia and Terentia." *Antichthon* 18:78–101. Reprinted in Rawson 1986: 111–115.

Dixon, S. 1988. *The Roman mother.* London: Croom Helm.

Dixon, S. 1992. *The Roman family.* Baltimore and London: Johns Hopkins University Press.

Dixon, S. 1997. "Conflict in the Roman family." In *The Roman family: Status, sentiment, and space*, ed. B. Rawson and P. Weaver, 149–167. Oxford: Oxford University Press.

Dixon, S. 2001a. *Reading Roman women: Sources, genres, and real life.* London: Duckworth.

Dixon, S., ed. 2001b. *Childhood, class, and kin in the Roman world.* London: Routledge.

Dixon, S. 2001c. "The 'other' Romans and their family values." In *Childhood, class, and kin in the Roman world*, ed. Suzanne Dixon. London and New York: Routledge.

Dixon, S. 2007. *Cornelia: Mother of the Gracchi.* London: Routledge.

Drabkin, I. E. 1944. "On medical education in Greece and Rome." *Bulletin of the History of Medicine* 15 (4): 333–351.

Ducat, J. 2006. *Spartan education: Youth and society in the classical period.* Cardiff: University of Wales Press.

Duncan Jones, R. P. 1974. *The economy of the Roman Empire: Quantitative studies.* Cambridge: Cambridge University Press.

Duncan-Jones, R. P. 1982. *The economy of the Roman Empire: Quantitative studies.* 2nd ed. Cambridge: Cambridge University Press.

Duncan-Jones, R. P. 1997. "The impact of the Antonine plague." *Journal of Roman Archaeology* 9: 108–136.

Edelstein, E. J., and L. Edelstein. 1945. *Asclepius.* Baltimore, MD: Johns Hopkins University Press.

Edmondson, J. 2004. "Family relations in Roman Lusitania: Social change in a Roman province." In *The Roman family in the Empire: Rome, Italy, and beyond*, ed. M. George, 183–229. Oxford: Oxford University Press.

Eger, A. A. 2007. "Age and male sexuality: 'Queer space' in the Roman bath-house?" In *Age and ageing in the Roman Empire*, ed. M. Harlow, M. and R. Laurence, 131–152. *Journal of Roman Archaeology* Suppl. Series 65.

Eichenauer, M. 1988. *Untersuchungen zur Arbeitswelt der Frau in der römischen Antike.* Frankfurt am Main, Bern, New York, and Paris: Peter Lang Verlag.

Ellis, S. P. 1988. "The end of the Roman house." *American Journal of Archaeology* 92:565–576.

Ellis, S. P. 1991. "Power, architecture, and decor: How the late Roman aristocrat appeared to his guests." In *Roman art in the private sphere: New perspectives* on the architecture and decor of the domus, villa, and insula, ed. E. K. Gazda, 117–134. Ann Arbor: University of Michigan Press.

Ellis, S. P. 2000. *Roman housing*. London: Duckworth.

Engels, D. 1980. "The problem of infanticide in the Greco-Roman world." *Classical Philology* 75:112–120.

Étienne, R. 1976. "Ancient medical conscience and the life of children." *Journal of Psychohistory* 4:131–161. First published as "La conscience médicale antique et la vie des enfants." *Annales de démographie historique* 9 (1973): 15–46.

Euben, J. P. 1997. *Corrupting youth: Political education, democratic culture, and political theory*. Princeton, NJ: Princeton University Press.

Evans Grubbs, J. 1993. "Constantine and imperial legislation on the family." In *The Theodosian Code: Studies in imperial law in late antiquity*, ed. J. Harries and I. Wood, 120–142. London: Duckworth.

Evans Grubbs, J. 1995. *Law and family in late antiquity: The Emperor Constantine's marriage legislation*. Oxford: Clarendon Press.

Evans Grubbs, J. 2002. *Women and the law in the Roman Empire: A sourcebook on marriage, divorce, and widowhood*. London and New York: Routledge.

Eyben, E. 1972. "Antiquity's view of puberty." *Latomus* 31:677–697.

Eyben, E. 1973. "Die Einteilung des menschlichen Lebens im römischen Altertum." *Rheinisches Museum für Philologie* 116:150–190.

Eyben, E. 1991. "Fathers and sons." In *Marriage, divorce, and children in ancient Rome*, ed. Beryl Rawson. Oxford: Clarendon Press.

Eyben, E. 1993. *Restless youth in ancient Rome*. London: Routledge.

Fagan, G. 1999. *Bathing in public in the Roman world*. Ann Arbor: University of Michigan Press.

Fantham, E., H. Foley, N. Kampen, S. Pomeroy, and H. A. Shapiro. *Women in the classical world*. New York and Oxford: Oxford University Press.

Fentress, E. 2000. "Introduction: Frank Brown, Cosa, and the idea of the Roman city." In *Romanization and the city: Creation, transformations, and failures*, ed. E. Fentress, 11–24. *Journal of Roman Archaeology* Suppl. 38.

Fentress, E. 2004. *Cosa V: An intermittent town. Excavations 1991–1997*. Ann Arbor: University of Michigan Press.

Feucht, E. 1986. "Geburt, Kindheit, Jugend und Ausbildung im Alten Ägypten." In *Zur Sozialgeschichte der Kindheit*, ed. Jochen Martin and August Nitschke, 225–265. Freiburg and Munich, Germany: Verlag Karl Alber.

Figueira, T. J. 1986. "Population patterns in late archaic and classical Sparta." *Transactions of the American Philological Association* 116:165–213.

Fildes, V. 1988. *A history of wet nursing: From antiquity to the present*. Oxford: Blackwell.

Finn, R. 2006. *Almsgiving in the late Roman Empire*. Oxford: Oxford University Press.

Finneran, N. 2005. *Alexandria: A city and myth*. Stroud: Tempus.

Flemming, R. 2000. *Medicine and the making of a Roman woman: Gender, nature, and authority from Celsus to Galen*. Oxford: Oxford University Press.

Forrest, W. 1980. *A history of Sparta: 950–192 BC*. London: Duckworth.

Foxhall, L. 1989. "Household, gender, and property in classical Athens." *Classical Quarterly* (n.s.) 39:22–44.

Frankfurter, D. 2005. "Beyond magic and superstition." In *Late ancient Christianity.* Vol. 2, *A people's history of Christianity*, ed. V. Burrus, 255–284. Minneapolis, MN: Augsburg Fortress Press.

Frasca, R. 1999. "Il profilo sociale e professionale del maestro di scuola e del maestro d'arte tra reppublica e alto impero." In *Magister: Aspetti culturali e istituzionali. Atti del convegno, Chieti 13–14 novembre 1997*, ed. Giulio Firpo and Giuseppe Zecchini, 129–158. Alessandria: Edizioni dell' Orso.

French, V. 1986. "Midwives and maternity care in the Graeco-Roman world." *Helios* 13:69–84.

Funari, P. P., R. S. Garraffoni, and B. Letalien, eds. *New perspectives on the ancient world.* Oxford: Archaeopress.

Gabelmann, H. 1985. "Römische Kinder in Toga Praetexta." *Jahrbuch des Deutschen Archäologischen Instututs* 100:497–541.

Gaffney, V., H. Patterson, and P. Roberts. 1997. "L'anfiteatro di Forum Novum." *Archeo* 16:10–11.

Gaffney, V., H. Patterson, and P. Roberts. 2001. "Forum Novum—Vescovio: Studying urbanism in the Tiber Valley." *Journal of Roman Archaeology* 14:59–79.

Gaffney, V., H. Patterson, and P. Roberts. 2003. "Forum Novum—Vescovio: From Roman town to bishop's seat." *Lazio e Sabina* 1:119–126.

Gaffney, V., H. Patterson, and P. Roberts. 2004a. "Forum Novum (Vescovio): A new study of the town and bishopric." In *Bridging the Tiber: Approaches to regional archaeology in the middle Tiber Valley*, ed. H. Patterson, 237–251. London: British School at Rome.

Gaffney, V., H. Patterson, and P. Roberts. 2004b. "Forum Novum—Vescovio. The results of the 2003 field season." *Lazio e Sabina* 3:109–114.

Gagarin, M., and D. Cohen, eds. 2005. *The Cambridge companion to ancient Greek law.* Cambridge: Cambridge University Press.

Gardner, J. 1986. *Women in Roman law and society.* London: Croom Helm.

Gardner, J. 1998. *Family and familia in Roman law and life.* Oxford: Clarendon Press.

Gardner, J., and T. Wiedemann. 1991. *The Roman household: A sourcebook.* London: Routledge.

Garland, R. 1990. *The Greek way of life from conception to old age.* London: Routledge.

Garland, R. 2001. *The Greek way of death.* New York: Cornell University Press.

Garnsey, P. 1991. "Child rearing in ancient Italy." In *The family in Italy from antiquity to the present*, ed. D. I. Kertzer and R. Saller. New Haven, CT: Yale University Press.

Gebbia, C. 2006. "La locatio-venditio dei pueri negli scrittori Cristiani d"Africa." In *Poveri Ammalati e Ammalati Poveri. Dinamiche socio-economiche, traformazioni culturale e misure assistenziali nell"Occidente Romano in età Tardoantica*, ed. R. Marino, C. Molè, and A. Pinzone, 67–76. Catania: Prisma.

George, M., ed. 2005. *The Roman family in the empire: Rome, Italy, and beyond.* Oxford: Oxford University Press.

Gil'adi, A. 1992. *Children of Islam: Concepts of childhood in medieval Muslim society.* Oxford: Macmillian.

Golden, M. 1979. "Demosthenes and the age of majority at Athens." *Phoenix* 33:25–38.

Golden, M. 1988. "Did the ancients care when their children died?" *Greece & Rome* 35:152–163.

Golden, M. 1990. *Children and childhood in classical Athens*. Baltimore and London: Johns Hopkins University Press.

Golden, M. 1997. "Change or continuity? Children and childhood in Hellenistic historiography." In *Inventing ancient culture*, ed. M. Golden and P. Toohey. London: Routledge. 176–191.

Golden, M. 2003. "Childhood in ancient Greece." In *Coming of age in ancient Greece: Images of childhood from the classical past*, ed. J. Neils and J. Oakley, 13–29. New Haven, CT: Yale University Press.

Golden, M., and P. Toohey, eds. 1997. *Inventing ancient culture*. London: Routledge.

Goodman, M. 2007. *Rome and Jerusalem: The clash of ancient civilizations*. Harmondsworth, UK: Penguin.

Goody, J. 1976. *Production and reproduction*. Cambridge and New York: Cambridge University Press.

Goody, J. 1983. *The development of family and marriage in Europe*. Cambridge: Cambridge University Press.

Gould, G. 1994. "Childhood in Eastern patristic thought: Some problems of theology and theological anthropology." In *The church and childhood*, ed. D. Wood, 39–52. Oxford and Cambridge, MA: Blackwell.

Gourevitch, D. 1989. "Les premières heures de la vie de l'enfant d'après Soranos d'Éphèse." *Histoire des Sciences Médicales* 23:225–229.

Gourevitch, D. 1995. "Comment rendre à sa véritable nature le petit monstre humain." In *Ancient medicine in its socio-cultural context*. Vol. 1, *Papers read at the congress held at Leiden University, 13–15 April 1992*, ed. Philip van der Eijk, Manfred Horstmanshoff, and Piet Schrijvers, 239–260. Amsterdam: Editions Rodopi.

Gourevitch, D. 1996. "La gynécologie et l'obstétrique." *Aufsteig und Niedergang des römischen Welt: II: Principate* 37 (3): 2083–2146.

Gourevitch, D. 2004. "Chirurgie obstétricale dans le monde romain." In *Naissance et petite enfance dans l'Antiquité: Actes du colloque de Fribourg, 28 novembre–1er décembre 2001*, ed. V. Dasen. Fribourg: Academic Press.

Gowland, R. 2001. "Playing dead: Implications of mortuary evidence for the social construction of childhood in Roman Britain." In *TRAC 2000. Proceedings of the tenth annual Theoretical Roman Archaeology Conference. London 2000*, ed. G. Davies, A. Gardner, and K. Lockyer, 152–168. Oxford: Oxbow.

Gowland, R. 2007. "Age, ageism, and osteological bias: The evidence from late Roman Britain." In *Age and ageing in the Roman Empire*, ed. M. Harlow and Ray Laurence, 153–169. *Journal of Roman Archaeology* Supplementary Series 65.

Gratton, J., S. Huxlet, L. A. Karak, H. Toland, D. Gilbertson, B. Pyatt, and Z. Saad. 2002. "'Death more desirable than life'? The human skeletal record and toxicological implication of ancient copper mining and smelting in Wadi Faynam, southwestern Jordan." *Toxicology and Industrial Health* 18:297–307.

Green, M. J. 1995. *The Celtic world*. London: Routledge.

Gruen, E. 1974. *The last generation of the Roman republic.* Berkeley: University of California Press.

Guerreau-Jalabert, A. 2000. "Nutritus/oblatus: Parenté et circulation d'enfants au Moyen Age." In *Adoption et Fosterage*, ed. M. Corbier, 263–290. Paris: De Boccard.

Guijarro, S. 1997. "The family in first century Galilee." In *Constructing early Christian families: Family as social reality and metaphor*, ed. H. Moxnes, 42–65. London: Routledge.

Gundry-Volf, J. F. 2001. "The least and the greatest: Children in the New Testament." In *The child in Christian thought*, ed. M. J. Bunge, 29–60. Grand Rapids, MA, and Cambridge: Eerdmans.

Guroian, V. 2001. "The ecclesial family: John Chrysostom on parenthood." In *The child in Christian thought*, ed. M. J. Bunge, 61–77. Grand Rapids, MA, and Cambridge: Eerdmans.

Hajnal, J. 1965. "European marriage patterns in perspective." In *Population in history: Essays in historical demography*, ed. D. V. Glass and D.E.C. Eversley, 101–143. London: Edward Arnold.

Hales, S. 2003. *The Roman house and social identity.* Cambridge: Cambridge University Press.

Hall, E. 1989. *Inventing the barbarian: Greek self-definition through tragedy.* Oxford: Clarendon Press.

Hallet, J. 1984. *Fathers and daughters in Roman society.* Princeton, NJ: Princeton University Press.

Halsall, G. 1995. *Settlement and social organisation: The Merovingian region of Metz.* Cambridge: Cambridge University Press.

Halsall, G. 1996. "Female status and power in early Merovingian Austrasia: The burial evidence." *Early Medieval Europe* 5:1–24.

Halsall, G. 2004. "Gender and the end of empire." *Journal of Medieval and Early Modern Studies* 34:17–39.

Halsall, G. 2007. *Barbarian migrations and the Roman West 376–568.* Cambridge: Cambridge University Press.

Ham, G. 1999. "The Choes and Anthesteria reconsidered: Male maturation rites and the Peloponnesian wars." In *Rites of passage in ancient Greece: Literature, religion, society*, ed. M. W. Padilla, 201–218. Lewisburg: Bucknell University Press.

Handel, G., ed. 2006. *Childhood socialization.* 2nd ed. New Brunswick and London: Aldine Transaction.

Handley, M. 2000. "Inscribing time and identity in the kingdom of Burgundy." In *Ethnicity and culture in late antiquity*, ed. S. Mitchell and G. Greatrex, 83–102. London: Duckworth.

Hands, A. R. 1968. *Charities and social aid in Greece and Rome.* London: Thames and Hudson.

Hänninen, M. L. 2005. "From womb to family. Rituals and social conventions connected to Roman birth." In *Hoping for continuity: Childhood, education, and death in antiquity and the Middle Ages*, ed. K. Mustakallio, et al., 49–59. *Acta Instituti Romani Finlandiae XXXIII*. Rome: Institutum Romanum Finlandiae.

Hanson, A. E. 1987. "The eight months child and the etiquette of birth: *Obsit Omen!*" *Bulletin of the History of Medicine,* 61 (4): 589–602.

Hanson, A. E. 1994. "Obstetrics in the *Hippocratic Corpus* and Soranus." *Forum* 4 (1): 93–110.

Hansen, M. H. 1997a. "Preface." In *The* polis *as an urban centre and as a political community,* ed. M. H. Hansen, 5–7. Copenhagen, Denmark: Kgl. Danske Videnskabernes Selskab.

Hansen, M. H. 1997b. "The *polis* as an urban centre: The literary and epigraphic evidence." In *The* polis *as an urban centre and as a political community,* ed. M. H. Hansen, 9–86. Copenhagen, Denmark: Kgl. Danske Videnskabernes Selskab.

Harders, A. C. 2008. *Suavissima Soror: Untersuchungen zu den Bruder-Schwester-Beziehungen in der römischen Republik.* Munich, Germany: Verlag.

Harig, G. 1971. "Zum Problem 'Krankenhaus' in der Antike." *Klio* 53:179–195.

Harlow, M., and R. Laurence. 2002. *Growing up and growing old in ancient Rome*: A life course approach, London: Routledge.

Harlow, M. and R. Laurence, eds. 2007. *Age and ageing in the Roman Empire. Journal of Roman Archaeology* Suppl. Series 65.

Harlow, M., and R. Laurence. 2008. "The representation of age in the Roman Empire: Towards a life course approach." In *New perspectives on the ancient world,* ed. P. P. Funari, R. S. Garraffoni, and B. Letalien. Oxford: Archaeopress.

Harlow, M., and R. Laurence. in press. "Betrothal, middle childhood, and the life course." In *Ancient marriage in myth and reality,* ed. L. Larsson Lovén and A. Strömberg.

Harlow, M., R. Laurence, and V. Vuolanto. 2007. "Past, present, and future in the study of Roman childhood." In *Children, childhood, and society,* ed. S. Crawford and G. Shepherd, 5–14. BAR International Series 1696. Oxford: Archeopress.

Harris, W. V. 1982. "The theoretical possibility of extensive infanticide in the Greco-Roman world." *Classical Quarterly* 32:114–116.

Harris, W. V. 1994. "Child-Exposure in the Roman Empire." *Journal of Roman Studies* 84:1–22.

Harris, W. V. 2007. "The late republic." In *The Cambridge economic history of the Greco-Roman world,* ed. W. Scheidel, I. Morris, and R. Saller. Cambridge: Cambridge University Press.

Harrison, A.R.W. 1968. *The law of Athens: The family and property.* Oxford: Clarendon Press.

Hartog, F. 1988. *The mirror of Herodotus: The representation of the other in the writing of history.* Berkeley: University of California Press.

Haynes, I. P. 2001. "The impact of auxiliary recruitment on provincial societies from Augustus to Caracalla." In *Administration, prosopography, and appointment policies in the Roman Empire. Proceedings of the First Workshop of the International Network 'Impact of Empire' (Roman Empire 27 BC–AD 406), Leiden, June 28–July 1, 2000,* ed. L. De Blois, 62–83. Amsterdam: J. C. Gieben.

Hemelrijk, E. A. 1999. *Matrona Docta: Educated women in the Roman elite from Cornelia to Julia Domna.* London: Routledge.

Henneberg, M., and R. J. Henneberg. 1998. "Biological characteristics of the population based on skeletal remains." In *The chora of Metaponto: The necropolis*, ed. J. C. Carter, 503–559. Austin: University of Texas Press.

Henry, M. 2008. *Neaera*. London: Routledge.

Herlihy, D. 1995. *Women, family, and society in medieval Europe*. Providence, RI: Beghahn Books.

Hill, J. D. 2001. "Romanisation, gender, and class: Recent approaches to identity in Britain and their possible consequences." In *Britons and Romans: Advancing an archaeological agenda*, ed. S. James and M. Millett, 12–18. York, UK: Council for British Archaeology Research.

Hodkinson, S. 1986. "Land tenure and inheritance in classical Sparta." *Classical Quarterly* 36:378–406.

Hodkinson, S. 1989. "Inheritance, marriage, and demography: Perspectives upon the success and decline of classical Sparta." In *Classical Sparta: Techniques behind her success*, ed. Anton Powell. London: Routledge.

Hodkinson, S. 2004. "Female property ownership and empowerment in classical and Hellenistic Sparta." In *Spartan society*, ed. J. Figueira. Swansea: Classical Press of Wales.

Holloway, S. L., and G. Valentine. 2000. "Children's geographies and the new social studies of childhood." In *Children's geographies: Playing, living, and learning*, ed. S. L. Holloway and G. Valentine, 1–26. London: Routledge.

Hong, S., J. P. Candelone, C. C. Patterson, and C. F. Boutron. 1994. "Greenland ice evidence of hemispheric lead pollution two millennia ago by Greek and Roman civilizations." *Science* 265:1841–1843.

Hong, S., J. P. Candelone, C. C. Patterson, and C. F. Boutron. 1996. "History of ancient copper smelting pollution during Roman and Medieval times recorded in Greenland ice." *Science* 272:246–249.

Hopkins, K. 1965. "Contraception in the Roman Empire." *Comparative Studies in Society and History* 8:124–151.

Hopkins, K. 1987. "Graveyard for historians." In *La mort, les mortes et l'au-delà dans le monde romain*, ed. F. Hinard. Caen, France: Centre de publications de l'Université de Caen.

Hopkins, K., and G. Burton. 1978. *Conquerors and slaves*. Cambridge: Cambridge University Press.

Horden, P. 1993. "Responses to possession and insanity in the earlier Byzantine world." *Social History of Medicine* 6 (2): 177–194.

Horden, P. 2006. "How medicalised were Byzantine hospitals?" *Medicina e Storia* 10:45–74.

Horden, P., and N. Purcell. 2000. *The corrupting sea: A study of Mediterranean history*. Oxford: Blackwell Publishing.

Horn, C. B. 2005. "Children's play as social ritual." In *Late ancient Christianity*. Vol. 2, *A people's history of Christianity*, ed. V. Burrus, 95–116. Minneapolis, MN: Augsburg Fortress Press.

Horstmanshoff, H.F.J. 1995. "Galen and his patients." In *Ancient medicine in its sociocultural context*, ed. P. J. van der Eijk, H.F.J. Horstmanshoff, and P. H. Schrijvers. Amsterdam and Atlanta: Rodopi Press.

Houby-Neilson, S. 2000. "Child burials in ancient Athens." In *Children and material culture*, ed. J. Sofaer Deverenski. London: Routledge.

Huebner, S. 2007. "'Brother-Sister' marriage in Roman Egypt: A curiosity of human-kind or a widespread family strategy?" *Journal of Roman Studies* 97:21–49.

Humbert, M. 1972. *Le Remarriage à Rome*. Milan: Guiffre.

Hummel, C. 1999. *Das Kind und seine Krankheiten in der griechischen Medizin: Von Aretaios bis Johannes Aktuarios (1. bis 14. Jahrhundert)*. Frankfurt am Main, Germany: Peter Lang.

Hunter, D. 2007. *Marriage, celibacy, and heresy in ancient Christianity: The Jovinianist controversy*. Oxford: Oxford University Press.

Huskinson, J. 1996. *Roman children's sarcophagi: Their decoration and social signifi-cance*. Oxford: Clarendon Press.

Huskinson, J. 1997. "Iconography. Another perspective." In *The Roman family in Italy: Status, sentiment, space*, ed. B. Rawson and P. Weaver, 233–238. Oxford: Clarendon Press.

Huskinson, J. 1999. "Women and learning: Gender and identity in scenes of intellec-tual life on Roman sarcophagi." In *Constructing identities in late antiquity*, ed. R. Miles, 190–213. London: Routledge.

Huskinson, J. 2005. "Disappearing children? Children in Roman funerary art of the first to the fourth century AD." In *Hoping for continuity: Childhood, education, and death in antiquity and the Middle Ages*, ed. K. Mustakallio, et al., 91–104. *Acta Instituti Romani Finlandiae* XXXIII. Rome: Institutum Romanum Finlandiae.

Huxley, G. 1962. *Early Sparta*. Cambridge, MA: Harvard University Press.

Huys, M. 1996. "The Spartan practice of selective infanticide and its parallels in ancient utopian tradition." *Ancient Society* 27:47–74.

Innes, M. 2007. *The sword, the book, and the plough: An introduction to early medi-eval Western Europe 300–900*. London: Routledge.

Invernizzi, A. 2002."Des enfants condamnés à travailler ou des enfants actuers économiques et sociaux? Eléments de dé-construction des discours sur le travail des enfants." In *Regards croisés sur la naissance et la petite enfance. Actes du cycle de conférences "Naître en 2001,"* ed. Véronique Dasen, 153–168. Fribourg: Editions Universitaires Fribourg Suisse.

Ioppolo, G. 1992. *Le Terme del Sarno a Pompei*. Rome: L'Erma di Bretschneider.

Jackson, R. 1988. *Doctors and diseases in the Roman Empire*. Norman and London: University of Oklahoma Press.

Jaczynowska, M. 1970. "Les organizations des iuvenes et l'aristocratie municipale." In *Recherches sur les structures socials dans l'antiquité classique*, 265–274. Paris: Antiquité Tardive.

James, A., and A. James. 2004. *Constructing childhood: Theory, policy, and social prac-tice*. Houndmills, UK: Palgrave Macmillan.

James, A., and A. Prout. 1990. *Constructing and reconstructing childhood: Contempo-rary issues in the sociological study of childhood*. London: Falmer.

James, E. 2004. "Childhood and youth in the early Middle Ages." In *Youth in the Mid-dle Ages*, ed. P. J. Goldberg and F. Riddy, 11–24. York, UK: York Medieval Press.

Jameson, M. H. 1990. "Domestic space in the Greek city-state." In *Domestic architecture and the use of space*, ed. S. Kent, 92–113. Cambridge: Cambridge University Press.

Janssen, R. M., and J. J. Janssen. 1990. *Growing up and getting old in ancient Egypt*. London: Rubicon Press.

Jenks, C. 1996. *Childhood*. London: Routledge.

Jensen, R. M. 2005. "Baptismal rites and architecture." In *Late ancient Christianity*. Vol. 2, *A people's history of Christianity*, ed. V. Burrus, 117–144. Minneapolis, MN: Augsburg Fortress Press.

Jewell, H. M. 2007. *Women in dark age and early medieval Europe c. 500–1200*. Basingstoke, UK, and New York: Palgrave Macmillan.

Johnston, S. 2001. "Charming children: The use of the child in ancient divination." *Arethusa* 34 (1): 97–118.

Jones, A.H.M. 1940. *The Greek city from Alexander to Justinian*. Oxford: Clarendon Press.

Jones, A.H.M. 1964. *Later Roman Empire*. 3 Vols. Oxford: Blackwells.

Joshel, S. 1986. "Nurturing the master's child: Slavery and the Roman child-nurse." *Signs* 12:3–22.

Joshel, S. 1992. *Work, identity, and legal status at Rome: A study of the occupational inscriptions*. Norman and London: University of Oklahoma Press.

Just, R. 1989. *Women in Athenian law and life*. London: Routledge.

Kagan, D. 2003. *The Peloponnesian War: Athens and Sparta in savage conflict 431–404 BC*. London: Harper Collins.

Kah, D., and P. Scholz, eds. 2004. *Das hellenistische Gymnasion*. Berlin, Germany: Akademie Verlag.

Kalogeras, N. 2005. "The role of parents and the kin in the education of Byzantine children." In *Hoping for continuity: Childhood, education, and death in antiquity and the Middle Ages*, ed. K. Mustakallio, et al., 133–143. *Acta Instituti Romani Finlandiae XXXIII*. Rome: Institutum Romanum Finlandiae.

Kapparis, K. 2002. *Abortion in the ancient world*. London: Duckworth.

Kaster, R. A. 1983. "Notes on 'primary' and 'secondary' schools in late antiquity." *Transactions of the American Philological Association* 113:323–346.

Kaster, R. A. 1988. *Guardians of language: The grammarian and society in late antiquity*. Berkeley and Los Angeles: University of California Press.

Keay, S. (1996). "Tarraco in late antiquity." In *Towns in transition: Urban evolution in late antiquity and the early Middle Ages*, ed. N. Christie and S. T. Loseby, 18–45. Aldershot, UK: Scholar Press.

Keay, S. J., and N. Terrenato, eds. 2001. *Italy and the West: Comparative issues in Romanization*. Oxford: Oxbow Books.

Kennell, N. M. 1995. *The gymnasium of virtue: Education and culture in ancient Sparta*. Chapel Hill: University of North Carolina Press.

Kennell, N. M. 2006. *Ephebia: A register of Greek cities with citizen training in the Hellenistic and Roman periods*. Hildesheim, Zurich, and New York: Olms-Weidmann.

Kertzer, D. I., and R. P. Saller, eds. 1991. *The family in Italy from antiquity to the present*. New Haven, CT: Yale University Press.

King, A. C. 2001. "The Romanization of diet in the western empire: Comparative archaeozoological studies." In *Italy and the West: Comparative issues in Romanization*, ed. S. J. Keay and N. Terrenato, 210–223. Oxford: Oxbow Books.

King, H. 1983. "Bound to bleed: Artemis and Greek women." In *Images of women in antiquity*, ed. A. Cameron and A. Kuhrt, 109–127. London: Routledge.

King, H. 1990. "Making a man: Becoming human in early Greek medicine." In *The human embryo: Aristotle and the Arabic and European traditions*, ed. G. R. Dunstan. Exeter, UK: University of Exeter Press.

King, H. 1998. *Hippocrates' women: Reading the female body in ancient Greece*. London: Routledge.

King, H. 2004. *The disease of virgins: Green sickness, chlorosis, and the problems of puberty*. London: Routledge.

King, P. D. 1972. *Law and society in the Visigothic kingdom*. Cambridge: Cambridge University Press.

Kleijwegt, M. 1991. *Ancient youth: The ambiguity of youth and the absence of adolescence in Greco-Roman society*. Amsterdam: Gieben.

Kleiner, D.E.E. 1977. *Roman group portraiture: The funerary reliefs of the late republic and early empire*. New York: Garland.

Kleiner, D.E.E. 1978. "The great friezes of the Ara Pacis Augustae." *Melanges de l'Ecole francaise de Rome. Antiquite* 90:753–785.

Kleiner, D.E.E. 1992. *Roman sculpture*. New Haven, CT: Yale University Press.

Kokkinos, N. 1992. *Antonia Augusta: Portrait of a great Roman lady*. London and New York: Routledge.

Kuefler, M. 2007. "The marriage revolution in late antiquity: The Theodosian Code and later Roman marriage law." *Journal of Family History* 32:343–370.

Kukofka, M. 1993. "Die paidivskoi im System der spartanischen Altersklassen." *Philologus* 137:197–205.

Kyle, D. 2006. *Sport and spectacle in the ancient world*. Oxford: Blackwell.

Lacey, W. K. 1980. *The family in classical Greece*. Reprinted with corrections from the 1968 edition. New Zealand: Auckland University.

Laes, C. 2003. "Desperately different? The use of *delicia*-children in the Roman household." In *Early Christian families in context: A cross-disciplinary dialogue*, ed. D. Balch and C. Osiek, 298–325. Chicago: Erdmans.

Laes, C. 2004. "Romeinse 'paedagogi' tussen minachting en waardering. Een voorbeeld van *differential equations*." *Handelingen van de Koninklijke Zuid-Nederlandse Maatschappij voor Taal-en Letterkunde en Geschiedenis* 58:161–180.

Laes, C. 2005. "Childbeating in antiquity: Some reconsiderations." In *Hoping for continuity: Childhood, education, and death in antiquity and the Middle Ages*, ed. K. Mustakallio, et al., 75–90. *Acta Instituti Romani Finlandiae XXXIII*. Rome: Institutum Romanum Finlandiae.

Laes, C. 2006a. "Children and office holding in Roman antiquity." *Epigraphica* 66:145–184.

Laes, C. 2006b. *Kinderen bij de Romeinen. Zes eeuwen dagelijks leven.* Louvain, Belgium: Davidsfonds.

Laes, C. 2007. "Schoolmasters in the Roman Empire: A survey of the epigraphical evidence." *Acta Classica* 50:109–127.

Laes, C. 2009. "The educated Roman midwife: An example of differential equations." In *Hippocrates and medical education. Selected papers read at the XIIth International Hippocrates Colloquium, Universiteit Leiden, 24–26 August 2005,* ed. Manfred Horstmanshoff. Leiden, Netherlands: Brill.

Laes, C. Forthcoming. "Pedagogues in Latin inscriptions." *Epigraphica* 70.

Laes, C., and J. Strubbe. 2008. *De jeugd in het Romeinse rijk.Jonge jaren, wilde haren?* Louvain, Belgium: Davidsfonds.

Lambert, S. 1993. *The phratries of Attica.* Ann Arbor: University of Michigan Press.

Lambrechts, P. 1957. "L'importance de l'enfant dans les religions à mystères." In *Hommages à W. Déonna* (Coll Latomus 28), 322–333. Brussels, Belgium: Société d'Études Latines de Bruxelles.

Landau, J. M. 1986. "Kuttab." In *The encyclopedia of Islam.* Vol. 5. Leiden, Netherlands: Brill.

Laslett, P., ed. 1972. *Household and family in past time: Comparative studies in the size and structure of the domestic group.* Cambridge: Cambridge University Press.

Laurence, R. 1994. "Rumour and communication in Roman politics." *Greece and Rome* 61:62–74.

Laurence, R. 2000. "Metaphors, monuments, and texts: The life course in Roman culture." *World Archaeology* 31:442–455.

Laurence, R. 2006. "21st Century TRAC: Is the Roman battery flat?" In *TRAC2006. Proceedings of the Fifteenth Annual Theoretical Roman Archaeology Conference,* ed. B. Croxford, H. Goodchild, J. Lucas, and N. Ray, 116–127. Oxford: Oxbow.

Laurence, R. 2007. *Roman Pompeii: Space and society.* London: Routledge.

Laurence, R. in press. "Investigating the emperor's toga—Privileging images on Roman coins." In *Dress and identity,* ed. M. Harlow. Oxford: Archaeopress.

Lavan, L. 2003. "The political topography of the late antique city: Activity spaces in practice." In *Theory and practice in late antique archaeology,* ed. L. Lavan and W. Bowden, 314–339. Leiden, Netherlands: Brill.

le Bohec, Y. 1994. *The imperial Roman army.* London: Batsford.

Lefkowitz, M. R. 1981. *Heroines and hysterics.* London: Duckworth.

Lefkowitz, M. R., and M. B. Fant. 1992. *Women's life in Greece and Rome. A source book in translation.* London: Duckworth.

Lemaire, A. 1981. *Les écoles et la formation de la Bible dans l'ancien Israel.* Fribourg and Göttingen, Germany: Vandenhoeck & Rupprecht.

Lendon, J. E. 1997. "Spartan honor." In *Polis and Polemos,* ed. Charles D. Hamilton and Peter Krentz. Claremont, CA: Regina Books.

Lepelley, C. 1996. "La Survie de l'Idée de Cité Républicaine en Italie au Début du VIe Siècle, dans un Édit d"Athalaric Rédigé par Cassiodore (*Variae* IX.2)." In *La Fin de la Cité Antique et le Début de la Cité Médiévale,* ed. C. Lepelley, 71–83. Bari, Italy: Edipuglia.

Leven, K. H. 1991. "Thukydides und die 'Pest' in Athens." *Medizin historisches Journal* 26:128–160.

Leven, K. H. 1995. "*Athumia* and *philanthropia,* social reactions to plagues in late antiquity and early Byzantine societies." In *Ancient medicine in its socio-cultural context,* ed. P. J. van der Eijk, H.F.J. Horstmanshoff, and P. H. Schrijvers. Amsterdam and Atlanta: Rodopi Press.

Lewis, N., Y. Yadin, and C. Greenfield. 1989. *The documents of the Bar Kokhba period in the Cave of the Letters.* Jerusalem: Israel Exploration Society.

Liebeschuetz, J.H.W.G. 1991. "The end of the ancient city." In *The city in late antiquity,* ed. J. Rich, 1–49. London: Routledge.

Liebeschuetz, J.H.W.G. 2001. "The uses and abuses of the concept of 'decline' in later Roman history." In *Recent research in late-antique urbanism,* ed. L. Lavan, 223–245. *Journal of Roman Archaeology* Suppl. 42.

Liebeschuetz, J.H.W.G. 2003. *Decline and fall of the Roman city.* Oxford: Oxford University Press.

Lightman, M., and W. Zeisel. 1977. "*Univira:* An example of continuity and change in Roman society." *Church History* 46:19–32.

Lillehammer, G. 1989. "A child is born: The child's world in archaeological perspective." *Norwegian Archaeological Review* 22: 89–105.

Lillehammer, G. 2000. "The world of children." In *Children and material culture,* ed. J. Sofaer Derevenski, 17–26. London: Routledge.

Link, S. 2004. "Snatching and keeping: The motif of taking in Spartan culture." In *Spartan society,* ed. T. J. Figueira, 1–24. Cardiff: Classical Press of Wales.

Lintott, A. 1994. "Political history, 146–95 BC." In *Cambridge ancient history.* 2nd ed. Vol. 9, *The last age of the Roman republic 146–43 BC,* ed. A. Lintott and E. Rawson, 40–103. Cambridge: Cambridge University Press.

Lintott, A., and E. Rawson, eds. *Cambridge ancient history.* 2nd ed. Vol. 9, *The last age of the Roman republic 146–43 BC.* Cambridge: Cambridge University Press.

Longrigg, J. 2000. "Death and epidemic disease in Athens." In *Death and disease in the ancient city,* ed. V. M. Hope and E. Marshall, 55–64. London: Routledge.

Loseby, S. T. 1996. "Arles in late antiquity: *Gallula Roma Arelas* and *Urbs Genesii.*" In *Towns in transition: Urban evolution in late antiquity and the early Middle Ages,* ed. N. Christie and S. T. Loseby, 45–70. Aldershot, UK: Scholar Press.

Lutz, C. E. 1947. "Musonius Rufus 'the Roman Socrates.'" *Yale Classical Studies* 10:3–150.

MacDowell, D. M. 1986. *Spartan law.* Edinburgh: Scottish Academic Press.

MacPherson, R. 1989. *Rome in involution: Cassiodorus' variae in their literary and historical setting.* Poznaň, Poland: Uniwersytetu im. Adama Mickiewicza w Poznaniu.

Maffi, A. 2005 "Family and property law." In *The Cambridge companion to ancient Greek law,* ed. M. Gagarin and D. Cohen, 254–265. Cambridge: Cambridge University Press.

Manca Masciadri, M., and O. Montevecchi. 1984. *I contratti di baliatico.* Milan: Università cattolica del Sacro Cuore.

Mann, J. C. 1983. *Legionary recruitment and military settlement during the principate.* London: Institute of Archaeology.

Mantle, I. C. 2002. "The roles of children in Roman religion." *Greece & Rome* 49 (1): 85–106.

Manville, B. 1990. *The origins of citizenship in ancient Athens*. Princeton, NJ: Princeton University Press.

Marino, R., C. Molè, and A. Pinzone, eds. *Poveri Ammalati e Ammalati Poveri. Dinamiche socio-economiche, traformazioni culturale e misure assistenziali nell'Occidente Romano in età Tardoantica*. Catania, Italy: Prisma.

Marrou, H. 1964. *Histoire de l'éducation dans l'antiquité*. 2 vol. Paris²: Editions du Seuil.

Massaro, A. 1977. "'*Aniles fabellae.*'" *Studi italiani di filologia classica* 49:104–135.

Matthews, J. 2000. "Roman law and barbarian identity in the late Roman West." In *Ethnicity and culture in late antiquity*, ed. S. Mitchell and G. Greatrex, 31–44. London: Duckworth.

Mattingly, D. 1997. *Dialogues in Roman imperialism: Power, discourse, and discrepant experience in the Roman Empire. Journal of Roman Archaeology* Suppl. 23.

Mattingly, D. 2004. "Being Roman: Expressing identity in a provincial setting." *Journal of Roman Archaeology* 17:5–25.

Mattingly, H., and E. A. Sydenham, eds. 1923. *The Roman imperial coinage*. London: Spink and Son.

Mayer, G. 1986. "Zur Sozialisation des kindes und Jugendlichen im antiken Judentum." In *Zur Sozialgeschichte der Kindheit*, ed. J. Martin and A. Nitschke, 365–389. Freiburg and Munich, Germany: Karl Alber.

McAuslan, I., and P. Walcot. 1996. *Women in antiquity*. Oxford: Oxford University Press.

McGinn, T. 1998. *Prostitution, sexuality, and the law in ancient Rome*. Oxford: Oxford University Press.

McGinn, T. 2004. *The economy of prostitution in the Roman world: A study of social history and the brothel*. Ann Arbor: University of Michigan Press.

McKeown, N. 2007. "Had they no shame? Martial, statius, and Roman sexual attitudes towards slave children." In *Children, childhood, and society*, ed. S. Crawford and G. Shepherd, 57–62. BAR International Series 1696. Oxford: Archeopress.

Meens, R. 1994. "Children and confession in the early Middle Ages." In *The church and childhood*, ed. D. Wood, 53–66. Oxford and Cambridge, MA: Blackwell.

Metzler, J., M. Millett, and J. Slofstra, eds. 1995. *Integration in the early Roman West: The role of culture and ideology*. Luxembourg: Musée National d'Histoire et d'Art.

Meyers, E. M. 1992. "The challenge of Hellenism for early Judaism and Christianity." *The Biblical Archaeologist* 55 (2): 84–91.

Mikalson, J. 1998. *Religion in Hellenistic Athens*. Berkeley: University of California Press.

Millar, F. 1981. "The world of the *Golden Ass*." *Journal of Roman Studies* 71:63–75.

Miller, T. 1997. *The birth of the hospital in the Byzantine empire*. 2nd ed. Baltimore, MD: Johns Hopkins University Press.

Miller, T. 2003. *The orphans of Byzantium: Child welfare in the Christian empire*. Washington, DC: The Catholic University of America Press.

Millett, M. 2001. "Roman interaction in north-western Iberia." *Oxford Journal of Archaeology* 20 (2): 157–170.

Milnor, K. 2005. *Gender, domesticity, and the age of Augustus: Inventing private life.* Oxford: Oxford University Press.

Moeller, W. O. 1970. "The riot of AD 59 at Pompeii." *Historia* 19:84–95.

Mommsen, T. 1884. "Conscriptionsordnung der römischen Kaiserzeit." *Hermes* 19:1–79.

Montserrat, D. 2005. "Carrying on the work of the Earlier Firm: Doctors, medicine, and Christianity in the *Thaumata* of Sophronius of Jerusalem." In *Health in antiquity*, ed. H. King. London and New York: Routledge.

Morgan, T. 1998. *Literate education in the Hellenistic and Roman worlds.* Cambridge: Cambridge University Press.

Morgan, C., and J. J. Coulton. 1997. "The *polis* as a physical entity." In *The polis as an urban centre and as a political community*, ed. M. H. Hanson, 87–144. Copenhagen, Denmark: Kgl. Danske Videnskabernes Selskab.

Morris, I. 1991. "The early *polis* as city and state." In *City and country in the ancient world*, ed. John Rich and Andrew Wallace-Hadrill. London and New York: Routledge.

Morris, I. 1999. "Archaeology and gender ideologies in early archaic Greece." *Transactions of the American Philological Association* 129:305–317.

Moscati, S. 1996. "Nuovi contributi sul 'sacrificio dei bambini.'" *Rendiconti dell'Accademia Nazionale dei Lincei, Classe di Scienze morali, storiche e filologiche*, 9th ser., 7:499–504.

Moxnes, H., ed. 1997. *Constructing early Christian families.* London: Routledge.

Mouritsen, H. 1988. *Elections, magistrates, and municipal elite. Studies in Pompeian epigraphy. Analecta Romana Instituti Danici Supplement* 15. Rome: Bretschneider.

Mouritsen, H. 1998. "The album from Canusium and the town councils of Roman Italy." *Chiron* 28: 229–254.

Mouritsen, H. 1999. "Electoral campaigning in Pompeii: A reconsideration." *Athenaeum* 87:515–523.

Murray, A. 1983. *Germanic kinship structure: Studies in law and society in antiquity and the early Middle Ages.* Toronto: Pontifical Institute of Medieval Studies.

Murray, O. 1993. *Early Greece.* 2nd ed. Cambridge, MA: Harvard University Press.

Mustakallio, K. 2005. "Roman funerals: Identity, gender, and participation." In *Hoping for continuity: Childhood, education, and death in antiquity and the Middle Ages*, ed. K. Mustakallio, et al., 179–190. *Acta Instituti Romani Finlandiae* XXXIII. Rome: Institutum Romanum Finlandiae.

Mustakallio, K. 2008. "The changing role of the Vestal Virgins." In *Official roles and private life of women in antiquity*, ed. Lena Larsson Lovén and Agneta Strömberg. Sävedalen, Sweden: Paul Åströms.

Mustakallio, K., J. Hanska, H. L. Sainio, and V. Vuolanto, eds. 2005. *Hoping for continuity: Childhood, education, and death in antiquity and the Middle Ages. Acta Instituti Romani Finlandiae* XXXIII. Rome: Institutum Romanum Finlandiae.

Naerebout, F., and H. Singor. 2008. *De Oudheid. Grieken en Romeinen in de context van de wereldgeschiedenis.* 8th ed. Amsterdam: Ambo.

Nathan, G. 2000. *The family in late antiquity.* London: Routledge.

Neils, J. 2003. "Children and Greek religion." In *Coming of age in ancient Greece: Images of childhood from the classical past,* ed. J. Neils and J. H. Oakley, 139–161. New Haven, CT: Yale University Press.

Neils, J., and J. H. Oakley, eds. 2003. *Coming of age in ancient Greece: Images of childhood from the classical past.* New Haven, CT: Yale University Press.

Nelson, J. N. 1994. "Parents, children, and the church in the earlier Middle Ages." In *The church and childhood,* ed. D. Wood, 81–114. Oxford and Cambridge, MA: Blackwell.

Nelson, J. N. 2002. "Family, gender, and sexuality in the Middle Ages." In *The Companion to historiography,* ed. M. Bentley, 153–176. London: Routledge.

Néraudau, J. P. 1984. *Etre enfant a Rome.* Reprinted in 1996. Paris: Les Belles Lettres.

Neumann, G., and J. Untermann, eds. 1980. *Die Sprachen im römischen Reich der Kaiserzeit.* Cologne, Germany: Rheinland Verlag.

Nevett, L. 1994. "Separation or seclusion? Towards an archaeological approach to investigating women in the Greek household from the fifth to the third centuries BC." In *Architecture and order: Approaches to social space,* ed. M. Parker Pearson and C. Richards, 98–112. London: Routledge.

Nevett, L. 1995. "The organisation of space in classical and Hellenistic houses from mainland Greece and the western colonies." In *Time, tradition, and society in Greek archaeology: Bridging the 'great divide,'* ed. N. Spencer, 89–108. London: Routledge.

Nevett, L. 1999. *House and society in the ancient Greek world.* Cambridge: Cambridge University Press.

Nevett, L. 2002. "Continuity and change in Greek households under Roman rule: The role of women in the domestic context." In *Greek Romans and Roman Greeks: Studies in cultural interaction,* ed. E. N. Ostenfeld. Aarhus, Denmark: Aarhus University Press.

Nicolet, C. 1980. *The world of the citizen at Rome.* Cambridge: Cambridge University Press.

Nicolay, J. 2002. "The use and significance of military equipment and horse gear from non-military contexts in the Batavian area: Continuity from the late Iron Age to the early Roman period." In *Kontinuität und Diskontinuität: Germania inferior am Beginn und am Ende der römishchen Herrschaft,* ed. T. Grünewald and S. Seibel, 345–373. Berlin, Germany: Walter de Gruyter.

Nippel, W. 1995. *Public order in ancient Rome.* Cambridge: Cambridge University Press.

Noy, D. 2000. *Foreigners at Rome: Citizens and strangers.* London: Duckworth.

Noy, D. 2007. "The life course of Jews in the Roman Empire." In *Age and ageing in the Roman Empire,* ed. M. Harlow and R. Laurence, 81–94. *Journal of Roman Archaeology* Supplementary Series 65.

Nutton, V. 1995. "Medicine in the Greek world, 800–50 BC," "Roman medicine, 250 BC to AD 200," "Medicine in late antiquity and the early Middle Ages." In *The Western medical tradition,* ed. L. I. Conrad, M. Neve, V. Nutton, R. Porter, and A. Wear. Cambridge: Cambridge University Press.

Oakley, J. H. 2003. "Death and the child." In *Coming of age in ancient Greece: Images of childhood from the classical past*, in J. Neils and J. H. Oakley, 163–194. New Haven, CT: Yale University Press.

Ober, J. 1989. *Mass and elite in democratic Athens*. Princeton, NJ: Princeton University Press.

Ogden, D. 1996. *Greek bastardy in the classical and Hellenistic periods*. Oxford and New York: Oxford University Press.

Oliver, B. 2000. "Jewelry for the unmarried." In *I Claudia II: Women in Roman art and society*, ed. D.E.E. Kleiner and S. B. Matheson. New Haven, CT: Yale University Art Gallery.

Orme, N. 2001. *Medieval children*. New Haven, CT, and London: Yale University Press.

Orme, N. 2006. *Medieval schools from Roman Britain to Renaissance England*. New Haven, CT, and London: Yale University Press.

Padilla, M. W., ed. 1999. *Rites of passage in ancient Greece: Literature, religion, society*. Lewisburg, PA: Bucknell University Press.

Parker, H. N. 1999. "Greek embryological calendars and a fragment from the lost work of Damastes, 'On the care of pregnant women and infants.'" *Classical Quarterly* 49: 515–534.

Parkin, T. G. 1992. *Demography and Roman society*. Baltimore, MD, and London: Johns Hopkins University Press.

Parkin, T. G. 2003. *Old age in the Roman world: A cultural and social history*. Baltimore, MD, and London: Johns Hopkins University Press.

Patlagean, E. 1977. *Pauvreté Économique et Pauvreté Sociale à Byzance 4e–7e Siècles*. Paris: Mouton.

Patterson, C. B. 1985. "'Not worth rearing': The causes of infant exposure in ancient Greece." *Transactions of the American Philological Association* 115:103–23.

Patterson, C. B. 1990. "Those Athenian bastards." *Classical Antiquity* 9:40–73.

Patterson, C. B. 1998. *The family in Greek history*. Cambridge, MA: Harvard University Press.

Peacock, D.P.S. 1982. *Pottery in the Roman world: An ethnoarchaeological approach*. London: Longman.

Petersen, J. M. 1994. "The education of girls in fourth-century Rome." In *The church and childhood*, ed. D. Wood, 29–38. Oxford and Cambridge, MA: Blackwell.

Phang, S. E. 2001. *The marriage of Roman soldiers*. Leiden, Netherlands, and Boston: Brill.

Phang, S. E. 2002. "The families of Roman soldiers (first and second centuries AD): Culture, law, and practice." *Journal of Family History* 27:352–373.

Pomeroy, S. 1975. *Goddesses, whores, wives, and slaves: Women in classical antiquity*. New York: Shocken Books.

Pomeroy, S. 1984. *Women in Hellenistic Egypt: From Alexander to Cleopatra*. New York: Shocken Books.

Pomeroy, S. 1994. *Xenophon Oeconomicus: A social and historical commentary*. Oxford: Clarendon Press.

Pomeroy, S. 1997. *Families in classical and Hellenistic Greece: Representations and realities*. Oxford and New York: Oxford University Press.

Pomeroy, S. 2002. *Spartan women*. Oxford and New York: Oxford University Press.

Pormann, P. E. 1999. *The Greek and Arabic fragments of Paul of Aegina's* Therapy of Children. MPhil diss., Oxford University.

Pormann, P. E. 2004. *The Oriental tradition of Paul of Aegina's* Pragmateia. Leiden, Netherlands: Brill.

Pormann, P. E., and E. Savage-Smith. 2007. *Medieval Islamic medicine*. Edinburgh, Scotland: University of Edinburgh Press.

Porter, H. 1999. "Greek embryological calendars and a fragment from the lost work of Damastes' *On the Care of Pregnant Women and Infants*." *Classical Quarterly* 49 (2): 515–534.

Preston, S. H., A. McDaniel, and C. Grushka. 1993. "New model life tables for high-mortality populations." *Historical Methods* 26:149–159.

Pulac, C. 1998. "The Uluburun shipwreck: An overview." *Journal of Nautical Archaeology* 27:188–224.

Raaflaub, K., J. Ober, and R. W. Wallace. 2007. *Origins of democracy in ancient Greece*. Berkeley and Los Angeles: University of California Press.

Radin, M. 1924. "The exposure of infants in Roman law and practice." *Classical Journal* 20:337–343.

Rajak, T. 2001. *The Jewish dialogue with Greece and Rome*. Leiden, Netherlands: Brill.

Rathbone, D. 1981. "The development of agriculture in the 'Ager Cosanus' during the Roman Republic: Problems of evidence and their interpretation." *Journal of Roman Studies* 71:10–23.

Ravegnani, G. 1983. *Castelli e città fortificate nel VI secolo*. Ravenna, Italy: Girasole.

Rawson, B. 1986a. *The family at Rome: New perspectives*. London: Croom Helm.

Rawson, B., ed. 1986b. "Children in the Roman *familia*." In *The family at Rome: New perspectives*, ed. B. Rawson, 170–200. London: Croom Helm.

Rawson, B., ed. 1991a. *Marriage, divorce, and children in ancient Rome*. Oxford: Clarendon Press.

Rawson, B. 1991b. "Adult-Child relationships in Roman society." In *Marriage, divorce, and children in ancient Rome*, ed. Beryl Rawson. Oxford: Clarendon Press.

Rawson, B. 1995. "From 'daily life' to demography." In *Women in antiquity: New assessments*, ed. R. Hawley and B. Levick, 1–20. London: Routledge.

Rawson, B. 1997. "The iconography of Roman childhood." In *The Roman family in Italy: Status, sentiment, space*, ed. B. Rawson and P. Weaver, 205–232. Oxford: Clarendon Press.

Rawson, B. 2001. "Children as cultural symbols: Imperial ideology in the second century." In *Childhood, class, and kin in the Roman world*, ed. Suzanne Dixon. London and New York: Routledge.

Rawson, B. 2003. *Children and childhood in Roman Italy*. Oxford: Oxford University Press.

Rawson, B. 2005. "The future of childhood studies in classics and ancient history." In *Hoping for continuity: Childhood, education, and death in antiquity and the middle ages,* ed. K. Mustakallio, J. Hanska, H. L. Sainio, V. Vuolanto. *Acta Instituti Romani Finlandiae* XXXIII: 1–12.

Rawson, B., and P. Weaver, eds. 1997. *The Roman family in Italy: Status, sentiment, space.* Oxford: Clarendon Press.

Rawson, E. 1969. *The Spartan tradition in European thought.* Oxford: Clarendon Press.

Remijsen, S., and W. Clarysse. 2008. "Incest or adoption? Brother-Sister marriage in Roman Egypt revisited." *Journal of Roman Studies* 98:53–61.

Revell, L. 2005. "The Roman life-course: A view from the inscriptions." *European Journal of Archaeology* 8 (1): 43–63.

Revell, L. 2009. *Roman imperialism and local identities.* Cambridge: Cambridge University Press.

Riccobono, S., ed. 1945. *Acta Divi Augusti.* Rome: Accademia Italica.

Riché, P. 1996. "La Représentation de la Ville dans les Textes Littériares due Ve au IXe Siècle." In *La Fin de la cité Antique et le début de la cité Médiévale,* ed. C. Lepelley, 183–190. Bari, Italy: Edipuglia.

Riddle, J. M. 1992. *Contraception and abortion from the ancient world to the Renaissance.* Cambridge, MA: Harvard University Press.

Rives, J. 1994. "Tertullian on child sacrifice." *Museum Helveticum* 51:54–63.

Rollet, C. 2001. *Les enfants aux XIXe siècle.* Paris: Hachette Littératures.

Rosenthal, F. 1941. "Some Pythagorean documents transmitted in Arabic." Part 2, "Plato's exhortation concerning the education of young men." *Orientalia* 10:383–395.

Rostovtzeff, M. 1900. "Pinnirapus iuvenum." *Romische Mitteilungen* 15:223–228.

Sallares, R. 2002. *Malaria and Rome: A history of malaria in ancient Italy.* Oxford: Oxford University Press.

Saller, R. P. 1984. "*Familia, domus,* and the Roman conception of family." *Phoenix* 38:336–355.

Saller, R. P. 1987. "Men's age at marriage and its consequences in the Roman family." *Classical Philology* 82:21–34.

Saller, R. P. 1991. "Corporal punishment, authority, and obedience in the Roman household." In *Marriage, divorce, and children in ancient Rome,* ed. Beryl Rawson. Oxford: Clarendon Press.

Saller, R. P. 1994. *Patriarchy, property, and death in the Roman family.* Cambridge: Cambridge University Press.

Saller, R. P., and Shaw, B. D. 1984. "Tombstones and Roman family relations in the principate: Civilians, soldiers, and slaves." *Journal of Roman Studies* 74:124–156.

Savunen, L. 1997. *Women in the texture of Pompeii.* Helsinki: University of Helsinki.

Schaps, D. 1979. *The economic rights of women in ancient Greece.* Edinburgh, Scotland: Edinburgh University Press.

Scheidel, W. 2001a. *Debating Roman demography.* Leiden, Netherlands: Brill.

Scheidel, W. 2001b. *Death on the Nile: Disease and the demography of Roman Egypt.* Leiden, Netherlands: Brill.

Scheidel, W. 2002. "A model of demographic and economic change in Roman Egypt after the Antonine plague." *Journal of Roman Archaeology* 15:97–114.

Scheidel, W. 2005. "Real slave prices and the relative cost of slave labor in the Greco-Roman world." *Ancient Society* 35:1–17.

Schmitt-Pantel, P. 1990. "Collective activities and the political in the Greek city." In *The Greek city from Homer to Alexander*, ed. O. Murray and S. Price, 199–214. Oxford: Clarendon Press.

Schroeder, J. A. 2004. "John Chrysostom's critique of spousal violence." *Journal of Early Christian Studies* 12 (4): 413–442.

Schwartz, S. 2001. *Imperialism and Jewish society 200 BCE to 640 CE*. Princeton, NJ: Princeton University Press.

Scott, E. 1995. "Women and gender relations in the Roman empire." In *Theoretical Roman archaeology: Second conference proceedings*, ed. P. Rush, 174–189. Aldershot, UK: Avebury.

Scott, E. 1997. "Introduction: On the incompleteness of archaeological narratives." In *Invisible people and processes: Writing gender and childhood in European archaeology*, ed. J. Moore and E. Scott, 1–12. Leicester, UK: Leicester University Press.

Seager, R. 1964. "The first Catilinarian conspiracy." *Historia* 13:338–347.

Severy, B. 2003. *Augustus and the family at the birth of the Roman Empire*. London and New York: Routledge.

Shahar, S. 1990. *Childhood in the Middle Ages*. London: Routledge.

Shaw, B. D. 1984. "Latin funerary epigraphy and family life in the later Roman empire." *Historia* 33:457–497.

Shaw, B. D. 1987. "The age of Roman girls at marriage: Some reconsiderations." *Journal of Roman Studies* 77:30–46.

Shaw, B. D. 2001. "Raising and killing children." *Mnemosyne* 54 (1): 31–77.

Shelton, J. 1988. *As the Romans Did: A sourcebook in Roman social history*. Oxford: Oxford University Press.

Shelton, J. 1990. "Pliny the Younger and the ideal wife." *Classica et Medievalia* 41:163–186.

Sissa, G. 1990. *Greek virginity*. Cambridge, MA: Harvard University Press.

Sissa, G. 1996. "The family in ancient Athens (fifth–fourth century BC)." In *A history of the family*. Vol. 1, *Distant worlds, ancient worlds*, ed. A. Burgière, C. Klapisch-Zuber, M. Segalen, and F. Zonabend, 194–227. Oxford: Polity Press.

Sluiter, I. 1988. "Perversa subtilitas. De kwade roep van de grammaticus." *Lampas* 21:41–65.

Smith, J. 2005. *Europe after Rome: A new cultural history 500–1000*. Oxford: Oxford University Press.

Smith, J. T. 1997. *Roman villas: A study in social structure*. London: Routledge.

Sofaer Derevenski, J. 2000. "Material culture shock: Confronting expectations in the material culture of children." In *Children and material culture*, ed. J. Sofaer Derevenski. London: Routledge.

Sofaer Derevenski, J. 2006. *The body as material culture: A theoretical osteology*. Cambridge: Cambridge University Press.

Sourvinou-Inwood, C. 1988. *Studies in girls' transitions: Aspects of the Arkteia and age representation in Attic iconography.* Athens, Greece: Kardamitsa.

Stafford, P., and Mulder-Bakker, A., eds. 2001. *Gendering the early Middle Ages.* Oxford: Wiley-Blackwell.

Staples, A. 1998. *From good goddess to Vestal Virgins: Sex and category in Roman religion.* London: Routledge.

Starr, C. 1986. *Individual and community: The rise of the polis, 800–500 BC.* New York: Oxford University Press.

Steedman, C. 1995. *Strange dislocations: Childhood and the idea of human interiority 1780–1930.* London: Virago Press.

Stortz, M. E. 2001. "'Where or when was your servant innocent?' Augustine on childhood." In *The child in Christian thought*, ed. M. J. Bunge, 78–102. Grand Rapids, MA, and Cambridge: Eerdmans.

Strauss, B. S. 1993. *Fathers and sons in Athens: Ideology and society in the era of the Peloponnesian War.* London: Routledge.

Stray, C. 1992. *The living word: W.H.D. Rouse and the crisis of classics in Edwardian England.* Bristol, UK: Bristol Classical Press.

Stray, C. 1998. *Classics transformed: Schools, universities, and society in England 1830–1960.* Oxford: Clarendon Press.

Strubbe, J.H.M. 1998. "Epigrams and consolation decrees for deceased youths." *L'Antiquité Classique* 67:45–75.

Swan, V. G. 1992. "Legio VI and its men: African legionaries in Britain." *Journal of Roman Pottery Studies* 5:1–33.

Tafazzoli, A. 1998. "Education II: In the Parthian and Sasasian periods." In *Encyclopaedia Iranica.* 8:2.

Tazelaar, C. M. 1967. "paides kai epheboi. Some notes on the Spartan stages of youth." *Mnemosyne* 20:127–153.

Todd, S. C. 2000. *Lysias.* Austin: University of Texas Press.

Tranoy, A. 1981. *La Galice Romaine: Recherches sur le nord-ouest de la péninsule ibérique dans l'Antiquité.* Paris: de Boccard.

Treggiari, S. 1991a. *Roman marriage: Iusti coniuges from the time of Cicero to the time of Ulpian.* Oxford: Clarendon Press.

Treggiari, S. 1991b. "Divorce Roman style: How easy and how frequent was it?" In *Marriage, divorce, and children in ancient Rome*, ed. Beryl Rawson. Oxford: Clarendon Press.

Trout, D. 2005. "Saints, identity, and the city." In *Late ancient Christianity.* Vol. 2, *A people's history of Christianity*, ed. V. Burrus, 165–187. Minneapolis, MN: Augsburg Fortress Press.

Uzzi, J. D. 2005. *Children in the visual arts of imperial Rome.* Cambridge: Cambridge University Press.

van der Eijk, P. J., H.F.J. Horstmanshoff, and P. H. Schrijvers, eds. 2005. *Ancient medicine in its socio-cultural context.* Amsterdam and Atlanta: Rodopi Press.

van Driel-Murray, C. 1995. "Gender in question." In *Theoretical Roman archaeology: Second conference proceedings*, ed. P. Rush, 3–21. Aldershot, UK: Avebury.

van Driel-Murray, C. 2002. "Ethnic soldiers: The experience of the lower Rhine tribes." In *Kontinuität und Diskontinuität. Germania inferior um Geginn und am Ende der römischen Herrschaft. Beiträge des deutsch-niederländischen Kolloquiums in der Katholieke Universiteit Nijmegen (27. bis 30.06.2001)*, ed. T. Grünewald and T. Seibel, 200–217. Berlin, Germany: Walter de Gruyter.

van Gennep, A. 1909. *Les rites de passage.* Paris: Emile.

van Minnen, P. 1995. "Medical care in late antiquity." In *Ancient medicine in its socio-cultural context*, ed. P. J. van der Eijk, H.F.J. Horstmanshoff, and P. H. Schrijvers. Amsterdam and Atlanta: Rodopi Press.

van Nieuwenhuizen, M., N. Brand, and J. M. Claassen. 1994. "Child psychology in the ancient world: Quintilian and Augustine on kindergarten education." *Akroterion* 39 (1): 12–26.

van Straten, F. 1994. "Images of gods and men in a changing society: Self-Identity in Hellenistic religion." In *Images and ideologies: Self-Definition in the Hellenistic world*, ed. A. Bulloch, et al., 248–265. Berkeley: University of California Press.

Vanderbroek, P. J. 1987. *Popular leadership and collective behaviour in the Roman republic.* Amsterdam: Geiben.

Veyne, P. 1990. *Bread and circuses.* London: Allan Lane.

Veyne, P. 2005. *L'empire gréco-romain.* Paris: Seuil.

Vilatte, S. 1991. "La nourrice grecque." *L'Antiquité classique* 40:5–28.

Vössing, K. 1997. *Schule und Bildung im Nordafrika der Römischen Kaiserzeit.* Brussels, Belgium: Collection Latomus.

Vössing, K. 2002. "Staat und Schule in der Spätantike." *Ancient Society* 32:243–262.

Vössing, K. 2003. "Die Geschichte der römischen Schule- ein Abriss vor dem Hintergrund der neueren Forschung." *Gymnasium* 110:455–497.

Vössing, K. 2004. "Koedukation und öffentliche Kommunikation—warum Mädchen vom höheren Schulunterricht Roms ausgeschlossen waren." *Klio* 86 (1): 126–140.

Vuolanto, V. 2008. *Family and asceticism: Continuity strategies in late Roman world.* PhD diss., University of Tampere, 2008.

Wacher, J., ed. 1987. *The Roman world.* London and New York: Routledge.

Walker, S. 1983. "Women and housing in classical Greece: The archaeological evidence." In *Images of women in antiquity*, ed. A. Cameron and A. Kuhrt, 81–91. London: Routledge.

Wallace-Hadrill, A. 1981. "Family and inheritance in the Augustan marriage laws." *Proceedings of the Cambridge Philological Society* 27:58–80.

Wallace-Hadrill, A. 1994. *Houses and society in Pompeii and Herculaneum.* Princeton, NJ: Princeton University Press.

Wallace-Hadrill, A. 1997. "Engendering the Roman house." In *I Claudia: Women in ancient Rome*, ed. D.E.E. Kleiner and S. B. Matheson, 104–115. New Haven, CT: Yale University Art Gallery.

Ward-Perkins, B. 1984. *From classical antiquity to the Middle Ages: Urban public buildings in northern and central Italy* AD *300–850.* Oxford: Oxford University Press.

Ward-Perkins, B. 1996. "Urban continuity?" In *Towns in transition: Urban evolution in late antiquity and the early Middle Ages*, ed. N. Christie and S. T. Loseby, 45–17. Aldershot, UK: Scholar Press.

Wasserstein, A. 1989. "A marriage contract from the province of Arabia Nova: Notes on Papyrus Yadin 18." *Jewish Quarterly Review* 80:93–130.

Watts, E. J. 2006. *City and school in late antique Athens and Alexandria.* Berkeley, Los Angeles, and London: University of California Press.

Wemple, S. F. 1981. *Women in Frankish society: Marriage and the cloister 500–900.* Philadelphia: University of Pennsylvania Press.

Whitley, J. 2001. *The archaeology of ancient Greece.* Cambridge: Cambridge University Press.

Wickham, C. 2005. *Framing the early Middle Ages: Europe and the Mediterranean 400–800.* Oxford: Oxford University Press.

Wickham, C. 2009. *The inheritance of Rome: A history of Europe from 400–1000.* London: Allen Lane.

Wiedemann, T. 1989. *Adults and children in the Roman Empire.* London: Routledge.

Wiedemann, T. 1996. "Thucydides, women, and the limits of rational analysis." In *Women in antiquity*, ed. I. McAuslan and P. Walcot. Oxford: Oxford University Press.

Wileman, J. 2005. *Hide and seek: The archaeology of childhood.* Stroud, UK: Tempus.

Willems, W.H.J. 1984. "Romans and Batavians: A regional study in the Dutch East River Area II." *Berichten van de Rijksdienst voor het Oudheidkundig Bodemonderzoek* 34:39–331.

Willemsen, A. 2003. *Romeins speelgoed. Kindertijd in een wereldrijk.* Zutphen, Netherlands: Walburg Pers.

Wiseman, T. P. 1994. "The Senate and the *Populares,* 69–60 BC." In *Cambridge ancient history.* 2nd ed. Vol. 9, *The last age of the Roman republic 146–43 BC,* ed. A. Lintott and E. Rawson, 327–367. Cambridge: Cambridge University Press.

Wood, D., ed. 1994. *The church and childhood.* Oxford and Cambridge, MA: Blackwell.

Wood, I. M. 2003. "Deconstructing the Merovingian family." In *The construction of communities in the early Middle Ages: Texts, resources, and artefacts,* ed. R. Corradini, M. Diesenberger, and H. Reimitz, 149–171. Leiden, Netherlands: Brill.

Woods, R. 1993. "On the historical relationship between infant and adult mortality." *Population Studies* 47:195–219.

Woods, R. 2007. "Ancient and early modern mortality: Experience and understanding." *The Economic History Review* 60:373–399.

Woolf, G. 1990. "Food, poverty, and patronage: The significance of the epigraphy of the Roman alimentary schemes in early imperial Italy." *Papers of the British School at Rome* 57:197–228.

Woolf, G. 2005. "Family history in the Roman north-west." In *The Roman family in the Empire: Rome, Italy and beyond,* ed. M. George. Oxford: Oxford University Press.

Wrigley, E. A., and R. S. Schofield. 1981. *The population history of England, 1541–1871: A reconstruction.* London: Edward Arnold.

Yarborough, L. O. 1993. "Parents and children in the Jewish family of antiquity." In *The Jewish family in antiquity,* ed. S. Cohen, 39–60. Atlanta: Scholars Press.

Yavetz, Z. 1963. "The failure of Catiline's conspiracy." *Historia* 12:485–499.

Younger, J. G. 1997. "Gender and sexuality in the Parthenon frieze." In *Naked truths: Women, sexuality, and gender in classical art and archaeology*, ed. A. O. Koloski-Ostrow and C. L. Lyons, 120–153. London: Routledge.

Zanker, P. 1998. *Pompeii: Public and private life.* Cambridge, MA: Harvard University Press.

Zienkiewicz, J. D. 1986. *The legionary fortress baths at Caerleon II: The finds.* Cardiff: Cadw, Welsh Historical Monuments.

Ziolkowski, A. 1993. "Urbs direpta, or how the Romans sacked cities." In *War and society in the Roman world,* ed. J. Rich and G. Shipley. London: Routledge. 69–91.

CONTRIBUTORS

Patricia Baker is a lecturer in the Department of Classical and Archaeological Studies at the University of Kent. She specializes in Greco-Roman medical history. Her publications include her monograph, *Medical Care on the Rhine, Danube, and British Frontiers from the First through to the Third Centuries AD* (2004).

Mary Harlow is a senior lecturer in ancient history in the Institute of Archaeology and Antiquity at the University of Birmingham. Her research focuses on social history, in particular the subjects of dress in antiquity and the Roman life course. Her publications include the book *Growing Up and Growing Old in Ancient Rome* (2002).

Christian Laes is an assistant professor in the departments of history and Latin at the Free University of Brussels and in the Department of History at the University of Antwerp. The history of children and childhood, including education, is the focus of his research. His monograph in Dutch will be published in English as *Outsiders Within: Children in the Roman Empire*.

Lena Larsson Lovén is a lecturer in the Department of Historical Studies at the University of Gothenburg. She is a specialist in Roman social history. She is one of the founders of ARACHNE—the Nordic Network for Women's Studies in Antiquity—which has produced a number of publications including *Public Roles and Personal Status: Men and Women in Antiquity* (2008).

Ray Laurence is a Professor of Roman History and archaeology at the University of Kent. His research is focused on social history and archaeology, particularly the city and the Roman life course. His previous publications include *Roman Pompeii: Space and Society* (2nd edition 2007).

Tim Parkin is professor of ancient history in the Department of Classics and Ancient History at the University of Manchester. His research has included the investigation of ancient demography and old age in antiquity. His publications include the monograph *Old Age in the Roman World: A Cultural and Social History* (2003).

Louise Revell is a lecturer in the Department of Archaeology at the University of Southampton. Her research engages with issues of identity and cultural change, in particular those that can be identified from the study of Roman public buildings and inscriptions. She recently published a monograph entitled *Local Identities and Roman Imperialism* (2009).

Jo-Ann Shelton is professor of classics at the University of California at Santa Barbara. She specializes in Roman social history and has written extensively on ancient attitudes to animals. Her publications include *As the Romans Did: A Sourcebook in Roman Social History* (1988).

Agneta Strömberg is a lecturer in the Department of Historical Studies at the University of Gothenburg. She is one of the founders of the ARACHNE—the Nordic Network for Women's Studies in Antiquity—and has particular expertise in the archaeology of archaic and classical Greece. Her publications include the volume *Gender, Cult, and Culture in the Ancient World from Mycenae to Byzantium* (2003).

Ville Vuolanto is a lecturer in the Department of History at the University of Tampere. His research focuses on the history of the family in the later Roman Empire. He also maintains the most extensive online bibliography for childhood in antiquity: *Children in the Ancient World and the Early Middle Ages—A Bibliography*.

INDEX